Rape Myths

FEMINIST DEVELOPMENTS IN VIOLENCE AND ABUSE

Series Editors: Dr Hannah Bows, Durham University (UK) and Professor Nicole Westmarland, Durham University (UK)

Feminist Developments in Violence and Abuse provides a feminist forum for academic work that pushes forward existing knowledge around violence and abuse, informing policy and practice, with the overarching objective of contributing towards ending violence and abuse within our society. The series enables academics, practitioners, policymakers and professionals to continually build and explore their understanding of the dynamics, from the micro to the macro level, that are driving violence and abuse. The study of abuse and violence has a large scope for co-producing research, and this series is a home for research involving a broad range of stakeholders; particularly those working in grassroots domestic and sexual violence organisations, police, prosecutors, lawyers, campaign groups, housing and victim services. As violence and abuse research reaches across disciplinary boundaries, the series has an interdisciplinary scope with research impact at the heart.

Available Volumes:

Victims' Experiences of the Criminal Justice Response to Domestic Abuse: Beyond GlassWalls
Emma Forbes

Understanding and Responding to Economic Abuse
Nicola Sharp-Jeffs

Forthcoming Volumes:

'Rough Sex' and the Criminal Law: Global Perspectives
Hannah Bows and Jonathan Herring

Not Your Usual Suspect: Older Offenders of Violence and Abuse
Hannah Bows

Gendered Justice? How Women's Attempts to Cope With, Survive, or Escape Domestic Abuse Can Drive Them into Crime
Jo Roberts

Rape Myths: Understanding, Assessing, and Preventing

BY

SOFIA PERSSON
Leeds Beckett University, UK

and

KATIE DHINGRA
Leeds Beckett University, UK

emerald
PUBLISHING

United Kingdom – North America – Japan – India – Malaysia – China

Emerald Publishing Limited
Emerald Publishing, Floor 5, Northspring, 21-23 Wellington Street, Leeds LS1 4DL.

First edition 2022

Reprints and permissions service
Contact: www.copyright.com

British Library Cataloguing in Publication Data
A catalogue record for this book is available from the British Library

ISBN: 978-1-80071-153-2 (Print)
ISBN: 978-1-80071-152-5 (Online)
ISBN: 978-1-80071-154-9 (Epub)
ISBN: 978-1-80071-155-6 (Paperback)

INVESTOR IN PEOPLE

This book is dedicated to all the women and girls who have been subjected to rape. We hear you; we see you; we believe you. Together we will build a society that does not justify, tolerate, or minimise men's sexual violence against women.

Contents

About the Authors

Sofia Persson, PhD, is a Senior Lecturer in Psychology at Leeds Beckett University, UK. She is a Chartered Psychologist with the British Psychological Society and a fellow of the Higher Education Academy. Her main research interests are blame attributions in rape cases and various forms of gender inequality. She is an Open Science advocate.

Katie Dhingra, PhD, is Reader/Associate Professor in Psychology at Leeds Beckett University, UK. She is a Chartered Psychologist with the British Psychological Society and a fellow of the Higher Education Academy. Her research largely focuses on the psychosocial mechanisms underlying suicide and non-suicidal self-injury. Additionally, she researches violence against women and children and psychological responses to trauma.

Acknowledgements

Sofia
I would like to thank my dad, who continues to be the most important person in my life – thank you for always being there for me whenever I need you. I would also like to thank Tom. Tom – thank you for everything, including for giving comments on an earlier draft of this book. Finally, I would like to acknowledge my cat Sukie, who is very small but incredibly loved.

Katie
I would like to thank my husband, Bill. He has been my rock – looking after our beautiful puppy, Poppy, so we could avoid asking for yet another extension (she thinks sleep is for wimps); for talking me through the rough times, of which there were many; and for allowing me to treat our home like a hotel (thank you and sorry). I could not have done this without you. I am also indebted to my parents and friends. Finally, I would like to express my sincerest gratitude to Tracy Levy Mulleague. No amount of 'acknowledgement' will repay the help and support that she has given, but I would like to say, 'thank you', nonetheless.

Sofia and Katie
We would like to thank Emerald Publishing Limited for the support they have provided in writing this book. Further, we would like to thank the editors of this book series, Dr Hannah Bows and Professor Nicole Westmarland for giving us the opportunity to contribute this book to *Feminist Developments in Violence and Abuse*. Here, we would also like to acknowledge the anonymous reviewers who provided incredibly valuable feedback and suggestions on our initial book proposal.

We are very grateful to the Centre for Psychological Research at Leeds Beckett University for a grant that enabled us to carry out original research for this book. We would also like to express our gratitude to the people who participated in our empirical research, which provided the foundation for this book. We are particularly grateful to the women who had been subjected to rape and provided data on their experience of reporting (or not reporting) to the police. We are incredibly thankful for the insights shared by these women, and we hope that their voices will contribute to improved provisions and justice for victim-survivors of rape. We would also like to acknowledge the organisations dedicated to supporting victim-survivors of rape, such as Rape Crisis England and Wales, and extend our sincere appreciation and thanks for all the important work that they do.

Chapter One

Introduction

Scope of the Problem

Sexual violence against women is a serious concern globally – this is one of the main reasons that we decided to write this book. A wealth of sources confirms that each year, a large number of women are subjected to rape and/or sexual assault. For instance, Rape Crisis England and Wales (2021) estimates that 20% of women in England and Wales have experienced sexual assault since the age of 16, and figures from Rape, Abuse, and Incest National Network (RAINN, 2021) suggest that one in six American women have been subjected to rape or attempted rape. Globally, the United Nations (UN Women, 2021) suggests that 30% of women have been subjected to physical or sexual violence. We note, however, that these figures are likely underestimations, as many women do not acknowledge experiences analogous to rape as being sexual violence or assault (see Chapter Four of this book). Perpetrators of rape are overwhelmingly male (ONS, 2019; UN Women, 2021) and typically known to the victim-survivor (e.g., ONS, 2019; Rape Crisis England and Wales, 2021), highlighting how sexual violence is both a result of and contributor to gender inequality. It is thought that only a minority of women who are subjected to rape report this to the police (Hohl & Stanko, 2015; RAINN, 2021; Rape Crisis England and Wales, 2021).

Despite the scope of the problem, legal provisions for women who report rape to the police are poor. In England and Wales, while reporting levels of rape are increasing, both prosecutions and convictions of rape cases are decreasing. Specifically, for the most recent figures in 2020, only 1.6% of recorded rapes resulted in a charge or a summons, and in 2019–2020, rape convictions fell to a record low (Crown Prosecution Service, 2020; George & Ferguson, 2021). The number of victim-survivors withdrawing support for the rape case once it has been reported has also increased to 41% (from 25% in 2015/2016; Molina & Poppleton, 2020). It is, therefore, established that 'attrition' in rape cases is significant (Kelly, Temkin, & Griffiths, 2006). Attrition refers to the process whereby cases drop out of the criminal justice system (CJS) at one of several points of exit from that system. Because of this, it is unsurprising that the most recent Victims' Commissioner's report into rape suggests that only a minority of the women surveyed believed

Rape Myths: Understanding, Assessing, and Preventing, 1–7
Copyright © 2022 by Sofia Persson and Katie Dhingra
Published under exclusive licence by Emerald Publishing Limited
doi:10.1108/978-1-80071-152-520220001

that they would receive justice by reporting a rape to the police, and that generally, victim-survivors of rape have low levels of confidence in the CJS. Here, we echo the serious concerns voiced by the Victims' Commissioner for England and Wales, Dame Vera Baird, in that we are 'witnessing (…) the decriminalisation of rape' (Siddique, 2020), and that myths and misconceptions about rape may be important in explaining this dire situation.

Stereotypes and misconceptions surrounding rape have long been thought to be implicated in the societal treatment of victim-survivors of rape, as well as in the lack of justice in rape cases (e.g., Schwendinger & Schwendinger, 1974). That these myths remain relevant in a contemporary context highlights a continuum in societal prejudices towards rape victim-survivors and suggests that these beliefs share common features. Initially formalised by Burt (1980), 'rape myths' sought to provide an integrated theory of the common properties of these prejudices and misconceptions surrounding rape. Burt (1980), as well as subsequent researchers (e.g., Bohner et al., 2009; Lonsway & Fitzgerald, 1994; Payne, Lonsway, & Fitzgerald, 1999), noted the societal functions of these beliefs as especially important, where these attitudes serve to justify and normalise sexual violence against women. The conceptualisation of 'rape myths' continues to be relevant today, where the endorsement of these beliefs and other victim-survivor stereotypes are thought to significantly contribute to continued high levels of victim blame, both in society more generally and within the legal system specifically. Because of the detrimental effects that these beliefs have on the lives of victim-survivors of rape, rape myths remain an important consideration for feminist theory on men's sexual violence against women.

Prevalence

Rape Myth Acceptance (RMA) prevalence estimates refer to the proportion of people who endorse rape supportive beliefs in a fixed period of time. Prevalence research methodology has been a topic of considerable international attention and debate, with no internationally agreed good practice and competing approaches present. How a survey is framed, the measured used (Lonsway & Fitzgerald, 1994), and other methodological factors (e.g., the number and wording of questions) affect individuals' responses, consequently rendering comparisons between studies both challenging and somewhat problematic. We discuss some of these issues throughout this book.

Overall Endorsement

A 2005 poll of 1,095 randomly selected adults in England and Wales found that between 22% and 37% held rape victim-survivor blaming attitudes across a range of situations (e.g., if a woman was drunk or had been acting flirtatiously; Amnesty International, 2005). Out of the categories of myths examined, the category most highly endorsed (in terms of blaming the victim-survivor) was if the woman failed to say 'no' clearly to the man (37%). Thirty-four percent of respondents believed that the woman was 'partially' or 'totally' responsible for being raped if she behaved in a flirtatious manner. A 2007 poll of 992 adults living in Scotland found similar endorsement rates (Scottish Executive/TNS System 3, 2007). Thirty one percent of respondents thought a woman can be at least partly responsible for being raped if she was flirting with the man (the item with the highest endorsement); and 18% believed that rape can be the woman's fault if she is known to have had several sexual partners (the item with the lowest endorsement). In a 2009 Ipsos Mori telephone poll of 915 adults, results indicated that there continued to be circumstances in which a large proportion of the population believed a woman should be held at least 'partly' responsible for being sexually assaulted or raped (Home Office, 2009). Out of the categories examined, endorsement was highest if the woman did not clearly say 'no' to the man (49% at least partially responsible) and lowest if a woman was out walking alone at night (14% at least partially responsible).

Although the findings outlined above are clearly related to rape myths, they did not use established and validated measures[1] of RMA, making findings difficult to compare with related studies. Temkin and Krahé (2008) provided information on acceptance of rape myths among the general population in the UK. In their online study of 2,176 adults, they found that 25.3% of participants scored above the midpoint (i.e., on the 'agreement' side of the scale) on the female precipitation belief scale, a subscale of Cowan and Quinton's Perceived Causes of Rape Scale (1997), and 44.4% scored above the midpoint of a 16-item version of the Acceptance of Modern Myths about Sexual Aggression (AMMSA) (Gerger, Kley, Bohner, & Siebler, 2007), which indicates more agreement than disagreement with the statements within that scale. Accordingly, rape myths – especially if measured with measures capturing subtle and less obvious stereotypical beliefs about rape – show substantial acceptance among members of the general population.

Although most RMA research has been conducted with college/university students, studies with other sample types generally find similar rates of rape myth endorsement (Edwards, Turchik, Dardis, Reynolds, & Gidycz, 2011). Gylys and McNamara (1996) found that 43% of US-based prosecuting attorneys sampled (n = 182) demonstrated a moderate to high level of RMA. Although minimal empirical research on rape myths within religious institutions exists, preliminary research suggests that some rape myths are endorsed by a substantial number of US clergy (Sheldon & Parent, 2002). However, 93% of the sample was female. Rape myths are also highly prevalent in a wide range of media content and directly affect consumers' attitudes towards rape (see Chapter Five).

Is the Prevalence Decreasing Over Time?

Given significant ongoing changes in society and increased awareness of men's sexual violence against women, we would also expect attitudes and beliefs about sexual violence to have changed over time, as reflected in reduced RMA. Somewhat surprisingly, there is little empirical research focusing on societal shifts in

---

[1]Validated measures are surveys and screening questionnaires that have been tested to ensure the production of reliable, accurate results.

RMA over time, and the methodological differences across studies make it difficult to compare endorsement rates of these beliefs across time (see Chapter Three).
Beshers and DiVita (2021) administered a scale intended to measure RMA (i.e., a
revised version of the Illinois Rape Myth Acceptance Scale (IRMAS)) to two samples of undergraduates at a US university, one in winter 2010 and the other in spring
2017. They found that scores on the revised IRMAS were significantly lower in 2017
than in 2010. Bryne, Petri, and Oh (2021) administered the Attitudes towards Rape
Victims Scale (ARVS) to two separate samples of college students from the same
university in the US and found evidence of a substantial decline in undergraduate
endorsement of rape myths from 1998 to 2018. Although these results may reflect a
decline in RMA, it is important to consider alternative explanations, e.g., the results
of both studies may in part reflect an increased awareness that it is not socially desirable to acknowledge beliefs that directly blame victim-survivors for their victimisation, excuse the perpetrators' behaviours, or trivialise the impact of sexual violence.
We seek to expand on some of these considerations throughout this book and comment on the prevalence and impact of RMA among different groups.

Focus and Definitions

The focus of this book is rape, broadly understood as penetration of the vagina
and/or anus with a penis without consent. In England and Wales, the Sexual
Offences Act (2003) expanded this definition:

> (1) A person [A] commits [rape] if:
>   (a) he intentionally penetrates the vagina, anus or mouth of
>   another person [B] with his penis;
>   (b) B does not consent to the penetration, and
>   (c) A does not reasonably believe that B consents.
> (2) Whether a belief is reasonable is to be determined having
>   regard to all the circumstances, including any steps A has
>   taken to ascertain whether B consents.
> (3) Sections 75 and 76 apply to an offence under this section.
> (4) A person guilty of an offence under this section is liable, on
>   conviction on indictment, to imprisonment for life.

Given the gendered nature of sexual violence, the focus in this book is on the
rape of women, as perpetrated by men. We acknowledge that sexual violence is a
pressing concern within groups outside of a heterosexual context, especially given
that groups with other gender identities and expressions can be among the most
vulnerable in society. The scope of this book is, however, limited largely to rape
perpetrated by men in a heterosexual context (which also reflects the research
base in this area). The fact that this book is about men's sexual violence against
women is not to suggest that men are not subjected to rape, that women do not
perpetrate sexual violence, or that sexual violence not perpetrated by men against
women is any less traumatic. Despite our focus, we hope that some of the implications of the findings reviewed may be of use outside a heterosexual context.

In describing rape, we have chosen to use the phrase 'subjected to rape'. This phrase acknowledges the forced and non-consensual nature of rape and is in line with terminology used by public health bodies such as the World Health Organization (WHO, 2021). Throughout this book, we have chosen to refer to women who have been subjected to rape as 'victim-survivors' of rape. The only exceptions are where we refer to research that has involved a pre-conceptualised idea or concept (e.g., the RMA domain of 'blaming the victim') or measurement of attitudes towards the victim-survivor (e.g., victim blame, victim culpability, victim responsibility, etc.), as we strive for an accurate representation of what previous research did and measured. Here, we acknowledge that phrases used to refer to women who have been subjected to rape not only describe these women as having been raped but also these labels come with connotations and may as such influence women's identities and outcomes following rape (Hockett & Saucier, 2015), including the support they receive.

In choosing the term 'victim-survivor', we drew on considerations by Thompson (2000) who introduced the 'victim-survivor paradox' where women may need to dynamically highlight or minimise the effects of rape to assume different identities, meaning that neither 'victim' nor 'survivor' is, in isolation, sufficient to capture the identities of women who have been subjected to rape. The women interviewed in the study by Thompson (2000) further stated that the way in which they described themselves varied, sometimes choosing the term 'victim' and sometimes choosing the term 'survivor' depending on the context. We acknowledge that while we needed to settle on an operational definition for this book, no single definition is perfect. Women who have been subjected to rape will inevitably have individual preferences about how they would like to describe themselves, and what they have survived (or even if they consider that they have survived and recovered from sexual violence). It is worth noting that CJS professionals refer to victim-survivors as 'complainants', but we feel this does not reflect the vulnerable position in which victim-survivors are situated.

Structure of this Book

Despite its long history and relative popularity as a research topic (as evidenced by recent meta-analytic research, e.g., Persson & Dhingra, 2020; Suarez & Gadalla, 2010), many questions regarding the nature, correlates, and assessment of rape myths remain unanswered. In this book, we review the available evidence on the topic of RMA and seek to provide a comprehensive answer to some of these questions. Here, we outline the theoretical background to rape myths and position this theory within feminist scholarship and activism. We also consider the many methodological issues involved in researching sexual violence attributions and provide a practical guide to those wishing to research and assess rape myths. Importantly, we seek to situate rape myths within a broader societal context of prejudices such as sexism and racism, to address *why* interventions to address sexual violence seem to fail to eradicate myths and misconceptions about rape. We further highlight gaps in past research and point towards future developments in the area. In this book, we include previously unpublished data (collected in

October 2021) highly relevant to the study of rape myths. Throughout all chapters, we consider practical implications of the findings reviewed for researchers and practitioners. Below is an outline of each of the six main chapters of this book.

Chapter Two serves as an introduction to the theory of rape myths and outlines how early feminist theorising into myths and misconceptions surrounding rape developed into the measurable construct of RMA. Here, we will stress that the feminist underpinnings of rape myths are crucial for understanding what they are as well as their purpose, especially in terms of how research into this area has sought to address the fundamental and persistent inequalities facing women in the context of sexual violence and rape. This chapter will further present different ideas about what rape myths 'are' and outline how these beliefs can be categorised into different domains or categories. Finally, we note that feminist theorising into sexual violence has traditionally failed to include the voices of women of colour, meaning that RMA is likely theoretically incomplete without considering its links with racism. Here, we make recommendations about how the theoretical basis of rape myths can be strengthened through also considering racist myths about victim-survivors and perpetrators.

Chapter Three focuses on the methodological background to, and assessment of, RMA and is intended to serve as a practical guide for those interested in assessing and researching rape myths. Here, we consider why it is advantageous to be able to measure RMA, and we also provide an overview of the ways in which this is typically achieved. In doing so, we detail the most commonly used scales for RMA assessment, including their psychometric properties and background. We further consider several other relevant variables often measured in conjunction with RMA. Finally, this chapter outlines some of the methodological challenges faced by researchers in this area, and we make several recommendations for how research methodologies can be improved. Here, we focus specifically on increased international collaboration and research transparency as two promising avenues going forward.

Chapter Four reviews the consequences of RMA on the CJS and women subjected to rape, and we further signpost how the impact of these myths could be mitigated. We note that rape myths play a major role at every stage of the CJS process, and that victim-survivor characteristics – especially the victim-survivor's relationship with the offender and whether the victim-survivor engaged in any 'risky' behaviour at the time of the rape – influence decision-making. Further, we examine the impact of RMA on juries and conclude that they may compromise their impartial position by infusing their assessment of a rape victim-survivor with their rape mythology. Here, we consider how the impact of prejudicial and stereotypical beliefs on verdicts could be reduced. We also argue that women's experience of the CJS is not only shaped by rape myths but also by age, ethnicity, social class, and disability. Consequently, improving the CJS response to rape will require a deeper understanding of wide-ranging and intersecting structural inequalities.

Chapter Five examines the perpetuation of rape myths in society, with a particular focus on the complex ways in which institutions who would – on the surface – disagree with the perpetuation of rape myths often maintain them. We also critically discuss some of the ways in which the media portray rape, since such portrayals have been shown to increase victim-survivor blaming and influence the way in which victim-survivors are perceived by the CJS and the general population more broadly. Within this section, we advance an outline of changes that could be made to improve prevention campaigns and media portrayals of sexual assault. Finally, we link the perpetuation of rape myths to the functions of rape myths, to explore *why* individuals and institutions appear reluctant to completely abandon these ideas, particularly regarding how truth is established and maintained.

Chapter Six draws on Burt's (1980) original considerations of the correlates of RMA and details the relationship between RMA and other types of prejudices ('-isms'). We pay particular attention to how *other* types of stereotypical beliefs may scaffold rape myths. Here, we argue that the many shapes of sexism present in society are key for maintaining and legitimising RMA, particularly through their cementing of gender differentiations and the backlash against feminism. We further note racism, classism, and ableism as relevant prejudices co-existing with the endorsement of rape myths and suggest that social dominance may be a general belief system underlying these beliefs. In doing this, this chapter finally notes that the failure to consider the societal context to RMA likely underlies the limited effectiveness of interventions developed to reduce these beliefs.

Chapter Seven examines whether rape myths can be prevented and, if already present, whether they can be changed. We outline some of the attempts to design rape myth prevention programmes and comment on their effectiveness. Placing rape myth prevention programmes within the context of theories of change, we consider some of the issues involved in using these strategies to impact deep-seated opinions. We argue that short-term interventions to lessen attitudes such as RMA are not a panacea, considering how pervasive and widely perpetuated these myths are. Here, we bring together considerations presented throughout this book and posit that so long as more benevolently sexist attitudes remain socially acceptable, interventions to reduce rape myths will have limited efficacy. We, therefore, conclude that wider discussions around sexist attitudes are necessary, and that sexual violence needs to be situated within wider gender inequality in society. A feminist context to these attitudes is, therefore, necessary, and we further propose ways in which research in this area can move forward to facilitate a reduction in RMA.

Chapter Two

Theoretical Background to Rape Myth Acceptance

Chapter Overview

The prevalence of, and responses to, rape have long been integral parts of feminist theory, where feminist scholars and activists have sought to address, and raise awareness of, rape prevalence and a lack of justice for women who have been subjected to rape. Because of this, Rape Myth Acceptance (RMA) is best understood by bearing its feminist foundations in mind. This chapter will situate rape activism within feminist theory and, in doing so, detail the theoretical background to, and development of, RMA. It will then provide a detailed outline of the conceptualisation of RMA as well as the different domains of rape myths and make suggestions about what rape myths 'are' based on the available research. Finally, this chapter will consider the limitations of feminist theory and RMA in the context of Black and South Asian feminist thought, and make recommendations about how theories of rape myths can incorporate intersectional considerations to improve the lives of *all* women.

The Importance of Feminism

The 1960s and 1970s saw a resurgence of organised feminism – the 'second-wave' women's liberation movement. The 'second-wave' asserted a woman's right to define her own sexuality and demanded: (a) equal pay for equal work; (b) equal education and job opportunities; (c) free contraception and abortion on demand; (d) free 24-hour nurseries; (e) financial and legal independence; (f) an end to all discrimination against women; and (g) freedom from intimidation by threat or use of violence or sexual coercion, regardless of marital status and an end to all laws, assumptions, and institutions that perpetuate male dominance and men's aggression towards women. Although rape (outside marriage) was illegal in the Western world during feminism's second-wave, feminists argued that the law did not go far enough (e.g., in the context of marital rape, which was still legal in the US and UK), and that de facto justice and social provision for

Rape Myths: Understanding, Assessing, and Preventing, 9–28
Copyright © 2022 by Sofia Persson and Katie Dhingra
Published under exclusive licence by Emerald Publishing Limited
doi:10.1108/978-1-80071-152-520220002

rape victim-survivors were lacking (Donat & D'Emilio, 1992). In particular, feminism's second-wave sought to emphasise that women's lived experience of gender inequality (including that of sexual violence) was key to improving conditions for women, and that current legal and social provisions centred the perspective of men (e.g., Davis, 1981/2019; MacKinnon, 1989/1991). Where feminism's first wave was largely focused on legal reform (e.g., women's right to vote and hold property), the second-wave (while also seeking to amend and expand rape legislation) sought to emphasise societal attitudes and rape stereotypes as important for understanding gender inequality (e.g., Brownmiller, 1975/1993). Specifically, although rape (outside marriage) was illegal, feminism's second-wave argued that sexist and permissive attitudes perpetuated sexual assault (especially within intimate relationships), and that negative stereotypes about rape victim-survivors largely prevented women from seeking justice in cases of rape, meaning current rape laws were in effect not implemented (MacKinnon, 1989/1991). As such, sexual violence was an important topic for second-wave feminist activism and led to considerable developments within feminist theory of rape. Many of the resulting considerations continue to be of relevance.

Rape and Feminist Theory

As noted above, sexual violence against women has long been an important part of feminist theory, and it continues to be highly relevant today. A major reason for this is the continued high prevalence of men's sexual violence against women (RAINN, 2021; Rape Crisis England and Wales, 2021), and the resulting impact on women's lives. Men's sexual violence against women also has broader political implications for how gender inequality is maintained. As sexual violence is a gendered crime both nationally (ONS, 2019; Rape Crisis England and Wales, 2021) and internationally (RAINN, 2021), understanding how it is perpetuated and responded to is integral to a feminist understanding of a gendered lived experience.

Feminist theorists (e.g., Brownmiller, 1975/1993) have suggested that the threat of sexual violence keeps all women in a state of fear and subjugation; this, therefore, contributes to an unequal power distribution between men and women more generally in society. Other feminist theorists, such as Davis (1981/2019) and Crenshaw (1989), have noted that the threat of rape enforces *all* forms of social hierarchies, including those based on ethnicity and social class. Elaborating on the point of social domination, MacKinnon (1989/1991) argued that raping with impunity is the ultimate index of social power and reflects a sexist society's punishment for being female, which links with Scully's (1990) notions of a kind of 'collective liability' for women. 'Collective liability' suggests that all people within a particular category are held accountable (liable) for the conduct of each of their counterparts. Thus, the victim-survivor of a violent act may merely represent the category of individual being punished (e.g., women). Theorists such as Dworkin (1987/2006) and Kelly (1987) have posited that heterosexual relationships (long-term relationships as well as briefer encounters between women and men) carry considerable potential for sexual violence, as this violence can take place outside the public realm.

Another important feminist concept that is highly relevant in the context of rape (especially within a relationship context) is that of 'the continuum of sexual violence' (Kelly, 1987). This concept suggests that sexual violence exists in many different forms and with differing prevalence rates. More common incidents that a majority of women have been subjected to might include verbal harassment and so-called grey[1] areas of sexual assault/violence (e.g., coercion and verbal persuasion to obtain sex) and less common incidents may include those that meet a legal, criminal definition of rape (Kelly, 1987). Importantly, viewing sexual violence as a 'continuum' allows for the recognition of the diverse range of sexual violence a woman might be subjected to in her lifetime, but emphasises the *shared meaning* underlying this violence and the detrimental effects that this can have on the lives of women. Kelly's (1987) research and resulting concept were also important in recognising that women's heterosexual encounters exist on a continuum from choice to force. In this, she argues against a binary view of women's sexual encounters with men and suggests that that these encounters cannot be neatly divided into 'consenting' or 'rape'.[2] Together, this leads to the conclusion that men's sexual violence against women has direct implications for women's lives as well broader political implications to entrench male structural power over women.

Rape and the Criminal Justice System

Sexual violence is also integral to a feminist understanding of the criminal justice system (CJS). The way(s) in which rape is responded (or not responded) to throughout the CJS (e.g., police, courts, prison, and probation service) illuminates the imagined objectivity of criminal law, and how contemporary justice practices may not be compatible with the needs of women. As originally highlighted by MacKinnon (1989/1991), and further elaborated on by Smith (2018), a passive, non-interventionist law can be construed as fundamentally patriarchal, as it assumes a level of equality between women and men in the social sphere. As the social sphere is not equal, the law merely reproduces these inequalities. This is exemplified by the law's limited practical understanding of consent and the

---

[1]Here, we acknowledge that referring to incidents of sexual violence as 'grey' is problematic, as it can fail to recognise and name sexual violence against women. The 'greyness' of these incidents can also be disputed given their detrimental impact on women, as well as the increased legal recognition of diverse expressions of non-consent. In her original study, Kelly (1987) refers to this category of events as 'pressure to have sex', and 83% of women had been subjected to this.

[2]More recently, the limits of 'consent' as a standard for women's sexual pleasure have been questioned by Angel (2021).

realities of sexual assault; this discrepancy between the law and women's lived experience has been a key focus of feminist anti-rape activism since the start of the second-wave of feminism and continues to be so today. Here, a useful example is the delayed criminalisation of marital rape in much of the Western world; marital rape was only criminalised in the UK in 1991 (Law Commission, 1992) and in 1993 in all US states (The National Center for Victims of Crime, 2004). Women have always known that sexual violence is possible within marriage, but the law, from a default male perspective, for a long time, failed to recognise this. It was only following intense feminist activism, along traditional feminist notions of consciousness-raising (MacKinnon, 1989/1991) that the law was changed.[3] Further examples of feminist initiatives in the context of the CJS have centred on practical court provisions for rape victim-survivors, the setting up of rape crisis centres, re-defining non-consent, and challenging the use of victim-survivors' sexual history in court (Donat & D'Emilio, 1992). Much of this activism remains ongoing and emphasises sexual violence as a key area for continued feminist involvement.

MacKinnon (1989/1991) advanced the notion of 'the legally perfect rape', which is a rape that fully adheres to stereotypical notions of a 'real rape', i.e., one that is perpetrated by a stranger, involves excessive physical violence (beyond the sexual violence already enacted), and is perpetrated against a woman society perceives as fully 'innocent' (i.e., White, modestly dressed, and sober; Estrich, 1987). Arguably, this is one situation in which 'truth' is gendered, where all women are measured against a hypothetical, non-existent, ideal. This gendered 'truth', it appears, is highly relevant to sexual violence and directly related to myths and misconceptions surrounding rape. As there are very high levels of attrition within the justice system (particularly when occurring between partners and spouses), it seems reasonable to question whether rape has effectively been decriminalised, as it seems to be an offence that many men can commit against many women with relative legal impunity. These concerns were echoed more recently by the Victims' Commissioner for England and Wales, Dame Vera Baird (Siddique, 2020). She based her comments on the experiences of the CJS among victim-survivors of rape (Molina & Poppleton, 2020), as well as on the low conviction rates for rape cases, and the collapse in rape prosecutions in all but the most severe cases. It is, therefore, likely that just as contemporary society looks back with scepticism to a time when marital rape was legal, future societies will be incredulous about how rape victim-survivors were legally managed in many Western countries today. We expand further on rape myths and the CJS in Chapter Four.

---

[3]Despite the criminalisation of marital rape, research with college students suggests that 9% of men and 5% of women believe that a husband's use of physical force to have sex with his wife does not constitute rape, and, in the same sample, 31% of men and 19% of women indicated that a husband having sex without his wife's consent does not constitute rape (Kirkwood & Cecil, 2001).

Rape Myths

'Rape culture' is central to the concept of rape myths. It refers to a social reality where it is assumed that 'sexual violence is a fact of life, inevitable as death or taxes' (Buchwald, Fletcher, & Roth, 1993). The term 'rape culture' itself indicates the need to understand rape *as* culture; as a complex social phenomenon that is not limited to discrete criminal acts perpetrated by a few individuals, but rather is the product of gendered, raced, and classed social relations that are central to patriarchal and heterosexist culture. Practically, a 'rape culture' contributes to, and maintains, permissive attitudes towards rape across societal institutions (e.g., courts) and contemporary culture (e.g., the media), creating an environment where sexual violence is normalised and the impact of sexual violence minimised. This is in line with feminist theorising on rape as regulated, rather than criminalised (Scully, 1990). Importantly, 'rape culture' theorising has greatly aided the identification of common myths and misconceptions surrounding rape, creating a foundation for the formal conceptualisation of rape myths.

The formalisation of rape myths into an integrated theory has been central to developments within scholarly research and feminist activism against rape culture. Informal theorising on myths about sexual violence has a relatively long history (e.g., Brownmiller, 1975/1993; Schwendinger & Schwendinger, 1974), with scholars agreeing that rape myths serve to perpetuate sexual violence against women, by exonerating the perpetrator and blaming the victim-survivor of rape. Drawing on this earlier theorising, rape myths were formally conceptualised by Burt (1980) who also argued that rape myths formed a set of attitudes, which could be measured as RMA (the measurement of this construct is further outlined in Chapter Three), i.e., the degree to which someone agrees with rape myths. Burt (1980) defined rape myths as beliefs about rape victim-survivors and perpetrators that were prejudicial, stereotyped, or false and contributed to an environment of victim blame.

The formalisation of rape myths was a seminal development for feminist anti-rape scholarly activism (and was, as such, of considerable importance to feminist theory more generally). However, at this time, the definition and measurement of rape myths remained vague. This is especially true for the concept of 'myths', which can be defined in a multitude of ways, and whether these beliefs are generally true or not was not considered. In response, Lonsway and Fitzgerald (1994) sought to establish a firmer theoretical concept, and stronger psychometric precision in concept measurement, particularly in response to the relatively subjective nature of the initial definition (e.g., the notion of 'myths' and their truth). They proposed a definition of rape myths, which is still widely used, namely, that rape myths are 'attitudes and beliefs that are generally false but are widely and persistently held, and that serve to deny and justify male sexual aggression against women' (Lonsway and Fitzgerald 1994; p. 134). Interestingly, this definition does not specify the content of rape myths (for example, 'attitudes about X or Y'), rather, content is defined only indirectly via the *functions* that rape myths are assumed to serve (i.e., to deny and justify male sexual aggression against women).

Although Lonsway and Fitzgerald (1994) argued that this lack of content speci-fication may facilitate an operational approach to rape myths, it may also make it challenging to differentiate rape myths from other types of beliefs (e.g., more general pro-violence attitudes). As discussed by Bohner et al. (2009), two aspects of this definition could be considered unnecessarily restrictive: (a) often it is dif-ficult, if not impossible, to determine if a specific rape myth meets the criterion of being 'false'; this is because it is not amenable to empirical falsification (e.g., 'Many women secretly desire to be raped'; Payne et al., 1999), because it is prescriptive in nature (e.g., 'A woman should be responsible for preventing her own rape'; Costin, 1985), or because it can be true under some circumstances or in certain cases (e.g., 'If a woman invites a man to her home for a cup of coffee after a night out this means that she wants to have sex'; Gerger et al., 2007); (b) the characterisation of rape myths as 'widely and persistently held' implies that a rape myth could lose its conceptual status as a rape myth if, over time, fewer people endorsed it.

Later work by Bohner et al. (1998) and Bohner et al. (2009) drew on the above considerations and moved rape myths further away from the concept of 'myths' and their veracity, proposing that rape myths are

> descriptive or prescriptive beliefs about rape (i.e., about its causes, context, consequences, perpetrators, victims, and their interac-tion) that serve to deny, downplay, or justify sexual violence that men commit against women. (Bohner et al., 2009; p. 19)

Bohner and colleagues' definition addresses many of the issues present in Lon-sway and Fitzgerald's (1994) definition and can, as such, arguably be considered more precise.

Recent developments within this field of research have seen useful meta-ana-lytic research and systematic reviews on the prevalence and correlates of rape myths (e.g., Persson & Dhingra, 2020; Suarez & Gadalla, 2010), which have fur-ther strengthened the understanding of this topic. In a recent meta-analysis and systematic review of ours (Persson & Dhingra, 2020), we considered RMA in conjunction with sexism and the victim-perpetrator relationship (i.e., what, if any, level of acquaintance existed between victim-survivor and perpetrator prior to the assault) among 47 individual studies. Through our analyses, we found that RMA correlated with victim blame in rape cases generally but did not interact with the victim–perpetrator relationship. This indicates that RMA remains an important correlate of victim blame across contexts, and that this is not notice-ably impacted by the prior relationship between the victim-survivor and perpe-trator. Future meta-research on rape myths will likely produce further valuable insights on the topic. A central question in the development of rape myths as a theory remains, however: what is the substance of rape myths?

What is the Substance of Rape Myths?

Myths. Myths are stories that are based on tradition, and while they may have some factual basis, they are largely exaggerated and cannot generally be falsified. Importantly, myths serve societal and cultural functions, in perpetuating cultural beliefs and identity, alongside prescribing behaviours and ways of thinking. Lonsway and Fitzgerald (1994) propose three key aspects of myths: (a) they are false and widely held beliefs; (b) they explain cultural phenomena; and (c) they justify existing arrangements. This means that rape myths do, on the surface, align well with the concept of 'myths', as they (a) are widely held (and mostly inaccurate, although as mentioned above, it is not always possible to test the veracity of these beliefs); (b) explain rape and rape culture; and (c) justify the existing patriarchal order.

While Burt (1980) and subsequent researchers give little justification for the conceptualisation of rape myths as 'myths', their feminist history and roots in feminist research and activism signpost at least two reasons for why this was logical. First, defining these beliefs as 'myths' alludes to a possibility of busting them through feminist consciousness-raising and education, which were central tenets of second-wave feminism more generally. As such, a key objective in the development of rape myths was to raise awareness of the realities of rape as faced by women, and to debunk common misconceptions about the causes, nature, and consequences of rape, particularly in the context of victim precipitation.[4] Second, conceptualising these beliefs as myths captured their pervasive nature within wider American culture and sought to highlight American culture as inherently patriarchal, which links with the societal functions of myths more generally (Burt, 1980; White, Strube, & Fisher, 1998). This, therefore, suggests that RMA was distinctly conceptualised within a wider environment of feminist activism and scholarship, i.e., to illuminate and 'correct' the dominant cultural narrative on rape. As such, the emphasis on the mythical and false nature of these beliefs made sense as the research broadly aimed to make a political statement, which was important for the collective advancement of women's rights in the context of rape and sexual violence. While the mythical nature of rape myths may have been important for early scholarly developments on rape culture, later developments sought to increase the scientific credibility of the construct and position rape myths more firmly in psychological theory.

Stereotypes.   Theorising by Lonsway and Fitzgerald (1994) has been pivotal in locating rape myths as stereotypes, rather than myths. Stereotypes are widely held and oversimplified images or ideas and, therefore, apply well to the nature of rape myths (Stuart, McKimmie, & Masser, 2019). Lonsway and Fitzgerald (1994; alongside Payne et al., 1999) noted that rape myths function in a similar manner to stereotypes, as they are culturally relevant not to the extent that they are true, but rather in their psychological and societal functions (as further noted in the definition above: '... serve to deny and justify male aggression against women'). Moreover, the conceptualisation of rape myths as stereotypes highlights that any given rape case may or may not conform to these stereotypical beliefs, but the cases that do (and are, inevitably, less common than non-stereotypical

---

[4]Victim precipitation is defined as any behaviour by the victim-survivor that be construed as having contributed to the sexual assault or rape in some way.

cases) will be taken as representative of sexual violence more generally. This is true for the example rape myth outlined above (i.e., that women that invite men home for a cup of coffee after a night out may want to have sex; Gerger et al., 2007), where inevitably, this situation will hold true for some people under some circumstances. Another highly relevant example is the belief that false rape allegations are commonplace, which we argue is central to how rape myths are maintained in the Western world today (as further outlined below). There are a small minority (around 3%; Kelly et al., 2005)[5] of false rape allegations (and, as such, going against the earlier mythological definitions of rape myths as consistently false), but this minority of cases generally receive a disproportionate amount of attention (Banet-Weiser, 2021). This attention has the impact of inflating the importance of false allegations in the context of rape, as opposed to much more frequent occurrence of actual rape, which mostly goes unreported and unpunished. As such, it is not necessarily relevant whether individual rape myths have some factual basis (although we note that they often lack at least a consistent factual basis); more relevant instead is (a) how these myths are taken as representative of heterosexual relations and sexual violence against women; and (b) the impact these myths have on women's rights more generally. Consequently, conceptualising rape myths as stereotypes (as opposed to myths) seems prudent and places these beliefs firmly within social psychology.

A Cognitive Schema.   More recently, there have been suggestions that rape myths should be conceptualised as a cognitive schema (e.g., by Bohner et al., 2009; Krahé, Temkin, Bieneck, & Berger, 2008). A cognitive schema can be understood as a pattern of thoughts that organises information about the world and influences how external events are perceived. Importantly, in serving as a general guide for how events should be perceived, cognitive schemas speed up information processing by making assumptions about event characteristics and 'filling in' missing information. This likely goes some way towards explaining how humans can mentally organise and keep track of large amounts of external stimuli (Krahé et al., 2008).

As incoming information is processed in line with existing schemas (and, consequently, rarely challenge beliefs already present), schemas are pervasive and difficult to fully change. An important aspect of a schema is the way in which it connects various types of beliefs in a wide-reaching information structure. One aspect of a schema can thus be activated by highlighting another related aspect – this speeds up information processing, but it can also result in biased judgements. Here, it is relevant to make a distinction between data-driven processing and schema-driven processing, drawing on the social-cognitive model of schematic decision-making (Kunda, 1999). Schema-driven processing draws on a

---

[5]Although false allegations may be 3% of all rapes reported to the police, the fact that at least 90% of rapes are never reported to the police (and this is a conservative estimate) suggests that of all rapes (those reported and not reported to the police), 0.03% are false allegations. However, we note that concerns have been raised by Rumney (2006) about the weak evidence base used to arrive at this prevalence estimate.

general knowledge structure that is pre-existing and assimilates incoming information to fit with these structures. In contrast, data-driven processing involves careful examination of each individual fact, to reach a supposedly objective decision (Krahé et al., 2008). Whether decisions made by humans can ever be truly objective is of course questionable. Schemas may be particularly important when there is little concrete information available, and schematic processing seems to be especially strong in ambiguous situations, where the schema 'fills in' the information gap(s) (Eyssel & Bohner, 2010).

Conceptualising rape myths as a schema, therefore, seems to fit well with how rape myths impact blame attributions in rape cases; these attributions seem to draw on myths and misconceptions surrounding rape (schematic processing), as opposed to facts of the case itself (data-driven processing). An important indication of rape myths as involving schematic processing is how specific stereotypes about rape and victim-survivors can be activated by presenting information that is broadly related to a general stereotype of rape, without making explicit reference to a specific rape myth (e.g., Süssenbach, Bohner, & Eyssel, 2012). This is further exemplified in the importance given to certain aspects of the victim-survivor's behaviour (such as intoxication or a previous relation to the perpetrator) as well as the inferring of information about a rape case even where this information was never explicitly presented (e.g., victim-survivor promiscuity). Smith (2018) highlighted that indirectly activating rape myths remains a successful defence strategy in the context of rape cases in English courts. While the outright engagement with rape myths is generally prevented in UK courts[6], barristers can successfully activate these attitudes by drawing on other aspects of the victim-survivor's behaviour or character (e.g., mental health issues) to influence jury decision-making.

The above goes some way towards explaining the pervasive nature of rape myths. Researchers such as Krahé et al. (2008) have suggested that the provision of clearer information about rape (e.g., legal definitions) does not reduce schema-driven processing in rape cases, as new information is assimilated into existing knowledge structures. In fact, additional information may *increase* social judgeability (i.e., relying on naïve theories or judgments to make decisions about others), which has been proposed as a key mechanism behind the influence of cognitive schemas on attributions made in rape cases (Eyssel & Bohner, 2010). This would, therefore, suggest that feminist consciousness-raising and education on the nature of rape may, in isolation, have little impact on reducing rape myths. We elaborate on this further in Chapter Seven, where we consider the limited effectiveness of strategies to address sexual violence behaviours and cognitions. Finally, conceptualising rape myths as a cognitive schema also highlights the importance of situating rape attributions in a broader societal context, as schemas about rape will be closely related to schemas about heterosexual intimacy and hostile views of women more generally. We examine the relationship between rape myths and other '-isms' in Chapter Six.

---

[6]We note that the United Kingdom does not have a unified court system – England and Wales have one system, Scotland another, and Norther Ireland a third.

Different Types of Rape Myths

The first attempt at distinguishing between different types of rape myths was undertaken by Schwendinger and Schwendinger (1974), who outlined five types of rape myths. Lonsway and Fitzgerald (1994) also alluded to different types of rape myths, although these were given as general examples, rather than formalised categories. The separation of rape myths into related constructs was further advanced by Payne et al. (1999), who proposed seven distinct categories of rape myths, some of which are still used. This categorisation was a key development in feminist theorising into rape, as it allowed for a finer conceptualisation of rape myths, alongside greater validity[7] and the ability to accurately measure these attitudes. Theoretically, a structural investigation would allow researchers to examine how the acceptance of different domains of rape myths varies between groups (e.g., women and men), as the nature of the specific myths may mean that some are more readily accepted than others. For instance, men may be more likely to endorse myths that justify rape, whereas women may be more likely to endorse myths that deny their personal vulnerability to being raped (this is further examined in Chapter Five, where we consider the gendered functions of RMA). It should, however, be noted that the empirical evidence for different domains as measured by the available RMA scales (as further detailed in Chapter Three) is varied and inconsistent. Contemporary investigations into rape myths (e.g., Bohner et al., 2009) have, based on the research outlined below, generally agreed upon four domains of rape myths:

- *Disbelief in claims and severity of rape* (e.g., 'false rape allegations are commonplace', 'women tend to exaggerate how much rape affects them')
- *Exonerate the perpetrator* (e.g., 'most men are over-sexed', 'rape occurs when a man's sex drive gets out of control')
- *Only certain types of women are raped* (e.g., 'usually it is women who do things like drink or take drugs and sleep around that are raped')
- *Blame the victim for the rape* (e.g., 'women often provoke rape through their appearance and/or behaviour')

Each of these is outlined further below.

Disbelief in Claims and Severity of Rape.   This domain concerns beliefs that downplay the prevalence and severity of rape, thus capturing the original idea behind rape myths as a theory, which was centred on these myths being *untrue* (i.e., rape is evidently very prevalent, with traumatic impacts on victim-survivors). This domain was present in the very early theorising on rape myths, such as rape perpetration being 'virtually impossible' if women resist (Schwendinger

---

[7]Validity refers to whether a construct or concept is logically and factually sound. Generally, validity relates to whether the construct can be measured accurately, and whether the measurement instruments used measure the correct 'thing' (Buntins, Buntins, & Eggert, 2017).

& Schwendinger, 1974), and that women often 'cry rape' without any substance (Lonsway & Fitzgerald, 1994).

Importantly, this domain captures convictions that false rape accusations are commonplace, and that many rape accusations are unfounded. We argue that as these myths become subtler, and change shape to fit cultural narratives (McMahon & Farmer, 2011; Payne et al., 1999), the belief that women routinely lie about rape has emerged as important for understanding how these myths are reproduced in modern society. The centrality of these beliefs likely stems from how rape cases are managed through court proceedings (i.e., defence strategies: where a typical defence against a rape accusation would be to imply that 'nothing' happened; Smith, 2018), and perhaps most importantly, how rape acquittals are understood by the public. Specifically, there appears to be a general conflation of rape acquittals with false allegations (Huntington, Berkowitz, & Orchowski, 2022), meaning that the latter is perceived to be more prevalent that it really is (especially given the considerable number of rape allegations that are dropped or acquitted; see also Rumney, 2006). This further establishes the self-perpetuating nature of rape myths (Bohner et al., 2009; Sinclair & Bourne, 1998), where high levels of perpetrator acquittal (in combination with low reporting and prosecution levels) enforce the belief that rape is not very common, or serious, and that false accusations are routinely made (if judging by non-convictions). In turn, this contributes to the broader legal and societal landscape, where women are seen as untrustworthy and malicious liars, which further contributes to these low reporting, prosecution, and conviction levels (Smith, 2018; Wennstam, 2002).

That women routinely lie about rape has seen renewed relevance in light of far-right men's rights activism (Gotell & Dutton, 2016), which we discuss in more detail in Chapter Six. This domain has also been highly relevant in response to accusations of public figures assaulting women, where the men themselves, as well as their supporters, can claim that accusations of this kind are personal vendettas or political tactics (Banet-Weiser, 2021). Finally, the belief that false rape accusations are prevalent plays an important role in exonerating the perpetrator, both from an outsider's perspective and from the point of view of the perpetrator himself.

Exonerate the Perpetrator of Rape. This domain encompasses beliefs that serve to exonerate and absolve perpetrators of rape. This exoneration often reflects two common themes: an overactive male sex drive and perpetrator intoxication. The overactive male sex drive as a fundamental and biological truth is a powerful cultural narrative across contexts (Bergenfeld, Lanzas, Trang, Sales, & Yount, 2022; Hlavka, 2014) and links RMA with gender stereotypes more generally (also further explored in Chapter Six). These attitudes towards the male sex drive would, at its most extreme, suggest that rape occur only when men are no longer able to contain themselves due to sexual arousal. Contemporary expressions of these beliefs are, of course, rarely this extreme, but stereotyped views of men's sex drive as aggressive, uncontrollable, and overwhelming still exist in contemporary discourse on heterosexuality (Hlavka, 2014). This is further exemplified in the relative commonplace suggestion that legalised prostitution or Managed Zones (e.g., Holbeck in Leeds, UK) would reduce the prevalence of rape, as men would then have alternative routes to sexual release (e.g., Bass, 2017). The suggestion that prostitution may 'solve' the problem of the overactive male sex has a relatively long history, as noted already by Schwendinger and Schwendinger (1974). In a contemporary context, this is rarely suggested as an official policy, but the argument does still reappear in public debates surrounding prostitution (Bindel, 2019). The notion that prostitution could reduce sexual violence against women[8] should be regarded with extreme caution, as these arguments ultimately reinforce stereotypical views of male sexuality, which may ultimately be key to perpetuating and normalising sexual violence.

Intoxication as causing rape is another central aspect of perpetrator exoneration. The centrality of this premise becomes somewhat ironic, given that alcohol functions to *increase* culpability for women (as further outlined below). Alcohol as functioning to excuse behaviour that would not normally be engaged in while sober (particularly for men) is a powerful cultural trope (McMahon & Farmer, 2011) and spans many moral and legal transgressions (e.g., aggression, infidelity, racism, sexism, etc.). It may, however, be particularly relevant for sexual behaviour, given that alcohol is perceived to increase sexual arousal (and thereby links with notions of the male sex drive as uncontrollable). Here, some feminist sexual violence theorists (e.g., Scully, 1990) have suggested that alcohol is not in itself important, but is rather the form of exoneration taken by strong cultural imperatives to excuse male behaviour. In other words, as intoxication is a culturally acceptable excuse for poor behaviour, it serves as a convenient go-to for accounting for male sexual aggression and may be as important for society (in explaining sexual aggression) as it is for perpetrators themselves. This also links with the societal functions of rape myths as explaining and downplaying sexual aggression against women more generally (see also Chapter Five). By invoking cultural notions of intoxication, a perpetrator is thereby able to concede to varying degrees of sexual assault (if admitted to), while still maintaining that they are not, in fact, a 'rapist'. Rather, they can claim that they are someone who did something 'stupid' when drunk. In fact, positioning rape as a morally reprehensible crime, but denying themselves the label of 'rapist' (as exonerating factors meant that their offence did not meet the high threshold for rape) seems to be central for how perpetrators exonerate themselves (Scully & Marolla, 1984).

The male sex drive as uncontrollable, alongside alcohol as an inhibitor, is implicitly important to most legal definitions of rape, which rest upon the premise that the perpetrator acted intentionally, and importantly, *understood* that the victim did not consent (i.e., 'person A does not reasonably believe that B consents'; Crown Prosecution Service, 2017). While supposedly objective, this premise inevitably draws

---

[8]Many feminist theorists also regard prostitution itself as sexual violence against women (e.g., Bindel, 2019; Dworkin, 1993; Ekis Ekman, 2011). This is also the perspective taken by countries such as Sweden (and more recently, France), where buying sexual access to someone is illegal.

on cultural beliefs about what is reasonable (and not), which interacts with rape myths to produce considerable issues in convicting men of rape. In an in-depth observational study of rape trials in English courts, Smith (2018) noted that many acquittals rested upon an inability to establish that the perpetrator understood that the victim-survivor did not consent. However, the court simultaneously agreed that the victim-survivor was telling 'her' truth. She noted that rape myths were central in establishing this 'truth', whereby the threshold for establishing a 'reasonable under-standing of non-consent' was set high enough to see a great number of acquittals, even in cases of considerable victim-survivor vulnerability and disability. Recent sexual assault legislation in Sweden from 2018 has attempted to overcome this issue by introducing a lesser offence category of 'negligent rape' for cases where consent had not been established, but where the perpetrator had not intended to commit rape. Within this offence, the perpetrator is considered as having been negligent in attempting to establish this consent. This, therefore, lowers the threshold for situa-tions that can be considered rape (Åklagarmyndigheten, 2021). As such, this defini-tion of rape seems to be informed by women's lived experience of sexual violence, where the impact is severe *regardless* of the intention of the perpetrator (i.e., irre-spective of whether he acted with intent or not). As Swedish courts have already seen an increase in rape convictions following this new legislation (although convic-tions for the specific offence of 'negligent rape' remain relatively few in number), further developments associated with this category of offences will be highly rel-evant for feminist researchers to follow (Nationellt Centrum för Kvinnofrid, 2021).

Beliefs around perpetrator exoneration further result in the belief that 'real' rape is rare, as most men who rape can be exonerated and are, thus, not 'real' rap-ists. This notion was important for early theorising on rape myths, which argued that 'real' rape is perceived as a rare event, not committed by 'normal' men but by 'bad men' (Scully, 1990; Scully & Marolla, 1984), and this belief continues to be relevant today. That rape is perceived as being committed by 'other men' also highlights the links between RMA and racism, where these 'other men' are often proposed to be immigrants and/or men of colour (Davis, 1981/2019). As such, the beliefs outlined above are somewhat contradictory: oversexed men are at risk of committing sexual assault (which presumably would indicate that *all men,* to a certain degree, are capable of committing rape), but, at the same time, 'real' rape is rare and committed only by 'other men'. This, therefore, further buttresses ten-dencies to blame the victim-survivor (as detailed below), as there is an implication that women need to be mindful of sexually arousing men without the intention of having sex (particularly where intoxication is involved), as men who are aroused are seen to lose control over their actions.

Only Certain Types of Women are Raped.   This domain concerns stereotypi-cal beliefs about women who are subjected to rape as being fundamentally differ-ent to other women. As such, these beliefs create a distinction between women who are at risk of being subjected to rape, and women who are not at risk of being subjected to rape, as linking to the personal characteristics of the women in question. This further highlights how stereotypes are important for how RMA is maintained as a cognitive schema. Here, through behaviour or other personal characteristics (often linking with sexism, as well as racism), a minority of women are regarded as inherently at risk of being subjected to rape. This ultimately positions most women as 'normal'/not at risk, and therefore not vulnerable to being subjected to rape. Reasons *why* people may perceive a woman to be the 'type' to be subjected to rape include (but are certainly not limited to) the woman: knowing the perpetrator (Persson & Dhingra, 2020, 2021), working in prostitution (Sprankle, Bloomquist, Butcher, Gleason, & Schaefer, 2018), having extra-marital sex (Viki & Abrams, 2002), being non-traditional/gender non-conforming (Grubb & Turner, 2012), and being intoxicated (Gravelin, Biernat, & Bucher, 2018). Importantly, this 'typing' of women shows considerable fluidity and can be applied post hoc, meaning that any woman who has been subjected to rape can, through some perceived fault of her own, be construed as having been predisposed to being subjected to rape.[9] This further emphasises that the relative veracity of individual rape myths is irrelevant; inevitably, some women who meet the 'criteria' for being a 'typical' rape victim-survivor will be subjected to rape, but these cases are taken as representative of rape victim-survivors more generally, in line with the stereotypical nature of many rape myths.

Believing that only certain types of women are subjected to rape (leaving most 'normal' women protected from this risk) was important for early conceptualisations of rape myths (e.g., Lonsway & Fitzgerald, 1994; Payne et al., 1999), which highlighted how these beliefs serve as a psychological buffer to women, to obscure the nature and prevalence of sexual violence, and the fact that all women are potentially at risk of rape. Beliefs in this domain are, therefore, likely powerful motivators for women, as well as men, to believe in rape myths. We elaborate further on this in Chapter Five. There is considerable overlap between this domain and that of victim blame as there are usually strong elements of victim blame involved in characterising a woman as the 'type' to be raped.

Blame the Victim for the Rape.   Finally, and perhaps most prominently in the context of RMA, is the set of beliefs that blame the victim-survivor for the rape. These beliefs encompass attitudes that position the woman as the cause of rape, through a plethora of reasons (some of these are outlined above; for reviews, see Grubb & Turner, 2012, and Gravelin et al., 2018). In this sense, these beliefs both contradict and complement the exoneration of the perpetrator domain, where rape is seen as being driven by *male* behaviour (e.g., intoxication) or the innate features of men (e.g., a naturally high male sex drive). Consequently, male behaviour is regarded as an excuse for rape, whereas female behaviour is seen as a cause of rape, particularly through its *impact* on male behaviour (e.g., dressing provocatively can *cause* men to become oversexed and unable to control themselves). This further establishes the complex nature of rape myths and confirms that rape myths are not about truth per se, but rather about cultural narratives on how truth is established (MacKinnon, 1989/1991; Smith, 2018).

This domain, however, presents several theoretical and methodological difficulties, owing to its considerable overlap with the other three domains, as well as its

---

[9]An important reason for this is that victim blame can be inferred from many factors (Gravelin et al., 2018) and can as such tap into characteristics of almost all women.

overlap with other variables (e.g., victim and perpetrator culpability[10]) commonly measured in conjunction with rape myths. Specifically, 'blame the victim' overlaps with 'exonerate the perpetrator', as well as 'only certain types of women are raped'. In fact, the exoneration of the perpetrator domain largely rests on the behaviour of the victim-survivor (as causing the perpetrator to rape), and the positioning of only certain women as potential victim-survivors of rape almost always occurs through a constructed 'fault' of hers (e.g., sexual promiscuity). This, therefore, makes it difficult to theoretically separate these three constructs, as the blaming of the victim may be too 'noisy' throughout all aspects of rape myths. This is something researchers measuring RMA should bear in mind, and we will elaborate further on measurement difficulties in this area of research in Chapter Three.

Taken together, it is evident that the domain articulation of rape myths has been considerably improved with more recent investigations into the common features of rape myths. This has worked to considerably strengthen the theoretical power of rape myths and thus provided a useful tool for feminist researchers. While the current domains are of value, it is likely that further adjustments are necessary, particularly regarding the final category: 'blame the victim', as the breadth of this category and its overlap with the other categories present conceptual as well as practical difficulties. Currently, there is also a lack of empirical evidence supporting the articulation of the different domains of rape myths.

Rape Myths and Black and South Asian Feminist Thought

Much of the past theorising on rape, and particularly on the concept of rape myths, has come from a place of limited diversity, typically centring on the voices of White, academically educated women. Similarly, sample demographics of much of the original research on rape myths have also been restricted to White, university-educated participants (White et al., 1998), which is reflected in much of the research outlined above. This is an important limitation of rape myths as a theoretical construct, and it has also served to obfuscate differences in rape theorising between mainstream and Black and South Asian feminism (Collins, 1990/2009). Before proceeding, however, it is important to note that while Black feminism and South Asian feminism are of course distinct feminist movements in their own right, they share many similarities in critiquing dominant perspectives (e.g., mainstream feminism, as well as general anti-racism activism). Both groups of women can also be said to be positioned as 'outsiders-within' (Collins, 1990/2009; Lorde, 1984/2007) feminism as well as civil rights/anti-racism movements. South Asian feminist organising in the UK also drew considerable inspiration from Black feminist activism in the UK and US (Anitha & Dhaliwal, 2019), both in terms of fighting racism and in fighting for worker's rights, and in working

---

[10]For example, some of our data (Persson & Dhingra, 2021) on 252 participants indicate significant correlations between RMA and victim and perpetrator culpability. Specifically, as RMA increases, so does perceived victim culpability; conversely, as RMA increases, perceived perpetrator culpability decreases.

towards a more inclusive feminism. This, therefore, suggests that there is value in drawing parallels between these groups in the context of RMA theory, which we do in the sections below.

The limited diversity in rape myth research has been suggested to reflect past demographics of mainstream feminism (and academia more broadly), which has been (and still is) homogeneous in terms of social class and ethnicity. However, the over-representation of White rape myth researchers might also be explained by structural racism, rather than the quantity of researchers. This has also been an issue in psychological research and knowledge production more generally, where women of colour have largely been overlooked, unless focusing on pathology (Spates, 2012). Further, academic journals are dominated by White researchers, which has implications for who and what is included and excluded from the scientific record (Roberts, Bareket-Shavit, Dollins, Goldie, & Mortenson, 2020). This is incredibly problematic, as rape and the fear of rape are threats to *all* women and addressing sexual violence within society has great potential for improving the lives of women across social and ethnic groups. Indeed, improving provisions for rape victim-survivors (through strengthening feminist theory) may be of particular benefit to socially disadvantaged groups. These groups are likely to face considerable barriers to accessing publicly available resources and may have limited means and social capital required for navigating complex barriers to accessing support (Anitha & Dhaliwal, 2019; Gill, 2009). People belonging to disadvantaged groups are also susceptible to being subjected to situations (e.g., insecure housing; precarious employment) that can increase the risk of sexual violence (Davis, 1981/2019). As such, consideration of those who have not come from a place of privilege, even before being subjected to sexual violence, is necessary to strengthen theorising on rape, as captured in Crenshaw's (1989) notion of 'but for' privilege.[11]

As noted by Davis (1981/2019), the history of feminism has largely ignored the specific concerns of women of colour and working class women, and some feminist activism has been seen to lack practical utility beyond theory. The limited practical relevance of certain aspects of feminist activism also applies to more recent issues faced by South Asian women in the UK today (Anitha & Dhaliwal, 2019). There has, within mainstream feminism, been an assumption that all aspects of sexual violence affect *all* women in the same way, which is clearly not the case (Gill, 2009). This likely stems from how mainstream feminism has implicitly equated the experience of women to mean the experience of White women (Lorde, 1984/2007). Although mainstream feminism has traditionally been largely White, there has been important theorising on rape emanating from Black and South Asian feminism. These perspectives are pivotal when considering the history of anti-rape activism, and provide direction for how feminist thought can move forward in this area. We seek to highlight some of these issues below, although these are by no means extensive.

---

[11]Crenshaw's (1989) notion of 'but for' privilege is a critique of the singular strategy of using only sex or ethnicity to ascertain effects of discrimination. This 'but for' discourse centres those who would be privileged *but for* their ethnicity or sex and therefore makes invisible those with intersecting identities.

Intersectionality and Racist Victim Blaming. In her work (and as highly applicable to rape and victim-survivor blame), Davis (1981/2019) alludes to the concept of intersectionality, which was formally named and conceptualised by Crenshaw (1989) a few years later. Broadly, intersectionality emphasises the compounding effects of inequalities and oppressions that work together (as well as in isolation, as sometimes an individual will face specific prejudice based on mainly one identity) to put considerable pressures on individuals, as they experience prejudice and discrimination based on multiple identities. The combination of identities also creates new and highly specific stereotypes that only apply where identities intersect. An example in the context of rape is the highly specific nature of racist stereotypes about Black women's promiscuity and animalistic nature (Davis, 1981/2019; Collins, 1990/2009; Crenshaw, 1989). This does not originate solely from sexism or from racism (and, as such, is not applied to all women, or all Black people) but is a unique stereotype levelled at Black women specifically. This stereotype originates from a legal unwillingness to consider Black women victim-survivors of rape (in the context of past chastity laws; Cocca, 2004), which still has considerable implications for how Black rape victim-survivors are perceived, and how perpetrator defence strategies are negotiated in a court setting in the context of rape myths. Drawing on cultural stereotypes of Black women as promiscuous, emotional, and unreliable (Collins, 1990/2009), barristers habitually affirm these images depicting Black women as 'welfare queens' and 'jezebels', rendering their reports of violence dismissible (e.g., Taslitz, 1999).

Moreover, as noted by Smith (2018), the nature of RMA varies according to victim-survivor socio-economic status and ethnicity. Specifically, victim-survivor blame beliefs are particularly salient for working class and Black women, as prejudiced beliefs about these groups already include fecklessness, sexual promiscuity, and deceitfulness (Collins, 1990/2009). While these aspects of victim-survivor behaviour are certainly invoked for many women in the context of rape (regardless of class or ethnicity), they are particularly pervasive for socially disadvantaged groups. Relatedly, sexual violence against South Asian women has traditionally been viewed as a cultural and ethnic problem (as linking to racist perpetrator rape myths, further outlined below), which is regarded as separate from mainstream society (Anitha & Dhaliwal, 2019). This further emphasises the utility in considering rape myths as a cognitive schema; in rape contexts, it may only be necessary to activate beliefs broadly related to rape myths (e.g., racism, classism, ableism), and these can then indirectly activate interconnected beliefs about racist victim-survivor precipitation and blame. The concept of intersectionality does, as such, have considerable implications for RMA theory, as it highlights that diversifying feminism will not be sufficient to end violence against women or victim-survivor blaming (although diversifying feminism is of course necessary), but rather the need for future theory to fundamentally integrate and change the analytic framework for how rape myths are understood. Importantly, rape myths enforce male domination over women, but they also manifest general dominant group control over subordinated groups; as noted by Crenshaw (1989), in the context of women of colour, this dominant group may sometimes be male and sometimes White.

Apart from administering measures of RMA alongside measures of racism (e.g., the Modern Racism Scale; McConahay, 1983) and other forms of prejudice, there has been limited direct re-conceptualisation of RMA in the context of racism, and how it applies to people of colour specifically. A notable exception to this is White et al. (1998), who proposed a Black feminist model of RMA, focusing on how feminist and racial identity development impact RMA. The authors argue that depending on the stage someone is at in their feminist and racial identity model, they may view rape through the lens of racism or through the lens of sexism. If viewed mainly through the lens of racism, the issue of rape can be seen as divisive to the cause of Black activism and social advancement (and RMA is high), but if viewed through the lens of feminism, the issue of rape is not seen as divisive to social advancement, and RMA is low. This study provides a useful consideration of identity development within Black feminist activism, and importantly, the authors added several items to the RMA scale (as further outlined in Chapter Three; Burt, 1980) to reflect rape discourses in the African American community. Consequently, this study gives a useful indication of how RMA can be potentially re-conceptualised within a Black feminist context.

Racist Perpetrator Myths.   A relatively understudied aspect within mainstream RMA theory is the notion of the racist perpetrator myth. Black feminist thought has, however, long noted the racist undertones of many myths about perpetrators of rape (e.g., Davis, 1981/2019) and how rape myths have served to entrench racism as well as sexism. While on the surface this may appear to have few implications for rape victim-survivors, as outlined above, racism and sexism are interconnected, and if rape myths support racist myths (even if mainly about perpetration), this ultimately does a disservice to victim-survivors as well.

Specifically, racist rape myths position men of colour as the most likely perpetrators of rape, particularly in the context of White women. This links with historical notions of Black sexuality as uncontrollable; Black men as being seen as more likely to rape is, therefore, the 'twin myth' (Davis, 1981/2019) of Black women's perceived promiscuity. White et al. (1998) give an example of such a rape myth; 'Most rapes are committed by Black men'; this can easily be applied to a contemporary UK context, both in the context of individual men of colour and in how 'Asian grooming gangs' (i.e., men of primarily South Asian descent grooming young and vulnerable White women for sex, as coming to light in multiple locations throughout the UK) have been erroneously positioned as the main context of sexual violence perpetration against young women and girls (Cockbain, 2013). This further affirms the self-perpetuating notion of RMA and interlinked racism; both the CJS and the wider media pay more attention to perpetrators of colour, as opposed to White perpetrators. Because of this, men of colour are taken as representative of rape perpetrators more generally. Again, this further supports the relative irrelevancy of the veracity of rape myths; inevitably, there will be perpetrators from all ethnic groups, but the perpetrators that fit with cultural racist stereotypes will receive disproportionate attention.

The above further links with central tenets of rape myths more generally, where perpetrator exoneration to an extent relies on positioning rape as being committed by 'other' men, both in terms of deviancy as well as ethnicity. For instance, research by Bongiorno, McKimmie, and Masser (2016) suggests that people are more willing to be lenient towards a culturally similar perpetrator when the victim-survivor is counter-stereotypical (i.e., does not align with public stereotypes about typical victim-survivor behaviour). This, therefore, emphasises the interaction between myths about perpetrators and victim-survivors of rape. The way in which rape myths are moulded to align with other forms of oppression in society (e.g., racism) to serve sexist, as well as far-right agendas (both consciously and unconsciously), further emphasises the need for an intersectional conceptualisation of rape myths. Consequently, future rape myth research may need to incorporate a consideration of racist rape myths, as opposed to only measuring RMA in conjunction with other prejudices.

Finally, Crenshaw (1989) suggests that the history of persecuting Black men for sexual crimes they did not commit (as linking with the origins of the racist perpetrator myth) has contributed to some Black women viewing feminist theory with suspicion, and it may unfortunately prevent Black women from wanting to engage with feminist theory on the topic of rape. South Asian women in the UK may have similar reservations about White feminism more generally, and they may also be deterred from engaging with broader theorising on rape prevention because of racist perpetrator myths concerning South Asian men as the main perpetrators of rape and grooming in the UK (Anitha & Dhaliwal, 2019). In their Black feminist model of RMA, White et al. (1998) also stress that a historical understanding of racism is necessary to understand Black people's attitudes to rape. Finally, it is likely that, because of shared experiences of racism, women of colour share more political solidarity with men of the same ethnicity than White women do with White men. As such, while RMA measurement may need to be revised to account for racist dimensions of rape myths, feminist theorising into rape and rape prevention more generally should account for the historical context of rape among people of colour. The above also highlights the need to tackle general prejudice in the context of rape prevention, rather than focusing solely on rape myths and ignoring the broader societal contexts in which they are maintained. This is further considered in Chapter Six.

Ways Forward in Working with Rape Myths

1. Rape myths as a theory is firmly anchored in feminist scholarship and activism and is best understood with this context in mind. Further, rape myths are best understood as seeking to answer long-standing questions about the sexual violence facing women, and importantly, how this violence is perpetuated by, and perpetuates, gender inequality. Because of this, rape myth should continue to be a prioritised area of research for feminists.
2. Rape myths are best conceptualised as a cognitive schema, made up of stereotypical beliefs about the nature of rape, victim-survivors, and perpetrators. Future theoretical work should distance rape myths from the concept

of 'myths', as these are poorly defined and lack empirical utility. Future work should also focus less on the veracity of these beliefs and focus more on how stereotypical rape cases are taken as representative of rape more generally.

3. While the different rape myth domains have theoretical value, further empirical research is needed to establish the validity of these categories. Future research may need to focus on the domain of 'blame the victim' in particular and consider whether this may be too integral to the theory of rape myths to be considered a separate category of beliefs.

4. Rape myths will remain theoretically impoverished unless it is further considered in the context of racism, focusing specifically on an intersectional understanding of the experience and impact of sexual violence. For feminist scholarship on rape myths to be relevant to all women, racist rape myths about victim-survivors and perpetrators need to be considered for rape myth theory and incorporated into the measurement of RMA.

Conclusion

This chapter has examined the history of rape myths and its conceptualisation into the measurable construct of RMA. We conclude that it is necessary to position RMA within its feminist history to fully understand it as a scholarly theory and to regard it as a kind of consciousness-raising strategy with distinctly political implications of improving the lives of women. By reviewing the development of RMA into a multi-domain construct including various suggestions as to what rape myths 'are', we conclude that rape myths are best conceptualised as a cognitive schema made up of stereotypical beliefs about the nature of rape, victim-survivors, and perpetrators. It is, however, clear that rape myths as a theory is limited by its lack of engagement with Black and South Asian feminism. Here, we echo concerns articulated by Lorde (1984/2007, p. 117), in that 'ignoring the differences of race between women and the implications of those differences presents the most serious threat to the mobilisation of women's joint power', and we recommend that, to become relevant for the lives of all women, RMA as a theory must begin to incorporate intersectionality as a foundational principle.

Chapter Three

Assessing Rape Myths

Chapter Overview

This chapter provides an overview of how rape attributions are typically researched and situates RMA assessment within this context. Expanding on considerations from Chapter Two, we elaborate on why it has been important for feminists to develop a more precise assessment of rape myths. We further outline different approaches towards RMA assessment, focusing on the most widely used RMA scales. We then signpost other variables often measured in conjunction with RMA, and how these may be measured. We further consider some of the many challenges involved in researching rape attributions, as well as the specific issues involved in measuring RMA. Here, we make some tangible recommendations for future research in this area and exemplify this through a case study of a reproducible research project that we conducted on RMA.

An Overview of Research into Rape Attributions

Rape attributions are typically measured in an experimental (quantitative) context, which is true of RMA as well. While there has been insightful qualitative research on the topic of rape myths (e.g., Bergenfeld et al., 2022), as well as content analyses of rape myths on social media platforms such as Twitter (Stabile, Grant, Purohit, & Rama, 2019; Stubbs-Richardson, Rader, & Cosby, 2018), RMA conceptualised as an attitude is typically measured quantitatively, largely because assessing this attitude relies on it being *measured* (Suarez & Gadalla, 2010) rather than explored. This approach to rape myths may, therefore, be considered somewhat contradictory to traditional feminist research, which has historically prioritised qualitative scholarship (e.g., Collins, 1990/2009; Harding, 2004; Smith, 1989) in an effort to capture non-dominant perspectives. We note, however, that there is no one feminist perspective, and hence, no one feminist methodology, and agree with Kelly, Regan, and Burton's (1992) assertion that, 'what makes feminist research feminist is less about method used, and more how it is used and what it is used for' (p. 150). Consequently, it is possible that the development of RMA into a quantitatively measured construct (Burt, 1980) can, at least partially, account

Rape Myths: Understanding, Assessing, and Preventing, 29–51
Copyright © 2022 by Sofia Persson and Katie Dhingra
Published under exclusive licence by Emerald Publishing Limited
doi:10.1108/978-1-80071-152-520220003

for its current popularity as a research topic, as it allows for large-scale and efficient data collection through online platforms.

Experimental research into rape attributions has a long and situationally diverse history (Burt, 1980; Fakunmoju, Abrefa-Gyan, Maphosa, & Gutura, 2021). There are, however, many commonalities in how this research has been conducted, with slight variation(s) depending on the exact target variables. Typically, participants are presented with details of a rape case, which are manipulated according to research objectives (e.g., the victim–perpetrator relationship; victim/perpetrator intoxication). There may be some variation in how these cases are presented (e.g., video or audio material; fictitious court documents; staged victim testimonies; newspaper articles; Persson & Dhingra, 2020), but the most used method can arguably be said to be the vignette.[1] Advantages (Steiner, Atzmüller, & Su, 2017) of the vignette include the relative ease with which it can be produced and distributed (as opposed to say, a video, which would require actors and filming equipment), that it allows for the convenient manipulation of variables, as well as the fact that any extraneous variables[2] can be kept to minimum (e.g., victim-survivor appearance).[3] Any relevant moderating variables (i.e., variables that affect the strength and direction of a relationship between variables) are measured before the vignette and outcome variables (e.g., victim-survivor/perpetrator blame) are measured afterwards. Mediating relationships (i.e., mechanisms behind observed effects) can also be measured. Consequently, this method of conducting research can provide rich and informative data, which can address a multitude of research questions relating to rape attributions and stereotyping.

Research into RMA

One of the major consequences of formalising rape myths into a coherent theory was the ability for it to be measured as RMA, as Burt originally did in 1980. Rather than being purely theoretical or exploratory (e.g., as in Brownmiller's considerations on rape culture from 1975), this allowed for rape myths to be empirically researched, which in turn allowed for an integration of rape myths within psychological theory. Empiricism (i.e., where information is acquired by observation or experimentation) may be particularly important for feminist research (and as such for research into rape myths), as traditionally, feminist inquiry has not been taken seriously by the mainstream (Westmarland & Bows, 2018), and women's voices have often been sidelined in mainstream discourses

---

[1] A vignette is a short fictitious story about an event or situation, which can be altered to address variables of interest. See Figure 1 for an example.

[2] In an experiment, an extraneous variable is any variable that you are not investigating that can potentially affect the outcomes of your research.

[3] A vignette may not be automatically high in validity, and care needs to be taken in design and implementation (Steiner et al., 2017). We address this issue and make recommendations for how to improve the quality of rape attribution research in the sections below.

(Murphy et al., 2020). In other words, as feminist research has been accused of lacking objectivity (failing, of course, to recognise that all research inquiry is inherently subjective; D'Ignazio & Klein, 2020), the ability to implement feminist theory in empirical research may be particularly important.

Before proceeding, it is important to consider how RMA assessment relates to what rape myths are perceived as 'being', which we discussed in more detail in Chapter Two. What rape myths 'are' directly impacts the level at which RMA is measured, and how it is conceptualised in the context of experimental research. Burt's (1980) original conceptualisation operationalised RMA as an attitude (although see Chapter Two for other, related conceptualisations) located *within the individual*, which was considered relatively stable (outside the context of attempting to alter it in some way, following a targeted intervention). This continued being the way in which RMA was measured, where the underlying assumption was of RMA as a set of beliefs that impacted the way in which rape cases were perceived. In other words, someone's level of RMA was considered to generally predict their evaluation of different situations of rape and not the other way around. There have been attempts to conceptualise RMA as *externally* located, i.e., as a feature of the rape case itself (i.e., grading different rape cases as either low or high in rape myth alignment, e.g., Hockett & Saucier, 2015). However, this fails to account for how features of the rape case will be interpreted *differently* depending on someone's personal level of RMA. For instance, someone low in RMA would theoretically pay little attention to the level of intoxication of the victim-survivor or perpetrator, but someone high in RMA would view this as casting doubt on the woman's account. Moreover, in line with the schematic nature of rape myths, those high in RMA might fill in the gaps of a case with details affirming victim-survivor blame strategies (e.g., Eyssel & Bohner, 2010), further emphasising that the precise details of the case are less important here. As such, it is sensible to align research in this area with the original conceptualisation of rape myths, and measure RMA as an attitude, rather than as a feature of the rape case itself.

Why Measure Rape Myths?

As Burt (1980) noted, there are several advantages of treating RMA as a measurable construct. The measurement of RMA allows for an examination into the prevalence, antecedents, as well as consequences of these beliefs, all of which are important in a feminist context. First, establishing prevalence is a crucial aspect of raising awareness of the realities of sexual assault and rape facing women. Moreover, the measurement of rape myths allows for an examination into the context and antecedents of rape myths (i.e., what precedes and correlates with RMA), and what other constructs are important for understanding the maintenance of these beliefs. This accurately situates men's sexual violence against women within a broader structure of gender inequality and establishes that rape myth endorsing beliefs exist in the context of a patriarchal society. Finally, by measuring RMA, researchers can explore the consequences of these beliefs, at both individual and societal levels. This has resulted in a valuable expansion of feminist theory (e.g., in the exploration of how rape myths impact rape perpetration and perpetrator leniency), and it has also strengthened the feminist understanding of women's lived experiences of the criminal justice system (CJS). The identification of the negative consequences of these beliefs has prompted investigations into potential interventions to reduce RMA (e.g., Parratt & Pina, 2017). Although these interventions have been moderately successful (as further elaborated on in Chapter Seven), it does nonetheless provide a foundation for future research in this area as, ultimately, the objective is not merely to observe these misunderstandings about rape but to correct them. A full summary of why it is advantageous to be able to measure rape myths can be found in Table 1.

Table 1.   Why Measure Rape Myths?

• **Scientific credibility**

The formal measurement of RMA establishes scientific credibility and positions feminist research within empirical psychology and criminology.

• **Prevalence**

By measuring rape myths, the prevalence of RMA both generally and within specific groups (e.g., police, medical professions) can be explored. By doing this, rape myths are established as a problem in society, something that has the potential to attract much-needed funding for victim-survivor provision.

• **Antecedents**

By measuring RMA in conjunction with other relevant constructs (e.g., sexism, racism), a feminist context to these beliefs can be established. This allows for an expansion of the theory behind RMA and provides valuable knowledge on the societal biases that allow for the perpetuation and maintenance of rape myths.

• **Consequences**

The measurement of RMA has allowed feminist research to signpost the negative consequences of these beliefs (e.g., sexual violence perpetration, perpetrator leniency, etc.), something that further establishes the importance of exploring these attitudes. It also aligns with feminist traditions of centring women's lived experience of sexual violence.

• **Interventions**

Alongside knowledge on the societal context of these beliefs, RMA measurement allows researchers to explore the potential impact of interventions to reduce these attitudes.

How to Measure Rape Myths

RMA is traditionally assessed through a scale where items tap into central tenets of rape myths (as outlined in more detail in the previous chapter); there may be some variation here, as rape myth definitions and the conceptualisation of specific rape myth domains may vary between researchers. Some scales (e.g., the Acceptance of Modern Myths about Sexual Aggression (AMMSA) scale; Gerger et al., 2007) have also established their own domain categories, but the empirical support for these in a measurement context is currently scant. If implemented in experimental research, RMA is often treated as a moderator, or the research explores how RMA is associated with other variables (e.g., through correlational analyses) or how it may predict other variables (e.g., through regression analyses). While RMA can be used as outcome variable,[4] the degree to which RMA can change following experimental manipulation is currently unclear (as further elaborated on in Chapter Seven), meaning that the utility of this type of implementation is not yet firmly established. There are other variables (e.g., victim-survivor blame, sentencing decisions, etc.) that can be used as proxies for RMA and can function as suitable outcome variables, but there would likely be value in developing specific outcome-oriented RMA measures as well. Below is an outline of the most widely used RMA scales and their historical and contemporary contexts.

Rape Myth Acceptance Scale (RMAS; Burt, 1980).   The RMAS was the first scale specifically devised to assess RMA empirically and is still used widely today. A meta-analysis by Suarez and Gadalla (2010) noted that 74% of US and Canadian studies (*n* = 27) used the RMAS; our meta-analysis (Persson & Dhingra, 2020) found that 28% of studies measuring RMA in conjunction with the victim–perpetrator relationship used the RMAS. The scale was originally developed on 598 adult US women and men and has since been implemented in a wide array of contexts (i.e., in samples of students, adults drawn from the general population, therapists, police officers, offenders; Suarez & Gadalla, 2010). This scale contains 14 items (reduced from 19 items in Burt's original 1980 research), which are measured on 7-point (*strongly agree* to *strongly disagree*) and 5-point (*almost all* to *almost none;* or *always* to *never*) scales. Items do not tap onto any specific structure of RMA.

Costin R Scale (Costin, 1985).   The Costin R Scale draws on and extends work by Feild (1978). It consists of 20 items, which load onto three domains: (a) women's responsibility and causal role in rape, (b) the role of consent in rape, and (c) rapist's role and motivation. The initial sample used to devise the scale consisted of 762 university staff and students. The scale is answered on a 7-point scale; the original study did not specify the exact phrasing of the scale's response options, but that responses should ask for agreement or disagreement with the statements presented. This scale is used less often than the RMAS and the Illinois Rape Myth Acceptance Scale (IRMAS); none of the studies in Suarez and Gadalla's (2010) meta-analysis used this scale, as compared to 17% in our (Persson & Dhingra, 2020) sample.

---

[4]The effectiveness of a RMA-reducing intervention can be examined by comparing RMA scores of the same group before and after an intervention, or by comparing RMA scores between two different groups, where one receives the intervention, and the other does not (Flores & Hartlaub, 1998).

IRMAS (Payne et al., 1999).   Payne et al. (1999) identified several issues with earlier RMA scales such as the RMAS, which led to the development of the IRMAS. The IRMAS sought to provide a clearer conceptualisation of rape myths and addressed issues relating to wording and clarity, colloquialism, and response sets.[5] The IRMAS is still widely used (16% prevalence in the sample by Suarez and Gadalla, 2010, and 28% prevalence in Persson & Dhingra, 2020). The IRMAS was initially developed using 604 participants and then refined through five further studies. It consists of seven domains, which also serve as sub-scales: (a) she asked for it, (b) it wasn't really rape, (c) he didn't mean to, (d) she wanted it, (e) she lied, (f) rape is a trivial event, and (g) rape is a deviant event. These sub-scales clearly map onto the overall belief system underlying RMA as a theory, which suggests that this scale has good face validity. The longer version of the scale consists of 45 items, and the shorter version (IRMA-SF) consists of 20 items. Questions are answered on a 7-point scale (*not at all agree* to *very much agree*). Recent research (IRMA-S; Thelan & Meadows, 2021) has sought to further adapt the IRMAS to enable it to capture even subtler rape myths, but the results indicated only very modest variations in responding between the new measure (IRMA-S) and the original one.

AMMSA (Gerger et al., 2007).   The AMMSA was designed to account for a number of weaknesses of past scales, most notably the frequency of positive skews (i.e., that RMA scores cluster at the low end of the scale, indicating, not always accurately, lower levels of RMA), which Gerger et al. (2007) suggest is a result of the bluntness of many of the original RMA questionnaire items (e.g., 'A woman who is raped might as well relax and enjoy it' and 'Women often provoke rape through their appearance or behavior'). A central aim in the development of the AMMSA, therefore, was to account for the subtlety of modern RMA[6] as well as to provide more modern language, less reliant on colloquialism. The AMMSA was validated through four studies, on a total of 1,279 participants who were German and English speaking.

The AMMSA consists of 30 items and reflects 5 content domains: (a) denial of the scope of the problem, (b) antagonism towards victims' demands, (c) lack of support for policies designed to help alleviate the effects of sexual violence, (d) beliefs that male coercion forms a natural part of sexual relationships, and (e) beliefs that exonerate the perpetrator by blaming the victim or the circumstances. Like the IRMAS, these content categories reflect the underlying structure of rape myth beliefs, indicating good face validity. Some researchers (e.g., Thelan & Meadows, 2021) have, however, noted the considerable overlap between the AMMSA's content categories and general sexist beliefs (e.g., that male coercion

---

[5]Response sets refer to patters of responding to a questionnaire; these can range from the unbiased (and arguably more accurate) to response-based social desirability or malingering.

[6]An example of a contemporary and more subtle rape myth is one that blames victim-survivors for alcohol consumption, as opposed to more overt rape myths of the past that would *directly* blame victim-survivors for rape.

forms a natural part of sexual relationships) meaning that the scale may not exclusively measure RMA. This highlights many difficulties involved in measuring a construct embedded in sexism and negative views of women more generally. The scale is scored on a 7-point scale (*completely disagree* to *completely agree*). The AMMSA has been mainly used in Northern European contexts; none of the sampled studies in Suarez and Gadalla (2010) used this scale, as compared to 28% of the studies in our meta-analysis (Persson & Dhingra, 2020).

Updated Illinois Rape Myth Acceptance Scale (U-IRMAS; McMahon & Farmer, 2011; Payne et al., 1999). The U-IRMAS attempted to account for validity issues of the original IRMAS. These validity issues stemmed from the outdated nature of the original scale, which is perhaps to be expected given how old it is. McMahon and Farmer (2011) noted that the original language of the IRMAS now seems colloquial and dated, and that rape attribution measurements, by their very nature, require culturally appropriate language to be fully valid. With a specific aim to capture victim blame and subtle rape myths, the U-IRMAS was developed following focus groups with sexual violence professionals as well as undergraduates. The scale consists of five sub-scales (as based on the original IRMAS): (a) she asked for it, (b) it wasn't really rape, (c) he didn't mean to, (d) he didn't mean to (intoxication), and (e) she lied. The remaining IRMAS subscales were excluded. The splitting of 'he didn't mean to' into two domains signals the increased, and distinct, importance of male intoxication in exonerating the perpetrator. We discuss some of the potential reasons for this in Chapter Two. Research into the differential predictive validity (i.e., the extent to which these sub-scales are differentially related to other variables) of these seven factors is lacking, and the scale is usually treated as measuring a one-dimensional construct (i.e., overall RMA).

The scale consists of 22 statements; most are based on the original items in the IRMAS but modified to account for validity issues, and a minority are newly added items that aim to capture subtle rape myths. Questions are answered on a 5-point scale (*strongly agree* to *strongly disagree*). A higher score indicates a greater rejection of rape myths. The scale was validated on 900 undergraduate students. The scale is used less often than the RMAS and the IRMAS (Persson & Dhingra, 2020).

Other Relevant Variables

There are several additional variables that are typically measured in conjunction with RMA in the context of rape attributions. Below is an overview of some of the more common ones; this is of course not exhaustive, and variables measured will vary depending on specific research objectives.

Victim and Perpetrator Culpability. Often, RMA is measured in conjunction with attributions towards the victim-survivor and perpetrator of rape, most commonly in the context of vignette-based research, where participants are asked to attribute blame in a sexual assault case. This makes sense given the feminist foundations of rape myths, where a key objective has been to highlight the negative consequences of these beliefs; increased victim culpability and reduced perpetrator culpability (especially in the CJS) provide a clear indication of a lack of justice for rape victim-survivors. Meta-analytic research confirms that RMA is associated with increased victim culpability, and reduced perpetrator culpability (Persson & Dhingra, 2020; Suarez & Gadalla, 2010). Although it could be considered redundant to administer both victim and perpetrator culpability scales (as they could be regarded as mutually exclusive) typically, separate scales for victim-survivor and perpetrator are administered. Based on some of our own research (Persson & Dhingra, 2021), this seems to be the most prudent approach, as although victim and perpetrator culpability do correlate, it is not a perfect negative correlation.[7] This indicates that participants can hold both the victim-survivor and perpetrator culpable simultaneously, which, from a theoretical perspective, is relevant to capture.

In previous work of ours, we have noted that a major issue in rape culpability research is that 'culpability' or 'blame' have been conceptualised in a variety of ways (e.g., blame, culpability, responsibility, guilt, and control). This is an issue, as these variations may limit the degree to which findings can be compared across studies, as they may, ultimately, be measuring different attributions. While there is inconsistent evidence about the empirical difference between these conceptualisations (e.g., Gravelin et al., 2018; Richardson & Campbell, 1980; Shaver & Drown, 1986), recent exploratory analyses of ours (Persson & Dhingra, 2021) indicated that women subjected to rape were attributed significantly more control, than blame or responsibility. Here, our findings suggest that people might be more willing to think that the victim-survivor could have avoided the rape if she had acted differently, than to directly blame her, or hold her responsible for the offence, which likely links to the increasingly subtle nature of victim-survivor blame. This has considerable implications for RMA, as different rape myths may have the potential to contribute differently to attributed control, blame, and responsibility.

To account for this, recent research of ours (Persson & Dhingra, 2020, 2021) developed and validated separate three-factor victim-survivor and perpetrator culpability scales measuring overall culpability ratings, which were made up of separate constructs of blame, control, and responsibility. We drew on and adapted items from previous research in this area (see Persson & Dhingra, 2020, for an overview), and conceptualised victim-survivor culpability as the degree to which participants implicated the victim-survivor in the assault, and perpetrator culpability as the degree to which participants implicated the perpetrator in the assault. Items of *blame* tapped into beliefs that the victim-survivor/perpetrator should be blamed for the assault (e.g., 'The woman/man is to blame for these circumstances'); items of *responsibility* tapped into beliefs that the victim-survivor/perpetrator was responsible for the assault (e.g., 'The woman/man is responsible for what happened'); and items of *control* tapped into beliefs that the victim-survivor/perpetrator had control over the situation and the outcome (e.g., 'The situation was influenced by the woman/man'). To enhance the potential for

---

[7]We found a strong (but not perfect) negative correlation of −0.65 using a mixed-gender sample of 252 participants. This suggests that when perceived victim-survivor culpability increases, perceived perpetrator culpability decreases.

replicability (i.e., the degree to which new research can produce similar findings) and to refine the understanding of victim-survivor and perpetrator attributions, we recommend that future researchers are clear about the specific culpability constructs they measure. A final issue to bear in mind is whether victim-survivor culpability and RMA may have too much overlap to be meaningfully measured together. In other words, as victim-survivor blame/culpability is such a core aspect of RMA, measuring victim-survivor blame/culpability alongside RMA may add little to the overall findings, unless considered in combination with other variables.

Rape Proclivity (RP). Another relevant variable that is often considered in the context of RMA is RP,[8] which is a man's *own* self-reported propensity for sexual violence. As RMA justifies and minimises the effect of sexual assault along similar premises as Neutralisation Theory (Sykes & Matza, 1957), it makes sense to ask whether endorsing rape myths may have theoretical links with an inclination to perpetrate sexual assault, and we explore this link further in Chapter Five.

In past research, RP has been measured using a variety of items (e.g., Eyssel, Bohner, & Siebler, 2006; Masser, Viki, & Power, 2006) and it does, as such, suffer from similar measurement issues as culpability measures, where a lack of consistent construct operationalisation limits the degree to which findings can be compared across studies, thus impacting the potential for meta-analytic research on the topic. In addition, RP is potentially even less socially acceptable than attitudes relating to victim culpability, making it particularly difficult to measure. In our recent research, we attempted to account for this by keeping questions as subtle as possible,[9] and we recommend that future researchers do the same.

The Victim–Perpetrator Relationship. The victim–perpetrator relationship in rape cases is another relevant variable to measure alongside RMA. In general, the victim–perpetrator relationship is categorised as either stranger (never met prior to assault) or acquaintance (have met prior to assault). It is likely that the considerable breadth of the acquaintance rape condition has contributed to variability within this research area, as this category could span someone the victim-survivor has just met, to a partner or a spouse. Consequently, the most useful approach to examining the victim–perpetrator relationship in the context of RMA is to distinguish between different categories of known-perpetrators, particularly whether the victim-survivor was in a relationship with the perpetrator prior to the attack.

Past meta-analytic research (e.g., Grubb & Turner, 2012; Persson & Dhingra, 2020) indicates that the victim–perpetrator relationship influences a wide array of attributions in rape cases; a large evidence base has established that a woman who

---

[8]Example RP items from our own research asked participants' responses to a short story about a rape, e.g., 'Is it possible you could have somewhat enjoyed getting your way like the man in this situation?' and 'Might you have behaved like the man if you knew for certain no one would find out?'

[9]For example, we changed 'would you have ... [behaved according to some aspect of the rape perpetration described in a short story]' to 'is it possible you might have ... [behaved according to some aspect of the rape perpetration described in a short story]'.

knows her perpetrator is consistently blamed more for the assault than a woman who does not (e.g., Persson & Dhingra, 2020, 2021). This is potentially a result of a general societal reluctance to hold men who rape within intimate relationships fully responsible, as illustrated in the delayed criminalisation of marital rape (Smith, 2018). This also points to the pervasive legacy of a legal framework centring men's perspectives, as further discussed in Chapter Two. When it comes to the interaction between RMA and the victim–perpetrator relationship, it seems that RMA predicts victim culpability across relationship contexts, i.e., that those high in RMA blame the victim-survivor regardless of who the perpetrator is, and those low in RMA blame them consistently less (Persson & Dhingra, 2020).

Challenges in Sexual Assault Research

The following sections will outline some of the many measurement challenges involved in quantitative rape attribution research, before proceeding to the challenges more specific to the assessment of RMA. As a key objective for research into rape attributions is to improve provisions and justice for rape victim-survivors, it is crucial to, where possible, mitigate these measurement challenges so that findings can be robust and reliable.

Samples

Most past research into rape attributions (including that on RMA) has relied on student samples (Persson & Dhingra, 2020; Suarez & Gadalla, 2010). Rape myths as a theory was mostly developed using student samples (Burt, 1980), and as discussed above, most of the current RMA scales were validated on students. This is not necessarily an issue in terms of generalisability, as student samples do not automatically invalidate the research. Our recent meta-analysis (Persson & Dhingra, 2020) did not find that sample type moderated the effect of the victim–perpetrator relationship on victim blame, but here, we note that the relative scarcity of community samples (only five studies recruited community samples) made the comparison difficult, particularly in the context of significant methodological variation. We recently collected data specifically comparing student and non-student responses on the AMMSA (Gerger et al., 2007), which confirmed that scores do not differ notably between the two groups.[10] However, using predominantly younger student samples may mean that the body of research does not reflect the diversity of our culture. It may, in particular, make invisible the sexual violence perpetrated against older (60+ years) women, which has also been an issue in the implementation of the Crime Survey for England and Wales (CSEW)[11] (Bows & Westmarland, 2017).

---

[10]We collected data from 565 Prolific participants (students and non-students) in October 2021. These data are previously unpublished.

[11]The CSEW also fails to integrate other groups such as the homeless and the institutionalised.

Another issue in researching rape attributions and RMA is the limited statistical power of studies to detect a desired effect. In short, insufficient statistical power produces serious issues for the accuracy of findings across the social sciences, calling into question many previously established effects (Ioannidis, 2005), which includes research into rape attributions. The limited statistical power of included studies was noted in our recent meta-analysis (Persson & Dhingra, 2020). We found that very few studies reported power calculations, and we estimated, through a Sunset Funnel Plot (Kossmeier, Tran, & Voracek, 2020), that around half of the included studies had 50% or less power to detect the desired effect. This has serious implications for the validity of studies, as there may be considerable effects of rape myths on various behaviours and attitudes that sample sizes are too small to detect. A lack of statistical power also limits what is currently known about the effectiveness of rape myth-reducing interventions, which is concerning given that an important objective of RMA research is to reduce the prevalence of these beliefs.

Evidently, a key consideration for researchers in this area is to recruit well-powered samples, as this will improve the degree to which findings can reliably impact rape victim-survivor support and justice services. Online, wage-paying, recruitment tools (e.g., Amazon Mechanical Turk (MTurk) and Prolific) are recent and promising developments in psychological research more generally (Mason & Suri, 2012) and can go some way towards accounting for issues around power, with the added benefit of little missing data (Persson & Dhingra, 2021). These recruitment platforms typically allow researchers to set inclusion criteria (e.g., only male, heterosexual participants for a study on RP) and advertise their study to large groups of participants, who (in theory) decide to take part in the study based on the topic, as well as the advertised payment.

However, feminist researchers must bear data ethics in mind when using these platforms. Specifically, they should carefully consider to whom the data belong to, what type of information participants need in order to make informed choices about the sharing of their data, and what type of incentive for data sharing can be considered fair (D'Ignazio & Klein, 2020). From a worker's rights perspective, participants are crucial for research, and they need to be paid fairly and treated ethically. Several scholars (e.g., Gleibs, 2017; Hauser, Paolacci, & Chandler, 2019) have noted a multitude of potential issues (both relating to data quality and in the context of worker's rights) with the recruitment platform MTurk. These include (but are not limited to) (a) participants having little agency on the platform (i.e., they cannot always get in contact with researchers or support staff to query non-payments); (b) participants can be paid considerably less than the minimum wage; and (c) it can enforce existing power hierarchies by using a low-paid, often minoritised work force (Gleibs, 2017; Hauser et al., 2019). As worker's rights and equality should be central to feminism (Davis, 1981/2019), researchers in this, ultimately feminist, research area must bear these considerations in mind when implementing data collection. This can be achieved through avoiding ethically problematic recruitment platforms. We note that when used appropriately, Prolific can be a good alternative as this has positioned itself as more ethical towards its workers (e.g., by not allowing payments under £5/hour; this is increasing to £6 in April 2022, to reflect the increasing cost of living in the UK), but the ethicality of this platform will still rely on the *ethical engagement* from the researcher (e.g., through prompt release of payment, answering any participant queries arising throughout the process, and so on).

Vignettes

As noted above, vignettes are a key medium for researching rape attributions (Persson & Dhingra, 2020), and although they may theoretically have many advantages as compared to alternative experimental manipulation strategies (e.g., video reconstructions, fictitious court documents), there are several issues with how they are currently implemented. Vignette research, in general, often lacks information about how valid vignettes are; this applies to whether participants identify key manipulations (e.g., type of victim–perpetrator relationship, victim-survivor intoxication, etc.), as well as whether participants find the vignettes believable and credible in relation to what they seek to portray. In other words, if a vignette seeks to portray a rape case perpetrated by a woman's partner, do participants reading this vignette find the details of the situation to be believable, and do they clearly identify that the woman was assaulted by her partner (as opposed to a general acquaintance)? If information on validity is missing, it can be unclear whether reported study findings are attributable to the manipulations used, and importantly, what real-life implications the findings of vignette studies can have. Vignettes do tend to be reused across research projects, and while this provides a level of theoretical reliability,[12] it does not improve the practical implications of the vignettes if reusages of them do not address underlying issues regarding validity.

Another issue with the current use of vignettes is their variability, and the lack of standardisation of key variables (Persson & Dhingra, 2020). A relevant example from our own research is on the relatively well-researched area of the victim–perpetrator relationship (which is often examined together with RMA), where vignettes depicting the stranger rape and the acquaintance rape can *unintendedly* be dissimilar in aspects other than the relationship. At the more extreme end, this would include alcohol consumption in one vignette but not the other (even where this is not a variable of interest), but even minor variations such as the time of day can affect outcome variables such as victim-survivor culpability. This can therefore limit the degree to which findings are informative when considering the interaction between RMA and the victim–perpetrator relationship and other variables. Finally, many published papers contain little data on whether participants paid attention throughout the research questionnaires (e.g., RMA scales), including any vignettes they were presented with, again calling into question whether key manipulations are being appropriately implemented.

---

[12]Reliability is the degree to which materials can be reliably reused in similar contexts and have the expected impacts on results.

Clearly, vignettes can be a valuable tool for research into sexual assault and RMA, but they need to be used in ways that maximise their effectiveness and account for potential caveats. For a recent study on the victim–perpetrator relationship and RMA, we specifically developed six vignettes, mindful of the above considerations (Persson & Dhingra, 2021). These vignettes drew on contemporary features of sexual assault (e.g., in terms of settings, contexts, and victim-survivor and perpetrator names), and extraneous features of the vignettes (e.g., level of force used by perpetrator, victim-survivor resistance) were kept similar across conditions. These were initially assessed on a separate sample, asking participants to identify key manipulations[13] across the vignettes (e.g., type of victim–perpetrator relationship). Importantly, this study also asked participants to rate the degree to which the vignettes were believable and realistic. Five out of the six vignettes that we developed reached our pre-registered (i.e., as decided on before data collection began) level of acceptability, out of which four were later implemented in a subsequent study. We also included attention checks throughout the study and removed participants who failed these. In doing this, we could be more confident in our results, and it improved the degree to which findings could be argued to have real-life implications. These vignettes were published alongside our results, meaning that future researchers can reuse our validated vignettes.

Court Observations and Mock Juries

Mock juror studies intend to simulate the experience of sitting on a jury by asking participants to read, listen to, or watch trial materials and make judgements about the cases presented to them in various forms. The materials used are typically fictitious and significantly shorter in comparison with a real trial. Considerable variation between studies in terms of the level of realism and how this, in turn, affects generalisability (i.e., the extent to which their findings are likely to apply to real juries, deliberating in actual trials) has been noted in the literature (for a review, see Leverick, 2020). Indeed, critics have voiced concerns about the lack of realism characterising these studies and have questioned the relevance of the findings to jury decision-making in the real world. Importantly, however, Bornstein (1999) was able to alleviate a number of these concerns by showing that (a) mock juries composed of undergraduate students – as is typical in these studies – do not significantly differ in their decision-making to juries composed of individuals from the general population; and (b) that the method used to provide mock jury evidence (transcripts, videotapes) made little difference to mock jurors' judgements (see also Bornstein et al., 2017). Further, as research involving real juries is either prohibited or heavily regulated in most justice systems, there are few alternatives to jury simulation studies, making observation studies rare (Smith, 2018).

---

[13]Questions aimed at assessing whether participants can identify key manipulations of a study are sometimes referred to as 'manipulation checks'.

Open Science and Reproducibility

During the last few years, Open Science has become an increasingly relevant paradigm across psychology and criminology. Open Science (or Open Scholarship) refers to attempts to strengthen reproducibility and replicability[14] within science, to ensure findings are accurate, reliable, and valid (Kathawalla, Silverstein, & Syed, 2021). There are different strategies proposed to achieve this, but most typically strategies centre around an increased transparency in the scientific process, with the sharing of materials, data, and analytical approach. Transparent research practices are also sometimes referred to as 'reproducible research practices'. The Open Science movement has raised important questions about the validity and reliability of some of the past results in the social sciences (Ioannidis, 2005), and naturally, this has implications for research into rape attributions and RMA. While there has been considerable uptake of reproducible research practices across parts of the psychological research community, and increased interest in how to combine feminist scholarship with Open Science (e.g., Matsick, Kruk, Oswald, & Palmer, 2021), currently the uptake of these research strategies remains relatively limited within RMA research (Persson & Dhingra, 2020). As we expand on further in Persson and Dhingra (2020), data sets on RMA are rarely published alongside findings, and there is sometimes a lack of methodological detail (e.g., vignettes not being openly available). This is unfortunate, as the societal importance, as well as the practical relevance, of these topics should mean that attempts at improving the reliability and robustness of research practices should be encouraged. It is possible that the limited uptake is a side effect of the current diversity issues within the Open Science movement (Persson & Pownall, 2021). However, while there may be challenges involved for feminists engaging with the Open Science movement, there are several reasons why RMA researchers would benefit from engaging in core transparency practices, particularly in the open sharing of research data and materials. Two of these benefits are outlined below.

Sharing of Resources. As noted by Westmarland and Bows (2018) in their guide on research practices in the areas of gender, violence, and abuse, funding for feminist research priorities is scarce. Resultantly, sexual assault provision is chronically underfunded (Rape Crisis England and Wales, 2019) and, considering its considerable societal impact, not sufficiently prioritised. Feminist researchers have, therefore, often informally shared scarce resources (Westmarland & Bows, 2018). Open Science practices present an important opportunity to formalise data and resource sharing. The sharing of anonymised data would allow other researchers to make use of it, which could facilitate large, well-powered studies and, in doing so, address some of the issues already noted with sample power. The sharing of research materials would also have positive implications. As noted above, there is considerable variation in how rape vignettes are conceptualised,

---

[14]Reproducibility refers to the ability for researchers to reproduce original results with the original data. Replicability refers to the ability to replicate the original findings using new data (Plesser, 2018).

which could be readily addressed through publishing these vignettes alongside research findings. This way, valid vignettes can be reused and re-conceptualised, thus improving reliability across the field, as well as limiting the unnecessary redevelopment of new material for each additional study. However, if vignettes are reused *too many* times, they can also lose validity and reliability in cases where the same participants are re-exposed to them repeatedly.

Improving the Practical Utility of Findings. Reproducible research practices have the potential to strengthen methodologies (Hardwicke & Ioannidis, 2018; Scheel, Schijen, & Lakens, 2021) and can as such improve the practical utility of rape attribution research. This is highly relevant for RMA, as its feminist foundations mean that research ultimately seeks to improve conditions for women. Sexual assault and a lack of victim-survivor provision have increasingly been noted as serious societal problems (Molina & Poppleton, 2020), yet responses to these problems are not consistently informed by academia. While this is likely due to a variety of reasons (e.g., a limited political commitment to funding research), it may also be partially due to a confusion about which strategies to adopt, given the variability of some of the findings in this area. Here, scholarly research further risks being viewed as detached from reality, which can be compounded when research practices are too dissimilar to real-life situations. Increased robustness, therefore, would increase the confidence with which academic theories can influence policymakers, which, as we discuss in Chapter Seven, may be especially relevant for interventions to address sexual violence.

Current Challenges in Measuring RMA

Numerous researchers (e.g., Frazier, Valtinson, & Candell, 1994; Gerger et al., 2007; Hinck & Thomas, 1999; McMahon & Farmer, 2011; Thelan & Meadows, 2021) have noted that there are inherent measurement difficulties associated with researching RMA, which are further compounded by the general measurement issues in rape attributions as outlined above.

Some of the measurement difficulties involved in assessing RMA are outlined below, and we further suggest recommended directions researchers in this area can take mitigate these.

Choice of RMA Measure

A review of the rape myth literature (Lonsway & Fitzgerald, 1995) identified 24 different measures designed to assess RMA, all of which were found to vary in their definitions of the construct and representations of the domains (Lonsway & Fitzgerald, 1995). More recent meta-analytic research on RMA assessment (e.g., Suarez & Gadalla, 2010) suggested considerably fewer measures of RMA within their sample ($n = 6$), which would indicate an increasing consensus around how to measure rape myth endorsement and a greater attention to the quality of psychometric measurement. Despite this, there is evidently still variation in how RMA is measured, which can cause issues for prospective researchers, and those seeking to do meta-research. In particular, it can make comparisons between studies problematic, particularly as the scales can reflect subtle differences in the definition of rape myths, e.g., rape myths as 'false beliefs' (Lonsway & Fitzgerald, 1995) as compared to definitions that make no reference to the veracity of the beliefs (Bohner et al., 1998, 2009).

Some authors have also suggested that English translations of some of the more widely used scales (e.g., the AMMSA (Gerger et al., 2007), originally written in German) may be 'oddly worded' (Thelan & Meadows, 2021), although this appraisal is subjective and difficult to empirically assess. Translation issues were also noted in a Japanese application of the RMAS (Burt, 1980) by Uji, Shono, Shikai, and Kitamura (2007). Relatedly, an increasing body of research suggests that rape myths are not universal and may be culturally and contextually dependent – this would naturally impact the choice of RMA measure for applications outside a Western context. This raises questions about whether existing RMA measures can be directly implemented in other contexts, or whether researchers should develop country-specific RMA measures. For instance, Oh and Neville (2004) suggested that for rape myth measurement to be relevant to a Korean context, chastity ideology and patriarchal Confucianism need to be taken into account, and this was echoed in a Vietnamese context by Bergenfeld et al. (2022). Similarly, Xue et al. (2019) proposed a new factor structure for a Chinese version of the IRMAS (CRIMA), which adds a factor that emphasises rape as a violent event ('rape must involve violence'). Bergenfeld et al. (2022) suggested that RMA scale items measuring false rape allegation beliefs are not relevant in a Vietnamese context, as rape allegations are viewed as high in social cost and as such unlikely to be perceived as fabrications. The researchers do, however, note that as the stigma associated with being a rape victim-survivor decreases (resulting in more victim-survivors reporting the offence to the police), the perception that false rape allegations are common may increase. Aside from highlighting the cultural specificity of rape myths (and the inevitable impact on rape myth assessment), the above emphasises the dynamic nature of many of these beliefs, as further outlined below.

Subtlety, Wording, and Colloquialism

Attitudes to gender, sexuality, and sexual crime are dynamic and often bound to a specific time and place (Payne et al., 1999). In some respects, this is encouraging for feminist researchers, as it indicates that there has been (and can in the future be) considerable progress in changing attitudes towards gender and sexuality, alongside legal progress for justice provision for rape victim-survivors. An illustrative example of this is the criminalisation of marital rape in the UK and US (as further discussed in Chapter Two), which came about following considerable consciousness-raising efforts of feminists (Donat & D'Emilio, 1992). Prior to this, marital (or indeed general acquaintance) rape would rarely be taken seriously by the legal system and there was less public acknowledgement of rape as existing outside the context of assaults perpetrated by strangers. Although victim-survivors of known-perpetrator rapes are still blamed significantly more than those assaulted by a stranger (Persson & Dhingra, 2020; indicating the pervasive legacy of these attitudes), there is now an increased acknowledgement of ongoing consent as an important feature of *all* sexual relationships (Angel, 2021), which has impacted the expression of rape myths.

However, the dynamic nature of attitudes to sexuality and gender also presents challenges for feminist researchers seeking to examine exactly how common rape myths are and their most prominent features. As societal attitudes towards victim-survivors are becoming more liberal (in that it is less socially acceptable to engage in overt victim-survivor blaming), many of the stereotypes about rape and victim-survivors of rape are becoming less overt. This is, in turn, making measurement strategies increasingly blunt (McMahon & Farmer, 2011), and it is progressively more difficult to determine whether RMA is decreasing overall and/or in certain populations, or whether these beliefs are merely becoming subtler. A related consideration is the changing nature of rape myths, where certain beliefs become less important for the facilitation of the overall belief system, and others become more prominent. McMahon and Farmer (2011) suggested that alcohol as an excuse for poor behaviour is increasingly central to perpetrator exoneration, and we note in several sections of this book that the belief of false rape allegations as commonplace may be another especially central aspect of contemporary RMA, at least in a Western context.

Moreover, some widely used RMA measures are also problematic regarding item wording and clarity. The reliable and valid assessment of constructs depends on wording that is clear and uniformly understood by all participants, which is sometimes not the case with rape myth scales. For example, Burt's (1980) measure includes the following item:

> If a woman gets drunk at a party and has intercourse with a man she's just met there, she should be considered 'fair game' to other males at the party who want to have sex with her, whether she wants to or not.

This item is too complex to be answered reliably as it contains several separate ideas; endorsement could indicate agreement to any one of its component parts. Additionally, it describes a scenario that is too specific to be considered a common rape myth. Further, Bumby (1996) noted that approximately one third of RMAS items do not specifically measure rape myths. Rather, he explained, the RMAS appeared to reveal how people's biases regarding age, race, and gender affect their likelihood of believing a rape allegation. Further, it has been argued that the RMAS should be seen as a measure of acceptance of violence against women rather than of RMA as it is structured to take into account three factors: (a) denial of rape accusations, (b) victim's responsibility, and (c) rape claims seen as manipulation (Jones, Russell, & Bryant, 1998). This echoes criticisms of the AMMSA (Gerger et al., 2007) by Thelan and Meadows (2021) where items such as 'Most women prefer to be praised for their looks rather than their intelligence' are arguably more related to an appraisal of gender roles than rape. This highlights the many complexities involved in researching a construct so steeped in sexism.

Social Desirability

The research described so far, and in the remainder of this book, relies on individuals' self-reports of their RMA. Self-report measures operate at a conscious controlled level of processing, and while these can produce valuable data, they are prone to biases such as responding in a manner deemed favourable by others (i.e., social desirability). Socially desirable responding is an important bias to consider when examining rape myth endorsement as, unsurprisingly, individuals have been found to under-report stigmatising views and behaviours when asked to fill out self-report measures (Hockett, Smith, Klausing, & Saucier, 2016; Thelan & Meadows, 2021). This might be especially likely when responding to particular items that might attract criticism and judgement from others or when the person responding has a certain occupation (e.g., police officer). This means that self-report measures may not be able to detect certain rape myths (McMahon & Farmer, 2011).

Social desirability appears to depend on two factors, one relating more broadly to the cultural acceptability of certain attitudes (e.g., sexual violence prevention campaigns have made people more aware of what is socially permissible; Gerger et al., 2007; McMahon & Farmer, 2011),[15] and the other relating more specifically to individual personalities (i.e., a person's willingness to disclose attitudes that may go against prevailing norms in society). There is likely to be a degree of interaction between these two factors (i.e., the perception of the perceived social acceptability of certain attitudes and a person's individual willingness to disclose undesirable attitudes); some people may be willing to disclose attitudes that are perceived to be somewhat controversial (depending on the cultural context), whereas others have a considerably higher threshold for attitudes that they are willing to disclose and are less dependent on the cultural context. Social desirability as obscuring true levels of RMA will only become a more prominent issue as these attitudes become increasingly unacceptable in society; this will reduce most people's willingness to disclose these attitudes (i.e., increase cultural unacceptability), and higher levels of RMA will only be detected among those who have little concern for disclosing societally unacceptable attitudes.

While care needs to be taken to use RMA measurement strategies that accurately reflect the subtle, and perhaps covert, nature of rape myths (i.e., by avoiding 'obvious' phrasing; Gerger et al., 2007; Hinck & Thomas, 1999; McMahon & Farmer, 2011), an additional approach for accounting for social desirability is to include a measure of the degree to which participants strive to give socially desirable answers (i.e., the degree to which they attempt to manage their own impressions). Typically, this is achieved through the administration of impression management scales alongside the RMA scale and any other measures of relevance. Scores from the impression management scale can then be inputted in the statistical model being tested, to see whether it accounts for any of the effects. A commonly used example of an impression management scale is the Balanced Inventory for Desirable Reporting (BIDR; Paulhus 1991), with a shorter

---

[15]For example, participants may no longer directly state that women desire to be raped but instead indirectly blame rape victim-survivors based on their behaviours.

version more recently developed by Hart, Ritchie, Hepper, and Gebauer (2015).[16] Another way to circumvent the potential bias inherent in explicit measures of RMA is to use implicit measures to assess people's automatic, unconscious thoughts (Greenwald, McGhee, & Schwartz, 1998). Caution would, however, be needed in interpreting these studies, given concerns about the reliability and validity of the Implicit Association Test (IAT)[17] (Schimmack, 2021). Further work into the idea of implicit RMA, including the validity of this concept and the interaction between explicit and implicit RMA, is warranted.

Ways Forward

The dynamic nature of rape myths; the cultural variations in the relative importance or unimportance of specific beliefs about rape, victim-survivors, and perpetrators; the potential for wording issues and concept overlap; and social desirability all present challenges for researchers seeking to assess rape myths. Below we suggest some potential solutions for these issues relevant to researchers and practitioners in this area.

1. **RMA measures as 'work in progress'.** The dynamic nature of rape myths suggests that instruments used to assess RMA may need to be a work in progress (i.e., that these need to be regularly updated and revised to ensure relevancy based on demographic, generational, and sociocultural differences). It is, as such, unlikely that any RMA scale will completely stand the test of time (or place) but may need to be changed incrementally and reassessed on validity and reliability, particularly in the context of floor and ceiling effects (i.e., participants scoring towards the lower or higher end of a scale, respectively).[18] This issue has been recognised in other fields of study, including alcohol consumption (Reich, Ariel, Darkes, & Goldman, 2012). It is, therefore, imperative that researchers in this area collaborate internationally on developing relevant and theoretically grounded RMA scales, with strong reliability as well as validity, avoiding where possible the overlap with other constructs. In practice, this further emphasises the need for engagement with data transparency and the sharing of open resources. If RMA researchers are to effectively maintain and update measurement instruments, doing this openly and

---

[16]Items ask participants to indicate whether they engage in common undesirable behaviours (e.g., gossiping, lying, cheating, etc.); people are considered to manage their impression more if they score higher on the scale. While the original scale is somewhat dated, it appears that the behaviours included as items remain relatively stable as being typically engaged in (by everyone) but being considered undesirable.

[17] The IAT is a method for indirectly measuring the strengths of associations among concepts.

[18] Skewed distributions are problematic for researchers, as most statistical tests require a normal distribution of scores. Further, examining the effectiveness of interventions designed to reduce RMA would be difficult if scores are already clustered at the lower end of a scale.

collaboratively would be the most efficient and cost-effective. As such, it may not be feasible to strive for one 'perfect' and universal measure of RMA but to ensure that those available are valid, reliable, and culturally appropriate.

2. **Acknowledging the cultural sensitivity of rape myths**. When promoting open and transparent research collaborations on RMA scale development, it will be imperative to expand research collaborations to non-Western settings, to capture cultural variations of the rape myth belief system. Here, it would likely be advantageous to continue the ongoing work towards the development of country-specific and contextualised RMA tools, such as that by Bergenfeld et al. (2022), rather than simply translating those already available. Relatedly (and as we discuss further in Chapter Two), here it will also be important to consider the racist nature of many rape myths, both in terms of victims-survivors and in terms of perpetrators. Future RMA measures will benefit from incorporating an intersectional understanding of RMA, to capture how these beliefs often support racism as well as sexism. This will have the benefit of a more accurate measurement of RMA; while people with racist beliefs may score low on RMA using traditional scales, they will likely endorse racist rape myths about both victim-survivors and perpetrators. Currently, these beliefs are not captured by most contemporary RMA scales.

3. **Widening research methodologies**. It will also be necessary to move research methodologies beyond those with a quantitative focus only (i.e., incorporating qualitative *and* quantitative approaches, as well as meta-research) to study RMA. The combination of several approaches could provide researchers with a more nuanced understanding of modern expressions of rape myths and may capture attitudes that participants are hesitant to endorse on any individual scale, and patterns of responding. In their development of U-IRMAS, McMahon and Farmer (2011) implemented focus groups in their initial reassessment of the IRMAS, which yielded many useful considerations for their subsequent scale development. A relevant and collaborative extension of this could be to implement cross-institutional focus groups across research teams (e.g., by using the Delphi method[19]), to share results and experiences of RMA scale development. This was also the approach taken by Bergenfeld et al. (2022) in their investigation of rape myth beliefs in Vietnam. Incorporating a wider array of research methods would, therefore, have the benefits of improving the cross-cultural relevancy of RMA measures and ensuring that non-Western attitudes towards rape are accurately assessed using appropriate tools.

4. **Social desirability**. Finally, it is recommended that studies into RMA consistently include measures of participants' desire to manage their impressions (e.g., the BIDR-16; Hart et al., 2015) but bear in mind several caveats when doing so. First, it may be the case that participants are more willing to

---

[19]The Delphi method is a process used to arrive at a group opinion or decision by surveying a panel of experts. Experts respond to several rounds of questionnaires, and the responses are aggregated and shared with the group after each round.

disclose undesirable behaviours, than they are to disclose believing in rape myths, as there is increasing awareness that overt rape myths are societally unacceptable (Thelan & Meadows, 2021). This would create the impression that social desirability in the context of rape attributions is less of an issue. Relatedly, it is also possible that groups who believe very strongly in rape myths are unwilling to disclose undesirable behaviours but are willing to indicate their agreement with rape myths, thus creating a false impression that rape myths are underreported within the sample. Moreover, impression management scales only measure the latter half of the social desirability construct (i.e., individual willingness to appear in socially desirable ways) and not the degree to which rape myths themselves are considered socially unacceptable attitudes. It might, therefore, be prudent to include measures related to the endorsement of rape myths (e.g., measures of sexism) alongside any RMA scale, to obtain a more accurate picture of a person's overall belief system.

Case Study: A Reproducible and Transparent Investigation into RMA, Ambivalent Sexism, and the Victim–Perpetrator Relationship

As outlined above, there are measurement difficulties involved in RMA research, and the methodological variation present in past research can limit the practical implications of findings. Consequently, recent research of ours into the impact of the victim–perpetrator relationship on rape attributions (culpability ratings and RP), alongside the moderating influence of RMA and sexism, aimed to account for some of these past issues. In doing so, we also sought to implement a framework for reproducible research practices in this area and to signpost recommendations for the development of research methodologies. Below is an outline to the key steps we took in producing this framework.

1. Review of the literature

In our initial meta-analysis and systematic review (Persson & Dhingra, 2020), we highlighted previous findings in this area, focusing on what was generally agreed upon in the context of rape attributions and the victim–perpetrator relationship, but more importantly, key variations in findings across past research. We noted that, generally, a woman raped by a known perpetrator was blamed more than a woman raped by a stranger, and that RMA and aggressively sexist attitudes correlated with victim-survivor culpability across varying scenarios (as emphasising the above point about RMA generally predicting victim-survivor blame across different scenarios). What was less clear, however, was the degree to which variations in research methodologies were related to contradictions in findings, particularly in the context of acquaintance rape. Consequently, and in line with our specific aim of considering research methodologies, we also graded past research on various aspects of research design, implementation, and statistical analysis. From these findings, we concluded that there was a lack of data on vignettes used to research rape attributions, e.g., how these vignettes were developed, what specific details they contained (or omitted), and whether the vignettes were considered believable by research participants. Under-powered samples were also recurring themes in past research, potentially limiting the validity of findings.

2. Research design and material development

Drawing on the findings of this literature review, we then sought to design a study and develop materials that addressed some of these issues. We were particularly interested in developing rape vignettes and outcome measures that could be used in conjunction with RMA. Therefore, we designed contemporary and standardised vignettes and implemented these among community participants. An example vignette can be found in Fig. 1.

This resulted in five validated vignettes, with varying manipulations of key variables. We further drew on past research in this area, to develop victim-survivor and perpetrator culpability scales and a RP scale, materials which are of key relevance to use in the context of RMA. For our culpability scales, we included three constructs: responsibility, control, and blame.

3. Replication attempt

Following our material development, we implemented two separate studies in well-powered (as based on effects obtained in our literature review) community samples. We were particularly interested in clarifying inconsistencies in previous findings, especially in the context of whether minor variations in vignettes would impact results (they did), and whether there was a utility in measuring different culpability constructs (there was). Broadly, our research found that aggressively sexist attitudes such as RMA were consistently associated with both culpability (increased victim-survivor culpability and decreased perpetrator culpability) and RP, particularly in known perpetrator scenarios.

Amy is at home with her boyfriend Joseph, watching TV. They have had a nice evening, eating a meal that they cooked together. It is getting late, and Amy wants to get ready to go to bed – she has an early start at work tomorrow. As she is about to get up from the sofa, Joseph starts to kiss her. Amy says she is too tired, and continues to get up off the sofa. Joseph pulls her back down on the sofa, and starts pulling off her clothes, telling her how attractive she is. Amy says no, but Joseph continues anyway. Despite Amy's repeated objections, Joseph holds her down and has sex with her.

Fig. 1.   Example Vignette (Partner Rape; Persson & Dhingra, 2021).

4. Data transparency

Finally, we deposited our research materials in repositories on the Open Science Framework (OSF). This included the culpability and RP scales that we developed, alongside all manipulation check items. We also deposited the vignettes, together with the data on their validity (see: https://osf.io/92bq7/).

Conclusion

This chapter has sought to provide a methodological context to RMA assessment by situating it within the broader area of research into attributions in rape cases. It has also explored why it is beneficial to be able to measure rape myths. Of particular importance is how RMA measurement can provide a much-needed societal context to these beliefs, which is important for feminist researchers seeking to establish RMA as existing within a broader system of gender inequality and sexism. We have provided an overview of some of the most widely used RMA scales, including their theoretical background and psychometric properties. There are many challenges involved in attempting to measure RMA, and we emphasise the subtlety, cultural unacceptability, and contextual dependency of these attitudes as particularly important to consider. We have argued that it is highly relevant for researchers in this area to collaboratively engage with the Open Science movement, to ensure accurate and reliable findings with practical use. This will be crucial for improving the implementation of rape myth measurement cross-culturally, as currently, many of the more widely used RMA scales may be of limited relevancy in non-Western contexts. We conclude that current efforts to re-conceptualise (as opposed to simply translate) existing RMA measures for implementation in non-Western countries are promising avenues for continued future research.

Chapter Four

Consequences of Rape Myth Acceptance on the Criminal Justice System and Women Subjected to Rape

Chapter Overview

The adverse impacts of RMA are well documented, and the recent report by the Victims' Commissioner for England and Wales noted these beliefs as important for understanding women's experiences of the criminal justice system (CJS) (Molina & Poppleton, 2020). Rape myths can shift the blame from the perpetrator to the victim-survivor, demoralise victim-survivors, minimise the significance of the crime, and adversely affect how women who have been subjected to rape are treated within the CJS. Further, RMA can contribute to self-blame among victim-survivors and/or have others blame the victim-survivor for their victimisation, shift legislative and public priorities (e.g., rape prevention efforts/training), and influence whether individual women conceptualise themselves as a 'rape victim-survivor' (i.e., whether what they were subjected to was a 'real rape'). These myths also minimise the perceived reality and extent of violence against women, since by accepting certain falsehoods (e.g., rape as not being very severe or prevalent), many may not believe rape statistics are accurate and could view the emphasis being placed on rape as unnecessary. Within this chapter, we review the consequences of RMA on the CJS and women subjected to rape, and we further signpost how the impact of these myths could be mitigated within the CJS.

Rape Myths and Policing

Prevalence

Several studies have examined the overall prevalence of RMA in police officers (for a review, see Sleath & Bull, 2017). These studies generally highlight low levels of RMA, particularly in relation to victim-survivor blame (see also Garza & Franklin, 2021). Wentz and Archbold (2012), for instance, found that only 2% of their

Rape Myths: Understanding, Assessing, and Preventing, 53–82
Copyright © 2022 by Sofia Persson and Katie Dhingra
Published under exclusive licence by Emerald Publishing Limited
doi:10.1108/978-1-80071-152-520220004

sample of 100 police officers produced victim-blaming statements when asked to provide a definition of rape. Moreover, studies comparing police officers to other populations, such as undergraduate students, have found that overall RMA levels do not significantly differ between groups (Sleath & Bull, 2017). Examination of specific rape myths, however, highlights that UK police officers tend to subscribe to 'she lied' myths to a greater extent than psychology and law students, while endorsing 'she asked for it' and 'he didn't mean to' myths to a lesser extent (Sleath & Bull, 2017). Additionally, research has noted the endorsement of specific myths by police officers (even when overall RMA is low; Page, 2008, 2010). For example, although 93% of US police officers agreed that 'any woman can be raped', 19% stated that they were *unlikely* to believe a woman who disclosed marital rape, 20.1% indicated that women who dress provocatively are inviting sex, and 22.7% stated that any victim can resist a rapist if they want to (Page, 2010).

Overall, it is reasonable to conclude that while officers generally self-report low levels of RMA and are similar or slightly lower in their overall RMA levels to other populations, a substantial minority of officers exhibit some degree of agreement with such attitudes. Further, despite the largely encouraging nature of low overall subscription to rape myths, *any* endorsement of rape mythology is problematic for victim-survivors who formally report, as officers possess significant discretion in their decision-making in terms of suspect apprehension, the investigative progress, and case-processing outcomes (Angiolini, 2015; Sleath & Bull, 2012; Spohn & Tellis, 2012; Spohn, White, Tellis, 2014). Indeed, if an officer ascribes to the notion that a 'genuine' victim-survivor must have certain characteristics or behave in a certain way, there is a heighted risk of a hostile or dismissive reception if a victim-survivor deviates from this. This, in turn, increases the possibility of secondary victimisation (i.e., victim-blaming behaviours and practices engaged in by legal and medical personnel, which exacerbates victim-suriviors' trauma) and the potential that the case will be dropped (Hohl & Stanko, 2015). Brown and Horvath (2009) describe the impact of these myths on the CJS process and on victim-survivors, noting that 'rape myths become part of a self-supporting system whereby the absence of convictions supports the beliefs that women falsify claims or men's behaviour does not justify the charge' (p. 322). Accordingly, the consequences of police officers holding negative attitudes about women subjected to rape may be far greater than that of individuals within the general population.

Impact on Decision-Making

The impact of RMA on officers' reasoning and behaviour has been examined in several studies. For example, when examining officers' own definitions of rape, extra-legal factors (including those related to rape myths) are frequently present (Campbell & Johnson, 1997; Mennicke, Anderson, Oehme, & Kennedy, 2014; Spohn & Tellis, 2012). In other words, police officers' personal definitions of rape can deviate from those prescribed by legislation. Officers' classifications of rape allegations (as 'good', 'real', or 'legitimate') also appear to be guided by schematic thinking constructed around particular myths, which further emphasises the schematic nature of RMA. The presence of rape myth-related information, such as an unexpected non-verbal or emotional response to the assault (Ask & Landström, 2010; Bollingmo, Wessel, Eilertsen, & Magnussen, 2008; Maddox, Lee, & Barker, 2011; Venema, 2016), negative moral character or 'perceived immorality' (e.g., because of prior engagement in prostitution or involvement in the commercial sex industry, a criminal history, and a history of substance abuse; Page, 2008a, 2008b), voluntary alcohol consumption (Campbell, Menaker, & King, 2015; Schuller & Stewart, 2000; Sims, Noel, & Maisto, 2007), inconsistent statements (Alderden & Ullman, 2012), lack of injury (McMillan, 2018), delayed reporting of the assault (Beichner & Spohn, 2012), and a closer victim–perpetrator relationship (Felson & Pare, 2008) influence police officer assessments of victim credibility; all of which contribute to more negative officer assessments. Further, myths concerning adherence to societal norms of femininity, such as victim-survivor sexual promiscuity/history (Campbell et al., 2015) and profession (e.g., in prostitution; see Page, 2007, 2010), have been shown to influence how responsible victim-survivors are judged to be, as well as whether an incident is classed as rape (Venema, 2016). Additionally, myths relating to 'genuine' victim-survivor behaviour, notably the voluntary consumption of alcohol (Goodman-Delahunty & Graham, 2011; Schuller & Stewart, 2000), and the presence/absence, degree, and/or timing of resistance (Hine & Murphy, 2017; Venema, 2016) also have a considerable impact on officers' allocations of victim-survivor and perpetrator responsibility. Further, in semi-structured research interviews, victim-survivor intoxication was found to result in officers believing a case to be more ambiguous, not legitimate, or false (Venema, 2016). According to Beichner and Spohn (2012), however, current research has failed to determine which factors matter most in shaping perceptions of victim-survivors, limiting our understanding of how credibility is evaluated.

Finally, characteristics relating to the context of the rape, such as the closeness of the prior relationship between the victim-survivor and perpetrator demonstrate further significant effects among police officers. Acquaintance rape victim-survivors are blamed more, and acquaintance rape perpetrators blamed less than those involved in stranger rape (Areh, Mesko, & Umek, 2009; Hine & Murphy, 2017; Sleath & Bull, 2012). In addition, research has found that a prior relationship can lead to officers perceiving cases as ambiguous and not legitimate (Venema, 2016). Moreover, studies examining several myths in combination, for example, those concerning victim-survivor behaviour (reputation and initial point of resistance) and context (victim–perpetrator relationship), find that these myths operate both in isolation and in combination to influence officers' judgements (Venema, 2016).

Together, these studies indicate that when victim-survivors do not conform to rape stereotypes (i.e., do not meet the standard of an 'ideal' or 'righteous' victim), officers believe the victim-survivor less (Ask & Landström, 2010). Importantly, officers' perceptions of victim-survivor credibility also predict case progression and arrest, indicating that these cognitive biases have considerable practical implications for justice for victim-survivors of rape (Dewald & Lorenz, 2021). Specifically, some victim-survivors state that police discouraged them from reporting (Campbell & Raja, 2005) or were told their case was not sufficiently serious to warrant filing a report (Campbell, 2006). This suggests that perceived credibility may be a mediating factor between rape myths and the processing of cases (Garza & Franklin, 2021; Morabito, Pattavina, & Williams, 2019). In relation to the investigation of rape, research has shown that some police forces 'no-crime'[1] complaints if they suspect a false allegation or if the allegation is difficult to prosecute, without having obtained the required verifiable information to this effect. For instance, it has been consistently found that in cases where a relationship existed between the victim-survivor and the perpetrator prior to the assault, a 'no-crime' outcome is more likely. This is because prioritising cases that align with notions of the 'ideal' victim may increase the chance of achieving acknowledged measures of *success* in the professional environment (Beichner & Spohn, 2012), such as securing a conviction. Such an outcome provides officers with tangible symbolic capital (Chan, Devery, & Doran, 2016), which can enhance their sense of police identity with peers, supervisors, and themselves, and arguably, this is easier to achieve when there is a stereotypical perpetrator and victim-survivor. Convictions may also be important for the police as an institution, as successful prosecutions are viewed as signalling police effectiveness by the government as well as the public.

Implications for Training

In light of the research highlighting the detrimental effect of RMA on officers' decision-making, it is important to consider how to train officers most effectively on rape myths including the impact they can have on the investigative process. However, previous attempts to mitigate stereotypical beliefs about rape in police officers, either through specific attitudinal interventions or delivery of specialist training, have largely been ineffective (Parratt & Pina, 2017; Sleath & Bull, 2017). As outlined by Parratt and Pina (2017), although training appears to influence behaviour (e.g., leads to better questioning and officers being less likely to mention victim intoxication), it fails to alter levels of rape myths. Even when officers outperform in simulated interviews after training (e.g., Lonsway, Welch, & Fitzgerald, 2001), the knowledge obtained during training deteriorates over time, eventually having no influence on victim blaming. Such findings are worrying as it would seem reasonable to assume that specialist training would address negative attitudes about rape victim-survivors and misconceptions that may be held about rape. However, these findings could also indicate that rape myths have little behavioural impact (i.e., officers can become better at working with victim-survivors of rape even where RMA levels are not altered), but the fact that victim-survivors continue to be impacted by rape myths within the police (Molina & Poppleton, 2020) would unfortunately suggest that this is not the case.

One explanation advanced in the literature for the limited intervention efficacy is that the provision of face-to-face, extensive, long-lasting interventions (e.g., Darwinkel, Powell, & Tidmarsh, 2013) is impractical (because of, for example, reform, caseload, austerity, reduced resources, and the need for 'abstraction' from operational duties). However, while we contend that it is important that all officers receive training on the myths and fallacies surrounding rape, and the impact these

---

[1] 'No-crime' is where it is judged by the police that no crime took place.

may have on how they conduct themselves, it is important to recognise that RMA training alone may be insufficient in tackling negative beliefs on a permanent basis. Indeed, RMA does not exist in isolation, but instead exists within the context of broader sexist attitudes (Hine & Murphy, 2017; Chapter Six of this book). Therefore, efforts to reduce officer RMA may require consideration of the broader attitudinal context of RMA, rather than focusing on RMA as the sole issue. The pervasiveness of RMA in broader society would also explain *why* training effects dissipate over time, as officers are re-exposed to these beliefs on a regular basis.

In addition, there may need to be a consideration of the culture[2] and structures within which police decisions are made (Darwinkel et al., 2013), which continues to be criticised for being macho, lacking diversity, and having a command-and-control ethos. As Crank (2003) argues,

> humans operate within social institutions, and personal meanings and goals are predetermined by the values, constructions of knowledge, rational forms, cultural predispositions and categorisations of social and moral reality embodied in these institutions. (p. 196)

Relatedly, Stanko and Hohl (2018) have argued that the reason *why* police training has failed to adequately address sexual voice is because it is largely delivered by former operational officers and, therefore, is almost always based on 'craft'[3] (experience) rather than 'science' (academic research/evidence-informed): 'professional skill development … takes place inside policing, and rests on internal police knowledge, taking little account of other sources of information (and particularly independent academic evidence)' (p. 170). The approaches and techniques that are passed down to officers (from other officers) have rarely been tested or challenged by those outside of the police and there is little scientific research on how police training may work to change behaviour (Stanko & Hohl, 2018). Essentially, police train police, and any insights from research, force performance, or Her Majesty's Inspectorate of Constabulary and Fire & Rescue Services (HMICFRS) inspections are generally kept at arms' length. Because police

---

[2] According to Cockcroft (2020, p. 12), definitions of police culture

> highlight the informality of the culture within apparently regimented organisational environments, the presence of accepted world views that influence and shape practice, the ambiguous real-life application of formally prescribed work behaviours, informal ideas of what constitutes the police role and the professionalism with which it should be undertaken, the role of the police in maintaining order and the uniqueness of police culture to the police role.

[3] 'A craft is acquired and improved through practice, is taught by fellow craftspeople (police officers) who know about good practice of refined policing skills through their experience of field operations' (Stanko & Hohl, 2018, p. 9).

training is largely sealed off from outside scrutiny, there is little transparency, educational review, or accountability for what is being taught. Consequently, in passing down the 'craft' of policing, instructors may inadvertently perpetuate harmful stereotypes about rape victim-survivors.

The considerations above are also of relevance to the initial selection (and training) of specialist officers who deal with rape victim-survivors. In England and Wales, Specially Trained Officers (STOs; previously called 'Sexual Offences Investigation Trained' officers (SOITs)) are allocated to individuals when they report sexual crimes. These officers play a vital role in terms of case processing, supporting the investigation, and providing services directly to victim-survivors. Their interactions with victim-survivors are pivotal in ensuring prosecutorial success (Stanko & Hohl, 2018; Westmarland, Aznarez, Brown, & Kirkham, 2012) as well as other forms of 'justice' (McGlynn & Westmarland, 2019). The role of an STO is meant to be self-selecting and, therefore, voluntary. However, the Her Majesty's Crown Prosecution Service Inspectorate (HMCPSI, 2007) report noted that in several force areas, some officers felt pressured to agree to train for the role (because of the paucity of STOs) and that appropriateness for the role was rarely assessed. The literature reviewed above suggests that RMA levels could, and perhaps should, form part of the suitability assessment. This is particularly true considering that research has found no significant differences between officers who were specially trained (STOs) and those who were not in terms of victim-survivor blaming (Sleath & Bull, 2012) or credibility attributions (Goodman-Delahunty & Graham, 2011).

More research is, however, needed to examine whether RMA impacts rape case decision-making among STOs. While the research reviewed above suggests that RMA can have practical implications for victim-survivor provision among police officers, Rumney et al. (2019) caution against assuming that negative attitudes, where they exist, inevitably influence professional behaviour. Further, a study of detectives specialising in sexual assault cases suggested that even when detectives acknowledge rape myths as false, their behaviours towards victims in investigations do not align with this knowledge (Schwartz, 2010). Thus, there may be a disconnect between attitudes (implicit and/or expressed) and behaviour.

Rape Myths and Juror Decision-Making

It is widely acknowledged that juries are susceptible to 'extra evidentiary influences' (Devine, Buddenbaum, Houp, Studebaker, & Stolle, 2009), of which the adherence to RMA may be particularly problematic. Indeed, a considerable body of research indicates that rape myths affect jurors' evaluation of evidence and their decision-making in rape cases (for a review, see Leverick, 2020). This research has largely found that rape myths provide juries with 'socio-sexual scripts' about rape, perpetrators, and victim-survivors, relating, for example, to the communication of consent, the use of physical force, and typical victim-survivor and defendant behaviour, before, during, and after the rape (Ellison & Munro, 2009a; McGee, O'Higgins, Garavan, & Conroy, 2011).

Quantitative research using mock jurors[4] consistently finds that RMA scores significantly predict judgements about victim-survivor/defendant responsibility, victim-survivor/defendant blame, and, most importantly, verdict (Leverick, 2020). For example, Schuller and Hastings (2002) found that the more participants endorsed rape myths, the less credible/more blameworthy the victim-survivor was perceived to be. The opposite effect was found for the defendant, with greater endorsement of rape myths leading to the defendant being considered more credible and less blameworthy. In other words, two individuals presented with the same information could, depending on their RMA score, have different views on the extent to which a victim-survivor or defendant is to blame for the rape, and whether a guilty verdict should be returned. This is in line with schematic information processing more generally (e.g., Krahé, Temkin, & Bieneck, 2007), as new information tends to be assimilated into existing knowledge structures. Interestingly, research has also shown that even mock jurors who do not score highly on RMA scales that measure attitudes in the abstract (i.e., not in relation to a specific incident) can express highly problematic views (false and prejudicial beliefs about rape victim-survivors) when discussing a concrete case (Leverick, 2020). This would suggest the possibility that RMA scales may not always have strong predictive validity in court settings, and that these beliefs may need to be considered in terms of how they interact with characteristics of victim-survivors and perpetrators.

Consistent with the above, Temkin and Krahé (2008) found that identical case information was evaluated differently depending on jurors' RMA levels, with those evidencing higher RMA blaming the victim-survivor more and being less certain about the guilt of the defendant. Further, as noted by Devine et al. (2009) extra-evidentiary factors, including RMA, appear more influential when the available evidence does not point to a particular verdict. As such, when the evidence is ambiguous, jurors appear 'liberated' from the constraints imposed by the trial information and can – and do – give expression to extra-legal values (i.e., general beliefs, assumptions, and sentiments) when arriving at verdicts. This is highly problematic, as the vast majority of rapes contain features that would typically lead to the case being perceived as 'ambiguous' by outsiders (Rape Crisis England and Wales, 2021).

---

[4]Restrictions under Section 20D of the Juries Act 1974 in England and Wales (and Section 8 of the Contempt of Court Act 1981 in Scotland) specifically preclude asking jurors about 'statements made, opinions expressed, arguments advanced or votes cast by members of a jury in the course of their deliberations'. Mock juror studies simulate the experience of sitting on a jury by exposing participants to realistic trial reconstructions, conducted under experimental conditions, and then requiring them to deliberate in groups towards a verdict in accordance with the appropriate legal tests.

Specific Myths and Juror Decision-Making

Qualitative research also finds that during deliberations mock jurors frequently express problematic views about how 'genuine' rape victim-survivors would behave before, during, and after a rape. Further, some mock jurors tend to consider a broad spectrum of improbable scenarios that shift the blame from the accused to the victim-survivor (Finch & Munro, 2005). Three illustrative examples are provided, along with some other relevant findings on rape myths more generally.

Physical Resistance not Evident.   Research has documented a common belief on the part of mock jurors that a 'genuine' victim-survivor would fight back, leading to substantial defensive injuries, including internal trauma (Chalmers, Leverick, & Munro, 2021; Ellison & Munro, 2009a), even when the victim-survivor was heavily intoxicated during her victimisation (Munro & Kelly, 2009). Indeed, Ellison and Munro (2009a) found assumptions about resistance and injury to be 'so engrained they appear unshakable' (p. 299). These views are not limited to male mock jurors; women express such beliefs, contending that if they had been in the victim-survivor's place, they would have struggled more forcefully (Chalmers et al., 2021; Ellison & Munro, 2009b); that their own instinctive reaction 'as a woman' would be to fight back and inflict 'some kind of damage' on the perpetrator; and that they would be able to resist, even if the assailant was bigger and stronger than themselves (Chalmers et al., 2021). Acquittal verdicts have also been found to be frequently justified with reference to the absence of extensive and/or serious injuries. The myth about physical resistance during rape may be particularly problematic for Black women, as it is likely to be exacerbated by racial stereotypes about Black women being hostile and dominant (West, 2008) and loud and tough (Ghavami & Peplau, 2013), as stemming from extensive historical racism including colonisation and enslavement.

In contrast to the belief that a 'genuine' victim-survivor will physically resist an attack, an extensive body of literature has established considerable variation in reactions to traumatic events. For many individuals, a 'freezing' (also referred to as 'tonic immobility') or dissociative response is common (Marx, Forsyth, Gallup, Fusé, & Lexington, 2008). For instance, a study of 298 women who visited a Swedish emergency clinic for women subjected to rape found that 70% reported significant tonic immobility during the assault (Möller, Söndergaard, & Helström, 2017). An intentional and calculated decision not to physically resist in the hope of avoiding additional violence to oneself or others is also relatively common, although a lack of physical resistance can also lead to feelings of self-blame among victim-survivors (Gbahabo & Duma, 2021). Although some jurors have been found to challenge the view that there would be corroborative evidence of injury on either the victim-survivor or perpetrator, and acknowledge a woman could 'freeze', it appears that for some mock jurors the feasibility of a freeze response is less plausible in a 'non-stranger rape' (Chalmers et al., 2021; Ellison & Munro, 2009a). Further, even in cases where a freeze response was considered plausible, jurors were typically of the view that internal injury was still to be expected (Ellison & Munro, 2013), even though the absence of this is not indicative of consensual sex.

False Allegations are Routine.   Mock jurors often express views about the prevalence of false allegations of rape, stating rape allegations are often unfounded and false claims are easy to make (Chalmers et al., 2021). In Chalmers and colleagues' study, a mock juror commented that, 'there [are] hundreds of cases coming out where women have lied about rape' (2019, p. 14). Further, some jurors constructed a narrative whereby the victim might have made a false allegation because,

> [...] 'she wants her man to come back' (M01H), was 'obsessed' with the accused (M04F), might be a 'psycho bunny', out for revenge (M07F); or simply because 'women can be vindictive' (M04G), 'bad' or 'mad' (M06H). (2019, p. 14)

This further emphasises the link between RMA and negative stereotypes of women, which we discuss further in Chapter Six. However, in Ellison and Munro's (2013) mock juror study, some jurors questioned how realistic it was that a woman would put herself through the challenges of a criminal investigation and trial to merely 'get one over on someone, or to get back at someone' (p. 314).

Uncontrollable Male Sexual Urges and Sexual Miscommunication.   The notion that men are at the mercy of uncontrollable sexual urges has also been supported in mock juror studies, despite there being no scientific evidence for this being true (although some research within the sphere of 'scientific sexism' would argue to the contrary; Chapter Six). In such instances, jurors have expressed the view that the perpetrator may have genuinely (and reasonably) believed in consent. In Ellison and Munro's (2010) study, it was frequently expressed by mock jurors that because the perpetrator was 'so passionate and into it' or 'so transfixed', he would not be able to 'register what she was actually doing'. One juror, for example, stated that

> a woman can stop right up to the last second ... a man cannot, he's just got to keep going, he's like a train, he's just got to keep going. (p. 793)

This belief in uncontrollable male sexual urges was also evidenced in participants' responses to a pre-deliberation questionnaire. Forty-two percent of jurors agreed with the claim that 'rape happens when a man's sex drive gets out of control'; 50% agreed with the suggestion that 'men don't usually intend to force sex on a woman but sometimes they get too sexually carried away'; and 33% agreed with the statement that 'when a man is very sexually aroused, he may not even realise that the woman is resisting'. Importantly, especially in terms of research methodology, the authors note that these attitudes were less prevalent and asserted with less conviction in the questionnaires than appeared to be the case in the context of the jury deliberations. This suggests that during deliberations, jurors may be harsher on the victim-survivor and more sympathetic towards the defendant than their responses to quantitative measures of RMA may indicate. A similar disconnect between quantitative and qualitative endorsement has also been noted elsewhere (Zidenberg, Wielinga, Sparks, Margeotes, & Harkins, 2021), again highlighting the need for RMA research to use multiple methodological approaches.

Other Myths. Mock juror studies further suggest that jurors often hold other false beliefs about rape victim-survivors, including the expectation that a 'genuine' victim would quickly report an attack to the police (Smith, 2018) and would invariably be observably distressed (but not *too* distressed) while recounting events, both at the time of the incident and at trial (Taylor & Joudo, 2005).[5] Batchelder, Koski, and Byxby (2004), for instance, noted that it is a commonly expressed view that a woman who has been raped would always show distress after the incident. This view is problematic as victim-survivors are heterogeneous (Smith, 2018) and emotionality is not a reliable tool for evaluating credibility (Keogh, 2007; Sanders & Jones, 2007). Further, it has been suggested that victim-survivors may manage their emotions in court so that the defendant or the public gallery would not see them visibly upset (Konradi, 2007). Finally, previous jury decision-making research has also found that credibility evaluations of the victim-survivor are influenced by her clothing and character. In a meta-analysis including data from 28 studies, victim-survivors who wore revealing clothing were judged to be less respectable and were significantly more likely to be held responsible for instances of rape (Whatley, 1996).

Not only does RMA unintentionally influence jurors (e.g., because of ignorance about sexual violence contexts), research has also found that defence lawyers intentionally employ these beliefs to challenge and create doubt of a victim-survivor's account. A 2010 trial observation study (Temkin, Gray, & Barrett, 2018), for instance, found that defence counsel used these myths to distance the defendant and the case from the 'real rape' stereotype; to discredit the victim-survivor by emphasising aspects of her history, psychology, or character that would distance her from the image of the 'real rape' victim; and by emphasising aspects of the case that were consistent with rape myths. Similarly, two other observational studies (Adler, 1987; Lees, 2002) found that defence barristers drew on a wide range of rape myths in order to undermine the credibility of the victim-survivor, to blame her for the assault, and to make her appear unworthy of the protection of the law. Other studies (e.g., Zydervelt, Zajac, Kaladelfos, & Westera, 2017) have found that defence barristers continue to use rape myths during cross-examination by focusing on delayed reporting and the relationship between the parties after the offence. That defence barristers use rape myths (directly or indirectly) to their advantage during court proceedings has also been echoed in English court observations by Smith (2018). Thus, rape myths can be intentionally deployed to manipulate jurors' interpretations of the case. Therefore, when the defence counsel employs rape myths, they are reinforcing the beliefs of those who already hold such myths to be true, while also potentially raising doubt in the minds of those who generally do not. Thus, because of rape myths, credibility is rarely approved and difficult to secure.

---

[5]A woman can also be rendered non-credible as she becomes pathologised and psychiatrically labelled or if she is perceived as beyond treatment or help (Jordan, 2004).

Together, the findings of mock jury research suggest that jury deliberations in rape cases may be influenced by RMA and may proceed on problematic assumptions about rape and victim-survivors. This is concerning as it brings the impartiality assumption underlying juror decision-making into question (Burrowes, 2013). However, it is important to note that the inherent self-selection bias in mock juries may make them a poor proxy for real ones. Professor Thomas of University College London, for instance, has noted,

> regardless of how demographically representative a group of volunteer 'mock' jurors are, the very fact that they have volunteered to take part in a mock jury study means they cannot be representative of the vast majority of those who actually serve on juries in England and Wales. (2020, p. 27)

Further, despite stating that her research findings indicate that claims of widespread "juror bias" in rape cases are not valid (Thomas, 2020), her work has been critiqued on the basis of study design, the conflation of attitudes in relation to abstract versus applied rape myths, and misleading data interpretation (Daly et al., 2021).

Implications: Addressing the Impact of RMA on Court Cases

Several options to reduce the potential impact of prejudicial and stereotypical beliefs on juries exist. Below we consider a number of these, including possible pitfalls involved in employing them.

Policy Changes.   Several policy changes have occurred to try to tackle rape myths. The Sexual Offences Act (SOA) 2003, for instance, attempted to alleviate rape myths by clarifying issues around consent and allowing discussion of the defendant's actions as well as those of the victim-survivor. Most commentary has been supportive of these changes. McGlynn (2010), however, has argued that the new focus on 'reasonable belief' *increases* reliance on extra-legal factors. This is because, for example, victim-survivor behaviour is likely to influence whether a defendant's belief in consent can be considered 'reasonable'. Consequently, despite attempting to reduce the influence of rape myths at trial, then, the SOA 2003 may have had the opposite effect, encouraging their inclusion in jurors' decisions (Temkin & Ashworth, 2004). Further, a Home Office (2006) evaluation found that the SOA 2003 had not significantly improved conviction rates or accused men's accountability (McGlynn, 2010).

Although rape shield laws rely on the premise of assuring victim-survivors that irrelevant (e.g., past sexual history and/or sexual character) and untrue information about them will not be admitted (Haddad, 2005) and were implemented 'to deprive the jury of precisely the type of information that promotes rape myths' (Orenstein, 2007, p. 1599), these laws are routinely ignored with few, if any, consequences for the lawyers who violate them (see Orenstein, 2007). Orenstein (2007) notes that while rape victim-survivors need to be questioned in court, and the defendant has the right to a fair trial (see, for example, Article 6 of the European Convention on Human Rights (ECHR)), there is an inherent problem when the cross-examinations of rape victim-survivors are fundamentally degrading. Moreover, if the perpetrator is an acquaintance, the tendency is for the defence attorney to portray the rape as consensual sex, and that the victim-survivor is lying and making a false allegation. If the perpetrator is a stranger, the defence attorney portrays the victim as

> delusional (either mentally unsound or so terribly repressed she cannot confront her own complicity in having had sex), a vengeful liar, a gold digger, an attention seeker, or an unpaid prostitute. (Orenstein, 2007, p. 1603)

Other assessments of the impact of rape shield legislations are conflicting. Research and commentary by Kibble (2008) concluded that the judiciary are exercising appropriate discretion. Kelly et al. (2006) took the opposing view, noting that despite the implementation of special measures to improve victim-survivors' experience, sexual history is used to both undermine the credibility of the victim-survivor and to raise doubt in the jury's mind on the issues of consent.

Yet, irrespective of any shortcomings, it cannot be concluded that legislative changes will sufficiently address the impact of RMA on court cases. Negative social attitudes and RMA cannot be effectively redressed by statutory revision of the substantive law or by modifying rules of evidence or procedure, since this would not address the pervasive societal gender inequality. Further, any attempt to draft legislation impenetrable to bias would likely be rendered futile, as indicated by research highlighting the extent to which jurors are likely to fail to interact with the relevant sexual offences law and to make decisions without reference to the applicable legal test. Consequently, it is important to consider whether other measures can minimise the potential impact of RMA among jurors.

Juror Screening.   One potential strategy for reducing the impact of stereotypical and prejudicial attitudes about rape in trials would be to screen out potential jurors with high levels of RMA. Screening for attitudes, such as RMA, is permitted in some US states as part of the *voir dire* procedure (the process by which the suitability of prospective jurors may be assessed) and can lead to the disqualification of individual jurors. The purpose of this screening is to identify potential jurors who might introduce bias, either in favour of the accused (e.g., because of their adherence to RMA) or in favour of the alleged victim-survivor (e.g., because they have previously been subjected to rape themselves).

Unfortunately, there is limited empirical research examining the effectiveness of *voir dire* in detecting which prospective jurors are biased (Diamond & Rose, 2005). On the basis of their review of the evidence, Hans and Jehle (2003) concluded that traditional *voir dire* procedures involving a limited set of questions, posed by a judge, in a group setting, may be ineffective in identifying jurors with potentially biasing experiences and attitudes. This is because the prospective jurors may be reluctant to express attitudes (e.g., RMA) due to concerns over not appearing in a manner which is socially desirable (or sufficiently impartial) or because they are unaware of how much influence certain experiences can have over their future decisions. Research (e.g., Nisbett & Wilson, 1977) documents that many people are not conscious of the factors that significantly shape their attitudes and behaviour, which would also be in line with the schematic nature of RMA. Resultantly, Hans and Jehle (2003) favour expansive potential juror screening, in which individuals are questioned extensively (using a larger number and broader range of questions) by the judge and the attorneys individually and in confidence. They suggest this may encourage potential jurors' honesty and full reporting, as well as increase the ability to detect potential juror bias.

Further research is, however, required to decide whether screening out individuals with high RMA levels would be sufficient to effectively suppress the impact of RMA on jury decision-making. Appropriate and effective screening tools would also need to be developed. Moreover, given the societal pervasiveness of RMA (and its scaffolding within other types of common prejudices; Chapter Six), it is questionable whether it would even be possible to identify jurors who do not adhere to at least some of these beliefs. Finally, at present, in England and Wales, jury screening to exclude those individuals with biased attitudes to rape would run counter to current practice, where jury screening is strictly limited.

Juror Education and Guidance. In some countries, such as the US (e.g., Boeschen, Sales, & Koss, 1998) and England and Wales (Leverick, 2020), processes to educate jurors about the impact of rape, varying reactions to sexual violence, and general victim-survivor behaviour have been introduced. This introduction explicitly recognises that juror common knowledge about rape and the varied, often complex, behaviour of victim-survivors is limited and, moreover, likely to consist of erroneous stereotypes or unjustified beliefs about 'typical' responses. The effectiveness of juror education – in the form of directions from the trial judge, expert witness evidence, or information provision (e.g., a pre-trial video; The Gillen Review, 2019) – has, however, received little research attention (for a review, see Leverick, 2020). Findings of a study by Ellison and Munro (2013) suggest a 'thorough interrogation of prevailing expectations regarding socio-(hetero) sexual behaviour and communication is required' (p. 321), alongside efforts to educate jurors about the realities of rape.

In addition to possible challenges from the prosecution (i.e., objecting, or challenging narratives), judges in England and Wales can give directions to the jury at the beginning of the case or as part of the charge to the jury regarding the dangers of relying on stereotyped assumptions about rape (Judicial Studies Board, 2010). They are not, however, obliged to do so (Ellison & Munro, 2009a), which means that there is considerable potential for biases of the judges themselves to impact whether directions are issued. Ellison and Munro (2009) highlight that judicial directions on RMA can be positive because such comments seem to redress at least some unfounded assumptions and attitudinal biases (i.e., in terms of victim-survivor emotional demeanour and delayed reporting, but not a lack of physical resistance/injury),[6] but McEwan (2005) argues that judges rarely make use of these provisions and Smith (2018) found that judges' 'myth-busting' directions were challenged by the defence in their closing speech. Moreover, Carline and Gunby (2011) found that barristers were sceptical of increasing the number

---

[6]This of course leaves open the question of how to address the remaining prejudicial and stereotypical beliefs, which may result in jurors disbelieving a woman. The remaining myths, which are deeply problematic, appear unlikely to be countered through such means.

of judicial directions, arguing that they unduly complicate trials and 'push' jurors down a path to conviction. Despite this, according to Smith (2018), the directions may need to be more extensive in order to counteract the ways in which defence lawyers attempt to undermine them. Further, the timing of their delivery appears key, as Temkin (2010) noted that 'myth-buster' directions could reinforce rape myths if delivered only at the end of trial, because juries focus on the information that 'fits' with their interpretation of the evidence, again emphasising the schematic nature of RMA.

Importantly, despite some promising research findings (Ellison & Munro, 2009b), the degree to which jurors are both able to put such biases aside and are willing to do so remains unclear. Smith (2018) has also noted that because RMA is not necessarily about ignorance, the impact of knowledge-correcting information about the realities of rape may be limited. Further, even if juror training were introduced, this may not eliminate the impact of group processes that occur during deliberation (i.e., majority and minority influence and group polarisation, e.g., Castelli, Vanzetto, Sherman, & Arcuri, 2001), as well as bias in judgement as a product of social conformity. Further, people's explicit judgement may tell us little about their implicit assessment (i.e., their automatic unconscious thoughts) of a case – a potential entry point for unwanted biases (Süssenbach, Albrecht, & Bohner, 2017). Ellison, Munro, Hohl, and Wallang (2015) have also argued that eliminating jurors' reliance on case narrative, and the cognitive processes underpinning it, is not only an impossible task but also an undesirable one. This is because juries are used precisely because of their non-legalistic and common-sense rationality, which would call into question the purpose of juries in the first place.

Judges are also permitted to intervene when defence barrister questioning becomes inappropriate. However, there is considerable discretion in determining what kind of questioning is 'inappropriate', and Smith and Skinner (2012) found that judges rarely intervene. Ellison (2001) suggests that this may be because judges do not want to interfere in case the questions are part of the defendant's instructions to their barrister. In addition, Burton, Evans, and Sanders (2006) note that judges sometimes adhere to rape myths themselves and are part of a 'cooperative court culture' that promotes camaraderie, which can distort their views about what constitutes inappropriate questioning. Further, judges may see defence barristers as 'justified' in their intimidation tactics, since their priority is protecting the defendant. Judicial intervention can also be grounds for appeal against any subsequent conviction, which can make judges wary of being perceived as partisan.

A judge is also able to rule evidence as inadmissible. However, research examining the impact of inadmissible evidence has shown that, despite judges' instructions to disregard information during deliberations, such evidence continues to have an unfair influence on juror decision-making (e.g., Lieberman & Arndt, 2000). A meta-analytic review of 48 studies demonstrated that judicial instructions did not effectively eliminate the biasing impact of such evidence (Steblay, Hosch, Culhane, & McWethy, 2006). The authors concluded that contested evidence, later ruled inadmissible, in fact accentuates that particular evidence in the decision-making process.

Creation of a Specialist Court.   The Scottish government is relying on mock jury research to inform proposed changes to the CJS, including the potential introduction of a national, specialist sexual offences court. Core features in this type of court are the adoption of routine pre-recording of the evidence of victim-survivors, the use of trauma-informed practices and procedure, and requisite training (on sexual violence, including equality and diversity issues) for all participants. Specialist courts to address gender-based violence seem to have the potential for positive outcomes. One study (Cook, Burton, Robinson, & Vallely, 2004), following the introduction of domestic violence courts in England and Wales, found enhanced effectiveness of court and support services for victim-survivors, improved advocacy and information sharing, and increased levels of victim-survivor participation and satisfaction, which resulted in increased public confidence in the CJS.

Specialist rape courts could reduce the use of rape myths because the legal personnel involved would have more extensive training (thus removing lay participation from decision-making), closer links with support services, and greater familiarity with the issues surrounding sexual violence. Judges and prosecution barristers would also, therefore, arguably have a deeper understanding of the need for resisting stereotypes and to challenge their use though 'myth-busting'. In addition, Walker and Louw (2005) note that specialist courts in South Africa allow legal personnel to become experts in the complicated and often-changing laws surrounding sexual violence. This could mean, in England and Wales, that any policies or guidelines attempting to tackle the use of rape myths would be implemented more fully, and reducing the impact of RMA should be a key underpinning principle of these courts. Ultimately, though, Smith (2018) found that there may be limitations to the extent that victim-survivors can be protected from inappropriate questioning because of the need to ensure a fair trial.

Trials Before a Judge Sitting Alone.   Given the inadequacies of the deliberation process and limited scope for educating juries to counteract the adverse impact of RMA on jury decision-making (Lieberman & Arndt, 2000), another potential solution to the jury problem is the abolition of a jury in rape cases (Dripps, 2008; Finn, McDonald, & Tinsley, 2011). Indeed, an emergent body of prominent commentators and political figures view the jury as an inappropriate decision-maker in rape trials (Dripps, 2008). The argument for the abolition of the jury arises not out of antipathy to the jury as an institution but because of the unreliability of the jury within the context of sexual offences (Krahé & Temkin, 2009). Abolishing the jury may be necessary as a direct bypass of popular prejudice. The impact of the Internet and pre-trial coverage on jurors' knowledge of cases (i.e., knowing more about the victim-survivor and accused than is reasonably fair) has also been used in support of this argument.

We argue that *currently* this is not a realistic option, because in England and Wales, non-jury Crown Court trials only occur in cases where there is danger of jury tampering or where jury tampering has already taken place. Because of this, the removal of juries in sexual assault cases would need to take place within the context of a more general overhaul of the justice system. It can also be argued that there are political and philosophical justifications for juries (e.g., around citizen participation or 'community input' and the need to provide a check on state power;

Houlder, 1997), although again, the current utility of juries to provide justice for victim-survivors of sexual assault may be limited, particularly since the deliberation process is an inadequate safeguard against prejudicial decision-making.

Even if juries were to be removed, it still leaves the question of whether judges can weigh evidence correctly and fairly and remain unaffected by rape mythology. This was illustrated by a 2014 Canadian rape trial, during which a Federal Court Judge, Justice Robin Camp, caused controversy with his remarks about the victim-survivor in the case he was hearing. When the victim-survivor was testifying, he asked her why she 'couldn't just keep [her] knees together' or 'sink [her] bottom into the bathroom sink' to avoid being raped, and further criticised her for not screaming, saying, 'if you were ... frightened you could have screamed' (O'Neil, 2016). He also commented that 'sex is very often challenging', leaving a reasonable person with the impression that he was endorsing a 'problematic' (to borrow the Crown's adjective) view of sexual interactions between women and men that underlies many discredited rape myths. The verdict was overturned at Appeal, noting that Camp seemed to not understand the laws on consent and an alleged rape victim-survivor's sexual activity, and instead relied on discredited myths and stereotypes to guide his verdict (Markusoff, 2016).

Compulsory training for judges overseeing rape trials has been introduced in England and Wales to alleviate the use of myths by highlighting the realities of rape. Rumney and Fenton (2011) praised such training; for example, noting that it is well designed, delivered by experts, and offers practical advice about legal decisions. Importantly, though, Rumney and Fenton (2011) acknowledged that some legal professionals could attend training and would continue trying rape cases, even where their preconceptions remain unaltered (see also Angiolini, 2015). In addition, The Stern Review (2010) argued that training could perpetuate stereotypes if interpretations of the course materials are not checked. For example, Smith (2009) found that one barrister perceived his training as teaching him to *doubt* any victim-survivor who was emotionally distressed. Consequently, although training is likely to play a key role in addressing rape myths, it is not a simple or comprehensive answer (Smith, 2009).

Expert Witnesses.   Another option to neutralise rape myths is through the use of expert witnesses (Lonsway, 2005) in support of victim-survivors. Relevant expert witnesses would be those who can dispel myths and correct misinformation and incorrect narratives about violence against women and seemingly counter-intuitive responses (e.g., continued contact and habitation with the accused) and inexplicable behaviours linked to trauma (both at the time of the traumatic event and afterwards). Expert witnesses could, for instance, provide information about the common and diverse reactions to rape, the frequency of delayed reporting, or lack of physical resistance to the attack, and so on. Although the counter-intuitive expert evidence of psychologists and clinicians cannot be used simply to bolster the credibility of a particular victim-survivor, it can aid the restoration of the victim-survivor's credibility to a fair and impartial level. Because of this, it may also have the added benefit of validating the lived experience of victim-survivors of rape. Although this type of evidence is intended to 'neutralise' the victim-survivor's credibility, it has been argued that it may pose certain risks to the accused's right to a fair trial. As such, evidence can only be admitted after a careful assessment to ensure risks and benefits are balanced. However, it has also been argued that provided the expert does not meet with the woman and their testimony is not case specific, there would not be a question of the expert encroaching on the jury's role by appearing to vouch for the woman (Ellison & Munro, 2009b).

Research examining the effectiveness of expert witnesses in dispelling misconceptions is mixed. This type of evidence does seem to improve jurors' understanding of rape, leading to less biased perceptions (Ellison & Munro, 2009b). One study found that expert evidence that offered an opinion about whether the woman had been raped was more influential than expert testimony that presented research findings of discussed hypothetical examples (Schnopp-Wyatt, 1999). Further, it has been found that expert witnesses are effective at challenging stereotypes about delayed reporting and survivor demeanour (Ellison & Munro, 2009a, 2009b). However, research demonstrates that the evidence of a prosecution expert is swiftly diluted if the defence uses its own expert (for a review, see Temkin & Krahé, 2008).

Barrister Training and Challenging Narratives.   Training barristers about rape mythology is another potential option to mitigate against the impact of RMA in the courtroom, but this also assumes that RMA is about a lack of knowledge.[7] This training could take the form of encouraging awareness of the subtle ways in which myths are invoked and the misleading assumptions that arise from them, as well as enabling prosecution counsel to effectively myth bust (e.g., outline possible non-rational influences on the victim-survivor's behaviour and recognise the role of emotions, intuition, and context) and offer counter-narratives to those employed by the defence. Burrowes (2013), for instance, has provided guidance for prosecutors, giving them practical ways to shape the key narratives in rape cases that challenge common rape myths. Within this guidance, Burrowes argues that barristers should reframe rape myths as 'narratives' that support the case of the prosecution. Victim vulnerability (through intoxication, life circumstances, or other 'risky' behaviour), for instance, should be discussed in terms of the defendant targeting a person who is unlikely to report to the police, and unlikely to be believed if they did report. Burrowes further recommends challenging hindsight, since jurors tend to judge victim-survivors' actions without recognising that they did not know how events would unfold at the time.

It is worth noting, however, that myth-busting comments have been found to be easily undermined in trials by defence rhetoric about the burden and standard of proof (Smith, 2018). Such rhetoric presents the burden of proof as meaning that jurors should only critically evaluate the victim-survivor, not the defendant, and that jurors must be 100% certain about the victim-survivor's evidence in order

---

[7]RMA as being about knowledge production rather than ignorance is discussed by Smith (2018) and in other sections of this book.

to find the defendant guilty (Smith, 2018). Such interpretations might explain why research has suggested that victim-survivors feel that *they* are on trial rather than the defendant (Sanders & Jones, 2007). It is, therefore, likely that the practice of critically evaluating a victim-survivor's evidence using rape myths and ideas about how 'rational' people would act in the same situation will continue (Smith, 2018), which would undermine any myth-busters.

Training of barristers to challenge such narrative and address RMA may not, however, be straightforward. The Stern Review (2010) notes that training might perpetuate stereotypes if interpretations of the course material are not checked. For instance, Smith (2009) found, during interviews, that barristers perceived experience of trials to be more important than training courses. Consequently, while training may play a key role in tackling rape myths, it is not always a simple or comprehensive answer. Effective training, therefore, must have a clear, practical focus, so that barristers not only receive information about the realities of sexual violence but also know how to translate that information into good practice at trial. In addition, alongside tackling rape myth usage, there will need to be attendance to using techniques such as closed questions, leading questions, or a selective discussion of evidence; all of which could significantly affect trials (Smith, 2018). Further, although training barristers about the realities of rape may be essential for improving trials, this training will be unlikely to be wholly effective unless the underlying motivation to 'win by any legal means possible' (see Sanders & Jones, 2007) is also addressed. This again points to the possibility that the current legal system is not operating in the best interest of victim-survivors of sexual assault and rape, and it may also not be possible to completely insulate the legal system from societally pervasive attitudes such as rape myths.

Summary

Eliminating, or at least minimising, the impact of rape myths on court proceedings is clearly not simplistic. It is not possible to simply tell people that their assumptions and beliefs are incorrect and expect them to automatically change. Some problematic views may be more difficult to shift than others (especially considering their pervasiveness in society more generally) and consideration also needs to be given to the timing of any intervention and to its content. But this, it is argued here, may be the most appropriate strategy before more radical measures (e.g., elimination of a jury) are considered, alongside well-funded research that can rigorously assess the effectiveness of such interventions.

Impact of RMA on Women Subjected to Rape

In the following sections of this chapter, we examine the impact of RMA on women subjected to rape, paying particular attention to the associated impact on disclosures (both to formal support services and informal support networks), help seeking, and psychological well-being.

Policing: Disclosure, Engagement, and Secondary Victimisation

While not all interactions that victim-survivors have with the police are nega-tive, bad experiences are not uncommon (Molina & Poppleton, 2020). In a US study conducted by Campbell and Raja (2005), most victim-survivors reported that their interactions with the police, including questions about how they were dressed when they were raped and about their previous sexual history (both of which are tied to rape mythology), made them feel guilty, distrustful, depressed, and anxious. Similarly, Patterson (2011) found that a substantial proportion of US victim-survivors reported being told their story was 'unbelievable' (in other words, that they were lying); being asked questions related to their prior sexual history and how they were dressed leading up to their assault; and being told they would be charged with a crime if they did not provide an accurate story. Unsurprisingly, many of these victim-survivors stated that if they had known what the reporting experience would be like, they would not have pursued police involvement (see also Ministry of Justice and Home Office, 2021). Thus, while it could be argued that all of those who report a crime to the police should expect a certain level of questioning, the questions posed to women reporting rape appear excessive and exceedingly intrusive. Consequently, this questioning can lead to considerable distress, particularity when the 'truthfulness' of the account is ques-tioned and responses to disclosure reflect rape myths (Maier, 2008; Shaw, Camp-bell, Cain, & Feeney, 2017). In addition to extensive questioning, a full download of a woman's phone may take place, requiring the victim-survivor to hand over personal and sensitive data. It has been argued that these requests, or 'digital strip searches' as they are often described, further adversely impact the well-being of a victim-survivor (and remove one crucial way of accessing support); infringe a victim-survivor's right to privacy; and deter engagement with the criminal justice process (Ellison & Munro, 2009a, 2009b).

Victim blaming and sceptical reactions from the police inflict additional harm on victim-survivors, often referred to as 'secondary victimisation', and this harm is a risk factor for increased psychological distress (Campbell, Ahrens, Sefl, Wasco, & Barnes, 2001; Dworkin, Brill, & Ullman, 2019). Research also dem-onstrates that secondary victimisation decreases victim-survivor participation in the criminal justice process, reducing victims-survivors' willingness to cooperate with the police (via information sharing) and participate in the investigation and legal process (Lorenz & Jacobsen, 2021; Lorenz & Maskaly, 2018; Patterson, 2011a; Spohn et al., 2014). This may go some way towards explaining why there has, in England and Wales, been a recent increase in victim-survivors withdraw-ing support for the rape case once it has been reported to the police (Molina & Poppleton, 2020). Yet, when victim-survivors withdraw a complaint – most fre-quently for reasons such as not wanting to go to court, wanting to put the expe-rience behind them, threat of retaliation, non-supportive reactions from family and friends, self-blame for the assault, and/or secondary victimisation (Centre for Women's Justice, End Violence Against Women Coalition, & Rape Crisis Eng-land & Wales, 2020) – police tend to interpret the withdrawal as evidence of fab-rication (e.g., Campbell, 2006). Recently (October 2021), we collected data asking women who had been subjected to rape but not reported it ($n = 112$), why this was (see Fig. 2). As can be seen in this figure, the most common reasons were wanting to move on, the feared impact on mental health, and feelings of embarrassment. It is relevant to note that the least important reason for not reporting the rape to the police was a dislike or fear of the police, followed by a lack of trust in the police. Finally, among all women who had been subjected to rape ($n = 121$), RMA endorsement (as measured by the AMMSA; Gerger et al., 2007) was not predictive of whether or not they had chosen to report the rape to the police. However, the number of women in our sample who had chosen to report an incident of rape was exceedingly small ($n = 9$), making the comparison between these women and the non-reporting group difficult.

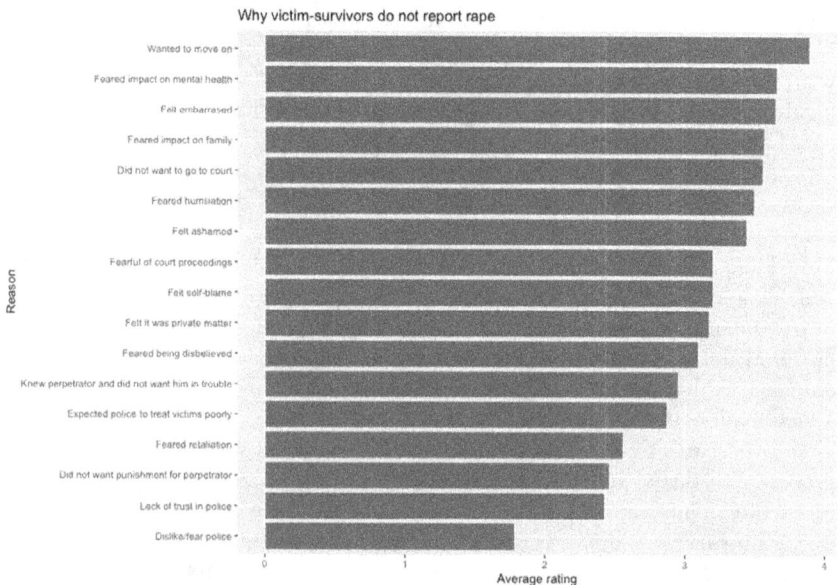

Why victim-survivors do not report rape

Fig. 2.   Reasons Why Women Did Not Report Rape. *Note*: These (not previously published) data were collected through Prolific on a sample of 298 women. Out of these women, 112 stated that they had been subjected to rape and chose not to report the offence to the police; these women were asked to rate how important 17 factors were in influencing this decision. Each item was rated 1 (*not at all important*) to 5 (*extremely important*). This figure illustrates mean responses for each of these factors.

Jordan (2004) identified a 'credibility conundrum' where police doubt a woman when she alleges rape but believe her retraction. This in turn contributes to the overestimation of false reports (Rumney, 2006) and decreases the likelihood that the perpetrator will be brought to justice, potentially allowing them to continue aggressing. Conversely, appropriate police responses (e.g., compassion and empathy, resource referral) can mitigate trauma, augment victim-survivor statements, and encourage continued victim-survivor cooperation during the investigation (Maddox et al., 2011; Patterson, 2011a). Consequently, it is clear that a 'positive' experience for the victim-survivor at the policing stage is of vital importance not only from the victim-survivors' perspective in terms of 'honouring the experience' and feeling heard (Ministry of Justice and Home Office, 2021; Stern Review, 2010) but also from an investigative and prosecution perspective. This may be particularly true for Black and minority ethnic (BME) rape victim-survivors, who experience higher rates of attrition and so have the least access to justice (Lovett, Uzelac, Horvath, & Kelly, 2007).

As well as affecting case progression, rape myths also impact the reporting behaviour of victim-survivors. Research indicates that reporting decisions are shaped by incident-related characteristics and contexts, including the perceived crime seriousness (i.e., whether it resulted in physical injuries, the presence of weapons, threats, or use of force), victim–offender relationship (i.e., acquaintance, stranger), offence location, and the voluntary consumption of drugs and/or alcohol. In other words, rapes that correspond to the 'classic rape scenario' (i.e., offences that resulted in visible injury, involved a weapon, were perpetrated by an unknown assailant, and occurred in an unfamiliar place) are more likely to be disclosed to the police (e.g., Felson & Pare, 2008; Fisher, Daigle, Cullen, & Turner, 2003; McGregor, Wiebe, Marion, & Livingstone, 2000). Fisher et al. (2003) found that over 42% of rape victim-survivors who did not report to the police cited that their primary reason for this was that they were unsure if a crime had been committed, as it did not contain stereotypical factors. This indicates that not only do rape myths inform society's and the CJS' response to victim-survivors of rape, but that these attitudes are also internalised by victim-survivors, resulting in women not reporting their victimisation because the incident was 'not serious enough', they are not sure that the crime or harm was intended, and they believe that there is a lack of proof that the rape happened (Fisher et al., 2003). Biased reporting may in itself lead to the perpetuation of rape myths, as more of the rapes that fit the 'real rape stereotype' will be made public than those that do not fit the stereotype (McGregor et al., 2000). It is also possible that men may target women whom they know will be reluctant to report rape (people seen as 'damaged goods'; Felson & Pare, 2008; Fisher et al., 2003), as they are aware that this will influence both initial reporting and police responses. This is not to imply that women are ever the cause or source of the abuse that they are subjected to, but to highlight that rape myths consistently work in favour of perpetrators of sexual violence, including in perpetration.

The impact of rape myths on reporting behaviour may be particularly relevant to certain groups of women. Sexual crimes and the subsequent need for assistance are not looked at similarly across cultural groups. For example, reporting may be particularly problematic for Black women (Munro & Kelly, 2009), because historically (and today) their claims of rape have not been taken seriously (Wyatt, 1992). Research on criminal justice outcomes shows that White suspects are more likely to avoid further investigation, especially if the victim-survivor is from a minoritised group, while perpetrators are more likely to be prosecuted if they are from a minoritised group (Hohl & Stanko, 2015). This serves to reinforce systemic racialised disparities within the justice system to minoritised women. In addition (and as outlined in further detail in Chapter Two), Black feminist theorists illustrate that the combination of racism and sexism has created oppressive images of Black women, which influence disclosure and reporting patterns when it comes to rape and sexual violence (Collins, 1990/2009). Olive (2012) states that when reporting rape, Black women must battle two myths: that they are promiscuous and that they are emasculating Black men by not giving them what they deserve. Similarly, Native American women have been historically described as 'rapable' because they were seen as dirty and the rape of a dirty body 'does not count' (Smith, 2005). Thus, other stereotypes may legitimize men's violence against women. With regard to controlling imagery and violence against Black women, Crenshaw (1993) argues that

> stereotyped representations encourage and incite violence against us. ... They create a dominant narrative that forces actual women of color to the margins of the discourse and renders our own accounts of such victimization less credible. (p. 113)

Distrust of criminal justice institutions may, however, be warranted, as BME victim-survivors have the lowest chance of conviction when they do engage with the CJS[8] (Hohl & Stanko, 2015b). This is most obvious when comparing convictions in rape cases involving Black victim-survivors with those involving White victim-survivors, where the conviction rates were 2.4% and 7.6%, respectively, between 2000 and 2002 (Munro & Kelly, 2009).

Delayed help-seeking and disclose was also found to be common among South Asian immigrant women in Toronto, mainly due to 'social stigma, rigid gender roles, marriage obligations, expected silence, loss of social support after migration, limited knowledge about available resources and myths about partner abuse' (Ahmad, Driver, McNally, & Stewart, 2009, p. 613). Myths about partner abuse included partner's use of alcohol as the sole cause of violence and partner's 'bad blood' or genetic reasons for violence. Cultural concepts concerning 'honour'[9] and 'shame' also shape victim-survivor approaches to reporting and seeking help (Gill, 2009). A woman is seen to risk her family's 'good name' by reporting her victimisation: she is seen to have acted in a shameful manner in making the report, as well as in being victimised in the first place. Indeed, family members often fear that a daughter's 'ruined' reputation following disclosure of rape will remain an ongoing threat to their familial honour (Phillips, 2010). Consequently, fears over alienation, isolation, and ostracism shape how South Asian women interpret what they have been subjected to and to whom they dare disclose having been subjected to rape (Gill & Harrison, 2019). Similarly, in Japanese culture, high value is placed

---

[8]We note that BME groups are under-represented within the CJS, implying this group is not seeking a justice response in the same way as White victim-survivors.

[9]'Honour' is usually regarded as a family's standing within the community as viewed through the lens of the family's control of 'their' women. This is because the actions of one member of the family are seen to reflect on all in collectivist societies (Gill & Harrison, 2019).

on endurance in the face of adversity, suffering is silence, sharing responsibility for 'unpleasant events' and defusing a situation to restore harmony (Dussich, 2001).

The decision not to report rape may have several consequences. At the most basic level, opting not to report rape precludes perpetrators' arrests, which in turn may limit the deterrent effect of the CJS and its ability to incapacitate offenders (Skogan, 1977). Moreover, women not reporting rape can also be said to impair the broader societal perspective of having a justice system that addresses rather than exacerbates inequalities. Not reporting rape also reduces the likelihood that victim-survivors will have access to victim-assistance services provided by the CJS. For example, victim-survivors in England and Wales cannot be compensated by the Criminal Injuries Compensation Authority (CICA)[10] if they do not report the crime to the police or do not cooperate with bringing the perpetrator to justice. Here, we do not in any way suggest that women are obliged to report rape, or that they are irrational if they choose not to. Ultimately, the responsibility for protecting women from sexual violence and bringing perpetrators to justice always lies with the CJS, and it is the duty of wider society to create a justice system where women can feel safe in seeking justice following rape.

Court

A considerable body of literature has looked at the impact of cross-examination on rape victim-survivors, as many women report feeling confused, humiliated, and silenced by the attack on their credibility (Ellison, 2001). It has, therefore, been argued that trials can lead to 'secondary victimisation' and victim-survivors have said they felt it was themselves, not the defendant, who was on trial, experiencing what has been termed as the 'second rape' (e.g., Campbell, 2008). Wheatcroft, Wagstaff, and Moran (2009) even found that some victim-survivors suffered flashbacks of their court experience because it was so traumatic. Consistently across studies, victim-survivors identify giving evidence as the worst part of their CJS experience (see Ellison, 2001), and fear about giving evidence at trial is one of the mostly commonly cited reasons for victim-survivor withdrawal of complaint (Ellison, 2001; Stanko & Williams, 2009). From our own data on victim-survivors of rape (Fig. 2), not wanting to go to court and being fearful of court proceedings were among the more commonly reported reasons for not reporting the rape to the police.

Further, when cases end in acquittals for allegations that deviate from stereotypical expectations and the 'real rape' scenario, victim-survivors are marginalised both individually and as a group (Taslitz, 1999). Larcombe (2002), however, argues that how a victim-survivor presents herself in court determines whether she is able to *resist* the defence's construction of her as sexualised, contradictory, or unreliable and whether she is silenced. In this context, 'successful' victim-survivors display self-assurance and take overt offence at (rather than being caught off guard by or accepting of) the defence's insinuations of contributory negligence, blame, and immorality. Larcombe (2002) suggests that a victim-survivor's rejection of the defence's propositions is important for being heard by the jury and to secure

---

[10]We note that both the eligibility criteria and CICS application process reinforce stereotypical beliefs about how victim-survivors of sexual offences 'should' behave.

convictions. Exhibiting resistance allows jurors, who are witnessing the second rape, to 'see' what happened on the earlier occasion. However, we argue that most women subjected to rape may not hold the necessary attitudinal and linguistic qualities for a resistive performance, which leaves them silenced. It also seems fair to suggest that victim-survivors needing to exhibit resistance to secure justice following a traumatic experience places an unfair burden on women who are already uniquely vulnerable. 'Social class' may also play a role here, as MacKinnon (2007) noted that legal rules and court norms are rooted in (White male) middle class values, meaning that any beliefs, experiences, or ways of communicating that diverge from the 'middle class norm' are trivialised or treated with suspicion. Similarly, victim-survivors with learning disabilities (e.g., low intelligence, autism) may struggle with detecting, understanding, and responding to defence questions (e.g., not resisting the implications of the questions) that challenge their testimony (Antaki, Richardson, Stokoe, & Willott, 2015). Thus, many women do not have 'full and equal participation' in the 'theatre of the trial', and aside from the influence of rape myths that negatively impact all women's credibility, some are inherently more believable than others due to prejudice.

It could be suggested that victim-survivors' perceptions of their treatment in the CJS are influenced by the verdict, and that negative perceptions arise when convictions are not obtained (Kebbell, O'Kelly, & Gilchrist, 2007). Convictions are not, however, always the most important outcome for women subjected to sexual violence (McGlynn & Westmarland, 2019). Participants in McGlynn and Westmarland's research coined the term 'kaleidoscopic justice' to 'capture the breadth, variety, complexity, and dynamism of sexual violence victim-survivors' understandings of justice', and this includes but also extends beyond the CJS (p. 19). Similar suggestions were put forward by Hill (2009), who argued that both criminal and non-criminal judicial responses are necessary to support minority women in the UK who are subjected to violent relationships. McGlynn and Westmarland' study (2018), and other studies on justice needs, have found that victim-survivors of sexual violence want meaningful consequences for, and the exposure of, perpetrators; to prevent future abuse from happening; acknowledgement of the harm they have experienced and recognition as survivors; prevention and education measures; assistance with rebuilding their lives; and procedural justice (i.e., to be treated with dignity and to have a voice in proceedings). Further, some women who are 'successful' (i.e., for whom a guilty verdict is obtained) may feel injustice and perceive their treatment during cross-examination negatively, which may work to reduce any future reliance on, and cooperation with, the CJS.

Formal and Informal Sources of Support

Victim-survivors, particularly women of colour (Thiara & Gill, 2010), may be further harmed if upon turning to the system for help they are met with secondary victimisation and rape myth endorsement (as well as other types of stereotyping) on the part of members of the helping professions. This can increase women's feelings of culpability and shame, causing them to feel invalidated, misunderstood, and judged. Further, victim-survivors are likely to become distrustful of others, making them reluctant to seek further help (Campbell et al., 1999;

Campbell & Raja, 1999). In line with this, most of the therapists surveyed in Campbell and Raja's (1999) study voiced a concern that interaction with community professionals can, at times, worsen the state of victim-survivors' mental health. This may, in part, be because therapists are sometimes unaware of their own RMA and may view victim-survivors as contributing in some way to their victimisation. Consequently, they may interpret victim-survivors' behaviours in problematic way(s) (e.g., by analysing a victim-survivor's reasons or motives for accompanying a romantic partner to his place, where she was then raped). For this reason, 85% of therapists expressed a belief that clinicians must be made more aware of the risks of secondary victimisation and its repercussions for the effectiveness of treatment, to avoid inflicting further harm on victim-survivors and to fully maximise the efficacy of therapy.

It is notable, however, that many victim-survivors experience mental health personnel as positive and supportive (Campbell, 1998). In addition, research examining victim-survivors' involvement with rape advocates suggests that those victim-survivors who have access to these personnel experience less distress and report better treatment by legal authorities (Campbell, 2006). This is perhaps because such professionals are able to counter any rape myths that victim-survivors may have internalised, leading to decreased feelings of self-blame and shame (Ryan, 2011).

An accumulating body of research has also examined the impact of informal sources of support's (e.g., rape victims-survivors' partners and family members) negative behavioural reactions to rape disclosures, which can be influenced by rape myths and other stereotypical beliefs. Such reactions include disbelief, suspicion, or blaming language when the victim-survivor discloses what they have been subjected to (Ullman, 2010); distraction/discouragement from talking (which has been termed 'silencing'); avoiding discussion about the rape(s); taking control from the victim-survivor for reporting the rape(s); and minimising the victim-survivor's reactions to the rape(s). Negative responses to disclosure may engender secondary victimisation (or re-traumatisation) in victim-survivors, an unfortunately common and harmful experience (Orchowski & Gidycz, 2012, 2015). Recent data collection of ours[11] did not find a relationship between women's scores on the AMMSA (Gerger et al., 2007) and whether they thought victim-survivors of rape should report to the police (as measured on a 5-point Likert-type scale). Participants did, however, not respond to a specific incident of rape, and it is possible that their answer on reporting/not reporting (and its relationship with RMA) would have been different if more context had been provided.

Mental Health and Well-Being

Rape myths can be detrimental to rape victim-survivors' mental health and well-being. Women who have been subjected to rape position themselves in relation

---

[11]These data were collected through Prolific on a sample of 173 women in October 2021 and have not been previously published.

to rape myths and victim blaming ideology, to both question the severity and reality of what they have been subjected to and assess how they are presenting themselves to others. Each encounter with others is potentially problematic and risky as it contains cultural presumptions and judgements that may confirm pre-existing feelings of self-blame and shame. Exposure to, and internalisation of, such myths may heighten a woman's inclination towards self-denigration and condemnation (e.g., 'How could I have been so stupid ... putting myself in such a situation, and allowing this to happen'; Ullman, 1996). Indeed, this tendency has been noted across varied cultural and ethnic backgrounds (Neville, Oh, Spanier-man, Heppner, & Clark, 2004). Being made to feel that the rape occurred because of the 'type of woman she is' (as directly linking with rape myth beliefs within the domain 'only certain women are raped', as further outlined in Chapter Two) frequently increases a victim-survivor's feelings of shame.

Rape myths can also promote beliefs that may discourage victim-survivors from disclosing the incident to others, thereby reducing their likelihood of obtaining the social and professional support that could facilitate their recovery (Botta & Pingree, 1997). For instance, as noted above, some myths may cause victim-survivors to doubt that what happened qualifies as a 'real rape', which may subsequently act as an internal barrier to help-seeking, as support services are thus viewed as being relevant for 'other women'. This problem appears to be espe-cially, although not uniquely, common among women who have been subjected to rape by an acquaintance, as well as among women of colour (Alvidrez, 1999; Ullman & Brecklin, 2002; Wyatt, 1992). Similarly, accusatory and/or demeaning social responses (e.g., from friends and family) may lead a substantial proportion of victim-survivors to isolate themselves from their close social network. This is because it is not uncommon for a victim-survivor to encounter blame from those closest to her in the form of dismay that she behaved in a certain way or failed to do something to protect herself (e.g., by engaging in 'unsafe' behaviour, such as drinking; by placing herself in 'unsafe' situations, such as bars or walking home alone; by wearing revealing clothes; or by behaving 'promiscuously'; Sheldon & Parent, 2002; Ullman, 1999). As Ahrens and Campbell (2020) noted, friends might have emotional reactions to a victim-survivor's rape disclosure (and it is likely that these reactions are informed by RMA) that interfere with their ability to provide support, which can lead to negative changes in the relationship. Shame among family members is also common, particularly, but not solely, if the victim-survivor belongs to an ethnic minority or has a low Socio-Economic Status (SES) (Alvidrez, 1999; Wyatt, 1992). It may take the form of urging the victim-survivor to remain quiet about her victimisation, pretending it never happened, or directly disgracing her for what has been done to her.

Self-Blame

Research shows that victim-survivors of rape tend to blame themselves for being raped. Obviously, self-blame is distressing, but it also inhibits victim-survivors from disclosing their victimisation, as they try to avoid receiving further blame reactions from others (Patterson, Greeson, & Campbell, 2009), a process Ullman (1996) described as 'avoidance coping'. When victim-survivors believe that their actions would be judged negatively by others, they are likely to internalise blame (see Finkelson & Oswalt, 1995). The propensity for self-blame contributes to poorer mental health and worryingly reduces the opportunity for victim-survivors to seek help. Self-blame has also been established as a critical factor for the establishment and maintenance of posttraumatic stress disorder (PTSD) after sexual violence (e.g., Peter-Hagene & Ullman, 2018). This self-blame tends to occur more often when victim-survivors were under the influence of alcohol at the time of the rape(s), and when they perceived that their own actions led to them being sexually victimised (behavioural self-attribution), again highlighting the links between self-blame and rape myths. Similarly, women who have been blamed by the police or CJS have been shown to also blame themselves (e.g., Fisher et al., 2003).

Finally, it is important to note that self-blame has been suggested to serve an important function for some victim-survivors (Koss & Harvey, 1991), in that it can provide some (albeit illusionary) sense of control over what they were subjected to, which can help to counteract feelings of helplessness. For example, if a rape victim-survivor believes that her behaviour contributed to her rape in some way, she can believe that changing this behaviour will prevent re-victimisation. This is true even though her behaviour had no rational relationship to the sexual violence and changing that behaviour would not protect her in reality (Branscombe, Owen, Garstka, & Coleman, 1996; Branscombe, Wohl, Owen, Allison, & N'gbala, 2003). Most contemporary research has, however, argued that counterfactual thinking and self-blame, even with the purpose of regaining perceived control over the sexual violence, results in reduced well-being and social isolation (Frazier, 2003; Koss, Figueredo, & Prince, 2002; Ullman, Townsend, Filipas, & Starzynski, 2007). Despite this, it is important to be aware of this potential protective function of self-blame and guilt. It also highlights the need for further research exploring the function(s) served by self-blame.

In terms of implications for therapy, any type of therapeutic intervention may be harmful to individuals if a therapist is unaware of their own prejudicial beliefs associated with rape. Further, irrespective of treatment modality, any intervention will likely be less effective if it fails to address the impact of rape myths on the victim-survivor's sense of self, including negative self-appraisals (i.e., feeling that her actions contributed to the victimisation), experiences of social condemnation (e.g., being made to feel culpable for the rape by friends and family members), and secondary victimisation by the CJS and/or other formal support systems. As such, it is likely that a consistent consideration of rape myths is necessary when working in a therapeutic context with women who have been subjected to rape.

Unacknowledged Rapes

Koss (1985) defined an unacknowledged rape victim as 'a woman who has experienced a sexual assault that would legally qualify as rape but who does not conceptualize herself as a rape victim' (p. 195). In these situations, victim-survivors often label their victimisation as a 'serious miscommunication' or 'bad sex' (Littleton, Axsom, & Grills-Taquechel, 2009; Littleton, Axsom, Breitkopf, & Berenson, 2006; Orchowski, Untied, & Gidycz, 2013). Although there are many reasons *why* a woman may not wish to consider that she has been subjected to rape (e.g., connotations of powerlessness or stigmatisation, being in a romantic relationship with the perpetrator), level of RMA also influences this labelling process (e.g., Orchowski et al., 2013; Peterson & Muehlenhard, 2004). For example, a woman who has not fought her attacker and also accepted the rape myth that a victim-survivor has to fight back for the offence to be classified as rape would be less likely to say she had been raped, even though, legally, she had been. A meta-analysis found that unacknowledged rape is quite common among adult women; the overall weighted mean percentage of unacknowledged rape was 60.4% (95% confidence interval [55.0%, 65.6%]; Wilson & Miller, 2016). In other words, around 60% of women who have been subjected to rape do not acknowledge that they have been raped.

The impact of RMA on rape acknowledgement is of importance because victim-survivors who do not label their victimisations as rape are unlikely to (a) report to the police (or delay reporting, increasing the time between the assault and their reporting of it, and thereby driving scepticism of their account; Capers, 2012); (b) seek mental and physical health services (and may not legally be entitled to it, as outlined further above); (c) participate in research, thereby leading to an underestimation of its true occurrence; or (d) communicate to others about what they have been subjected to (Littleton et al., 2006). They are also more likely to blame themselves for their victimisation (Miller, Amacker, & King, 2011) and are more likely to be revictimised (Littleton et al., 2009). Further, because we are not capturing a key subset of the affected population, our awareness and understanding of rape may be biased towards acknowledged rape victim-survivors and may not be representative of all rape victim-survivors.

How Disability and Perceived Social Class Affect CJS Experiences

Although research has examined the effects of race and ethnicity on CJS experiences and outcomes, there has been less consideration of how disabled people and the working class/those with low SES are vulnerable to discrimination within the CJS linked to rape myths and the impact this may have on engagement with the legal system. The findings discussed below suggest that these groups are likely to perceive the CJS as unfair or unable to meet their needs. There is also notable discrimination within rape trials against victim-survivors with mental health problems (Smith, 2018). Ellison et al. (2015) argue that this is because people requiring mental health treatments are assumed to make more false allegations, despite there being no evidence to support this claim. As further discussed in Chapter Six, myths around mental and physical disabilities can also be used to activate more direct rape myths in a court setting. In addition, Ellison (2009) notes that there are no systematic rules about when psychiatric evidence is relevant and, therefore, admissible at trial. Consequently, individual judges must rely on discretion, despite being likely to hold entrenched stereotypes about disability.

Moreover, research suggests that people from different perceived 'social classes' can have markedly different experiences of the CJS (Equality and Human Rights Commission (EHRC), 2010). MacKinnon (2007) notes that the law and legal rules are rooted in middle class values, meaning that a person's social class is likely to influence how they are treated and perceived by the CJS. Phipps (2009), for example, highlights the role of working class stereotypes; noting that juries often consider middle class notions of 'respectability' when determining victim-survivor credibility (see also Stevenson, 2000). Phipps (2009) advances, therefore, that working class women are perceived as being partly culpable for sexual victimisation because of reduced 'chastity' and 'femininity'. This also means that sexual history evidence is likely to have greater impact when linked with social class. Despite having the potential to mislead the jury, these narratives are justified by the adversarial imperative for each barrister to advance their client's case by any legal means, a practice that is clearly problematic in the case of rape trials.

Conclusion

The literature reviewed above is overwhelming in indicating that rape myths affect the way in which police officers and jurors evaluate evidence in rape cases. The research implemented on mock juries demonstrates that jurors' rape myth endorsement is related to judgements in individual rape cases, both in terms of the degree of culpability attributed to a rape victim-survivor and – more importantly – views about what the verdict should be. The extent to which RMA impacts real-life decision-making, is, however, unclear. The literature does suggest that juries may compromise their impartial position by infusing their rape mythology with their assessment of a rape victim-survivor, to the extent that an acquittal may be based on grounds other than the accused's factual innocence. As such, the jury can undermine the authority of the law and decriminalise rape. Further, a jury's failure to deliver an impartial verdict can lead to further victim-survivor distress. In addition, and as discussed in Chapter Five, the jury's verdict also contributes to the definition of what is considered 'real rape' (Sinclair & Bourne, 1998). For instance, as cases deviating from the 'real rape' stereotype are more likely to culminate in an acquittal decision, this verdict bolsters the widely held view that cases that do not closely resemble the stereotype are not really rape. Because of this, there is a pressing need to further our understanding of the 'jury problem'.

Central to the way(s) in which the CJS responds to incidents of rape are decisions around how credible the victim-survivor is. At every stage of the CJS process, from the initial reporting of the rape, rape myths appear to play a major role in establishing or denying this credibility. Research further suggests that not only are the outcomes of rape cases affected by legally relevant factors, they are also affected by legally irrelevant factors linked with rape myths. Consequently, for many victim-survivors, the CJS is not experienced as a site of protection but as a site of harm that compounds the distress associated with having been sub-jected to sexual assault. Formal and informal support systems have the potential to support victim-survivors through the CJS experience, but responses from these sources of support can also be affected by rape myth endorsement. Because of this, negative reactions from others can enhance feelings of shame and self-blame among victim-survivors of rape. We conclude that anyone working to support women who have been subjected to rape should consider their own belief in rape myths, as well as how rape myths may have impacted the victim-survivor's mental health and their experiences with the CJS.

Chapter Five

The Perpetuation and Functions of Rape Myths

Chapter Overview

This chapter will examine the perpetuation of rape myths in society, with a particular focus on the complex ways in which the institutions that we might expect to protect members of the general population against the effects of rape myths, may, in some cases, be central to their maintenance (Kitzinger, 2009). We argue that while most people and institutions would – on the surface – disagree with rape myths, they are often pervasively maintained, sometimes with the intent to protect women. Within this argument, we will present examples of sexual violence prevention campaigns that have been designed by police forces and authorities with the intention to prevent sexual violence by encouraging women to protect themselves (e.g., by changing their appearance, character, or behaviour), which we will argue ultimately blame women for being victimised. We will also critically discuss some of the ways in which the media portray rape, since such portrayals have been shown to increase victim-survivor blaming and influence the way in which victim-survivors are perceived by the criminal justice system (CJS) and the general population more broadly (Horvath, Hegarty, Tyler, & Mansfield, 2012; Hust, Rodgers, Ebreo, & Stefani, 2019; Kitzinger, 2009). Here, we will explore how rape myth-supporting media portrayals interact with stereotypes around perceived social class and ethnicity, to perpetuate myths around the rape of particular groups of women. This chapter will advance an outline of changes that could be made to improve prevention campaigns and media portrayals of sexual assault committed against women and girls.

Finally, we link the perpetuation of rape myths to the functions these myths serve, to explore *why* individuals and institutions appear reluctant to completely abandon these ideas, particularly regarding how truth is established and maintained (Smith, 2018). We focus specifically on rape myths as misguided intentions to protect women, the Just World Theory (e.g., Lerner, 1977, 1980), and the gender-specific functions of these attitudes (Bohner et al., 2009).

Rape Myths: Understanding, Assessing, and Preventing, 83–103
Copyright © 2022 by Sofia Persson and Katie Dhingra
Published under exclusive licence by Emerald Publishing Limited
doi:10.1108/978-1-80071-152-520220005

The Perpetuation of Rape Myths

Prevention Campaigns

Primary prevention interventions, often in the form of media campaigns, are frequently used to deter and inhibit sexual violence *before it occurs*. While this would, in theory, appear to be a sensible approach, many of these campaigns have been criticised for 'providing safety and awareness messages to women', which place 'the responsibility for being raped solely on women' (Stern Review, 2010, p. 52). Within these campaigns, the focus tends to be on the behaviour of women, implying (or even explicitly stating) that they are responsible for 'rape avoidance', while overlooking the actions, motives, and intentions of the perpetrator (Pease, 2014). Because of this, campaigns such as these link directly with the rape myth belief system, as, by positioning women as the 'solution' to the problem of rape, they also position them as the initial cause.

Some specific examples of these types of prevention campaigns include posters with slogans such as 'Don't be a victim, drink sensibly' (South Wales Police, 2011) and 'Avoid being a rape victim' (Warwickshire Police, 2013). Another example of a female-centric victimisation intervention is a poster by Sussex Police that informed women that '[m]any sexual assaults could be prevented' and advised them to '[s]tick together and don't let your friend leave with a stranger or go off on their own' (Sanghani, 2015; see also Brooks, 2011; Campbell, 2005). This implies that if a friend started the evening with you and is subsequently raped when later separated from you, the fault lies with you, again placing the cause of rape everywhere but with the perpetrator. Another campaign, 'Safe Night Out', by West Mercia Police (2012) included a webpage and a video of a victim-survivor encouraging women not to drink to excess in order to avoid victimisation. The posters showed a smiling woman in a club above another photo of the same woman barefoot and seemingly unconscious laying on the ground with the text: 'Don't let a night full of promise … turn into a morning full of regret. Drink sensibly and get home safely'. If the poster were about getting drunk to the point of falling over and/or passing out, we would agree that is arguably something a person would regret; if it is about being raped while drunk, 'regret' is entirely the incorrect word, as it implies culpability. West Mercia Police stated the campaign's aim was to 'distribute information showing potential victims how to avoid becoming vulnerable'. However, as with many other high-profile campaigns, the focus was entirely on the behaviour of women, with no reference to the responsibility men might have in such scenarios. Moreover, apart from this 'safety advice' drawing on central tenets of the rape myth belief system (e.g., 'only certain types of women are raped'), these ideas are also being communicated *within* a rape culture. In other words, even if the campaigns appeared seemingly objective to those who designed them, the messages cannot be isolated from the social context in which they are being delivered and heard. This context justifies, tolerates, and minimises sexual violence by men and differentially disbelieves and blames some women for the victimisation they are subjected to, which impacts how these messages are understood. We argue that because of this, anti-rape interventions such as the ones discussed above are likely important for understanding how RMA is maintained on both a societal and individual level.

Apart from their obvious links with central rape myth beliefs, the 'risk management' or 'rape avoidance' approaches to rape prevention discussed above are highly problematic for several reasons. First, the realities of sexual violence are misrepresented, as not even women who adhere to the 'safety advice' are rendered impervious to abuse (Powell & Henry, 2014). Indeed, the list of behaviours women are instructed to avoid is often so encompassing that 'we could remind women that taking their vaginas out [...] with them is "risky"' (Lawson & Olle, 2006, p. 50). Another issue with the victim-survivor-focused risk management approach is that it conveniently makes the perpetrators of rape invisible, at the same time 'denying women a right to be safe' (Lawson & Olle, 2006, p. 50). In other words, the focus is on the 'target' and 'guardianship' aspects of the crime while ignoring or minimising the responsibility of perpetrators and the cultural and social conditions that condone and support hegemonic beliefs and attitudes about gender, sexuality, and violence (Vetten, 2011). As Vetten (2011) argues, these interventions do not address rape causation but ask people (predominately women) to take responsibility for avoiding sexual violence or resisting sexual violence once it is already occurring through various self-defence methods. Importantly, without addressing the actual cause of rape (i.e., perpetrators), even if most women were to adhere to the 'safety advice', those who may not have the resources to do so (e.g., homeless women and other vulnerable groups) are left uniquely vulnerable to perpetrators who are arguably still seeking potential targets. Because of their lack of targeting the perpetrator (i.e., the *only* cause of the rape), these campaigns implicitly shift the risk of victimization onto women who may not be able to 'protect' themselves. Moreover, these campaigns also tell women that they cannot realistically expect any social structure or institution to act towards ensuring their safety.

It also cannot be overlooked that female-centric rape prevention campaigns are performative in nature, sending a message to the public about how key stakeholders (e.g., the Police, National Health Service (NHS)) view rape and the perceived solution(s) to reduce its incidence. As Mardorossian (2002) argues,

> Making women's behavior and identity the site of rape prevention only mirrors the dominant culture's proclivity to see rape as women's problem, both in the sense of a problem women should solve and one that they caused. (p. 755)

Such campaign messaging was also mirrored recently following the kidnap, rape, and murder of Sarah Everard; the Metropolitan Police Force, for instance, suggested that women who felt threatened by officers should 'wave a bus down' (Middleton, 2021).

Although not currently widespread in the UK, male-focused campaigns do exist (DeGue et al., 2014), including Police Scotland's (2021) campaign to reduce rape, serious sexual assault, and harassment, 'Don't Be That Guy' (https://that-guy.co.uk/). The campaign urges men to 'look in the mirror' and address behaviours that women find abusive, intimidating, or threatening. The actors in the video explain that gestures that some men may dismiss as 'innocent' can form part of a broader pattern of damaging behaviour. By highlighting the 'continuum of sexual violence' (Kelly, 1987; as further detailed in Chapter Two), the campaign correctly identifies sexual violence as existing in many forms, all of which have negative impacts on the lives of women. Importantly, the campaign's emphasis is on changing male behaviour, putting the focus on the only people responsible: the perpetrators.

Another good example is Rape Crisis Scotland's campaign, 'This is not an invitation to rape me' (Cameron & Murphy, 2009). The campaign materials comprised a series of posters, depicting women in different scenarios (e.g., a couple in a taxi passionately kissing and touching) with the same strapline featured on each poster, and was designed to encourage discussion and challenge attitudes. This series of posters clearly lays the responsibility for rape where it belongs – entirely with the perpetrator – and advances that there are no excuses when it comes to sexual violence. These campaigns (in contrast to the victim-survivor-focused ones discussed above) have the potential to make a possible perpetrator think twice about his behaviour, which would reduce the threat of rape for *all* women (not just the ones able to adhere to 'safety' guidance). An external evaluation of the Rape Crisis Scotland campaign found that it had been successful in stimulating debate, with 98% of those interviewed ($n = 686$) agreeing that the campaign tackled an important issue, and 16% stating that it would prompt them to consider their own attitudes towards rape (Progressive, 2008). While this creates optimism for the role of targeted public education campaigns, whether this translates to reducing sexual violence or improved outcomes for women subjected to rape is unclear. We explore the current evidence on sexual violence prevention campaigns further in Chapter Seven. Finally, despite the promising outcomes noted here, public bodies (e.g., Police forces, the NHS, Transport for London) persist in the use of female-centric interventions, which we argue needs to change.

Whether victim-survivor- or perpetrator-focused, many interventions take the form of 'threat campaigns'. Broadly, threat campaigns aim to produce behavioural change by engendering fear (threat) via emphasising the detrimental consequences that individuals may experience as a result of engaging in the depicted unsafe and/or illegal behaviours – such as negative health and/or legal repercussions (Lee & Krogh, 2005). This is problematic for sexual offences as it is men, not women, who are responsible for male violence, and there can be no effective deterrence without an effective threat of punishment (Carmody, 2003). Carmody (2003) argues that the high prevalence of sexual violence demonstrates that the threat of criminal sanctions is an inadequate prevention mechanism, which is further supported by the low detection, prosecution, and conviction rates for rape (Crown Prosecution Service, 2021; Molina & Poppleton, 2020; RAINN, 2021; Rape Crisis England and Wales, 2021). Even outside of the lack of legal repercussions for perpetrators or rape, it can also be argued that by focusing on individuals, anti-rape campaigns perpetuate stereotypical gender scripts, individualise the causes of sexual violence, and do little to tackle the wider factors underlying men's sexual violence. Further, they may produce a 'boomerang' or 'rebound' effect: eliciting the very attitudes and behaviours they were designed to inhibit (Bremh, 1966).

Summary. Much of the rape avoidance or safety advice for women implicitly makes women responsible for managing men's sexual aggression and reproduces many myths central to the rape myth belief system. Although warning women to avoid inviting rape through their dress or behaviour may be driven by a desire to reduce the incidence of rape, we agree with Campbell's (2005) assertion that it may inadvertently *increase* its incidence by reinforcing the rape myths that enable men to internally justify their actions and that impede efforts to bring perpetrators to justice. This forms part of the 'gendered configurations' that reify male dominance and female rapeability by constructing 'masculinity-as-aggressive' and 'femininity-as-vulnerable' (Campbell, 2005, p. 134), thus installing rape as a 'fixed reality', that can only be managed, not eradicated. We explore how gender differentiations may work to scaffold RMA in Chapter Six. Further, advice on how to avoid attracting the attention of male strangers also ignores the fact that most rapes are perpetrated by someone the victim-survivor knows (Rape Crisis England and Wales, 2021). Importantly, much of the advice offered is not evidence-based (i.e., not derived from, or tested by, empirical research) and, as noted above, offers no readily implementable course of action which could reasonably be expected to impact a woman's risk of being subjected to rape. Further, when women are held accountable for following safety advice, their practical interests are harmed, rendering them less likely, if they are raped, to receive supportive responses, assistance in bringing the perpetrator to account, or criminal compensation (e.g., Grubb & Turner, 2012; Stanko, 1996).

Echoing Lievore (2003), we call for comprehensive education strategies that inform the general population about the social and criminal definitions of sexual assault (challenging the erroneous and damaging 'real' rape stereotype); frame sexual assault as a community (rather than women's) issue; target the perpetrator's actions rather than the victim-survivor's; raise awareness about the multiple strategies of violence and coercion (addressing the belief that physical violence is the only form of coercion); and address the long- and short-term physical and psychological consequences of sexual assault.

Rape in the Media

Although most rapes never receive any publicity, the ones that do play an important role in shaping and maintaining individual as well as societal perceptions of sexual assault. This is because the media are a key arena in which rape is defined, and does, as such, shape our understanding of what is considered rape, who perpetrates it, and what factors contribute to its perpetration (Kitzinger, 2009). Further, media representations influence perceptions of victim-survivors and the likely psychosocial consequences of being subjected to rape (Mullin, Imrich, & Linz, 1996). Through its influence on public perception, news coverage of men's violence against women can affect public policy, and it can also facilitate the continued perpetration of violence. Because of this, the media are crucial for understanding how the rape myth belief system is maintained in society. The links between media reporting and rape myths have been supported by experimental research. Specifically, research found that the framing of rape in news stories directly affected college students' attitudes about rape, such that after reading stories which contained rape myths, college women and men were more likely to blame the victim-survivor (Franiuk, Seefelt, & Vandello, 2008). Further, in conditions where participants were exposed to rape myth-supportive articles as opposed to rape myth-challenging articles, participants were more likely to absolve the perpetrator of their crime (Franiuk, Seefelt, Cepress, et al., 2008).

Unfortunately, the media present a highly stereotypical view of rape, which often reinforces gendered myths and stereotypes that blame the victim-survivor and/or deny a claim of rape (Franiuk, Seefelt, & Vandello, 2008; Kitzinger, 2009). While the media of course shape representations in the first place, these representations are also *informed by* social attitudes such as criminal justice procedures (i.e., police and court responses, which are dominated by traditional patriarchal understandings of rape), institutional racism and sexism within the media industry, news values (such as the search for the sensational or 'click bait', covering controversial high-profile and/or contested cases rather than statistics about the prevalence of rape), and broader journalistic practices (e.g., production processes, agenda setting, and editing). Below we outline some examples of rape myths and how they are perpetuated in the media.

False Allegations are Routine.   As noted already by earlier rape myth researchers (e.g., Burt, 1980; Lonsway & Fitzgerald, 1994), the belief that women routinely lie about rape is exemplified by (and to a degree perpetuated through) the media paying considerable attention to rare false rape accusations and less attention to the actual prevalence of rape. In recent years, there continues to be a tendency for the media to focus on the issue of supposedly false allegations (e.g., through portraying men as distressed by false allegations; Banet-Weiser, 2021; Franiuk, Seefelt, & Vandello, 2008), rather than established facts about sexual violence (Reavey & Warner, 2003). Furthermore, even where false allegations have occurred, proven cases of rape typically do not receive the same amount of media attention (Belknap, 2010), which makes false accusations even more memorable.

Studies examining media reporting of false allegations highlight how such reporting follows problematic fault lines. For instance, there is a striking asymmetry in how the credibility of each side is assessed. The emotions of men are said to underlie their innocence, whereas the 'hysteria' of women is used to undermine their credibility (Kitzinger, 1998). The media attention to false allegations also speaks to the gendered nature and power of the media (Kitzinger, 2009). It has been suggested (e.g., Jordan, 2004) that media reporting of false rape allegations (or those believed to be) has become a 'fashionable area of inquiry and speculation', leading to extensive coverage and greater emphasis on these stories than when a man is convicted of rape.

The tendency to recall highly publicised cases and consider false allegations to be more common than they are is related to the 'availability heuristic' (Tversky & Kahneman, 1973). According to the availability heuristic, individuals estimate the likelihood or frequency of an event based on the ease with which relevant instances can be retrieved from memory: the easier it is to bring an example to mind, the more often that event is judged to occur. In the same way that people overestimate the likelihood that they might be a victim of a shark attack, because of how much media attention these attacks elicit, individuals overestimate the chances that a rape claim is false due to a very small number of highly publicised cases where there is evidence a woman lied or was mistaken (e.g., where DNA evidence runs counter to the allegation) or more common scenarios where acquittals were made (especially as the public may misunderstand acquittals and conflate them with false allegations; Huntington et al., 2022; Rumney, 2006).

The high-profile Mangum/Duke case,[1] where rape allegations were made by Crystal Mangum against lacrosse players at an elite private university (i.e., Duke University) in 2006 is a useful example of the media's tendency to inflate unfounded/dropped rape allegations (Taylor & Johnson, 2007), even though withdrawal of an accusation or dropping of a case do not indicate that it is false. In the Mangum/Duke case, the lacrosse team members were alleged to have raped Mangum, an African American woman working as a stripper; and the racial, gender, and class differences between Mangum and the accused, as well as Duke's affluent status, ignited a firestorm of media coverage (Phillips & Griffin, 2015). While the investigation was ongoing, there were new stories about Mangum's 'see-through' outfit at the party, her sexual history, her status as a teenage runaway, her mental health, her criminal history, and previous allegations of rape (Phillips & Griffin, 2015). Together, these stories rigorously attacked Mangum's character, undermining the possibility of taking her allegations seriously and assuming the players' innocence by default.

Similarly, when the case against basketball player Kobe Bryant was dropped in 2003, little attention was paid to the possibility that the intensive intrusive media coverage and related public backlash made continuing to press charges untenable for the 19-year-old victim-survivor. Studies of the media coverage surrounding the Kobe Bryant case showed that 10% of headlines featured a rape myth, as did the text of 42% of the articles (Franiuk, Seefelt, & Vandello, 2008). Cases where a rape allegation is dropped may even influence decision-making among public defenders (lawyers), and, as such, reduce even further the visibility of rape cases that are founded (McCannon & Wilson, 2019). Any time charges are dropped in a sexual assault case, or a defendant is acquitted, the rape myths used in that case are validated and it becomes even more difficult for future sexual assault victim-survivors to come forward with their claims. Media reporting of rape may be particularly important in influencing the decision of vulnerable victim-survivors to engage with the CJS (Murphy, Hine, Yesberg, Wunsch, & Charleton, 2021). Finally, the development of social media has further entrenched the media's role in perpetuating the belief that false rape allegations are commonplace, and Twitter seems to be especially important in sustaining the notion that women routinely lie about rape (Stabile et al., 2019).

---

[1]We refer to the case as the 'Mangum/Duke' case to mark Mangum's erasure, as the case is usually referred to as only the 'Duke' case.

The Nature of Rape and Victim-Survivors.   The nature of rape is also obscured in media reporting, and cases are rarely framed as problems of misogyny and the treatment of women. Terms such as 'had sex' and 'rough sex' are used, rather than rape. Relatedly, the media frequently portray women subjected to date rape as 'lying, vindictive shrews' and the perpetrators of rape as 'folk heroes – innocent boys tragically charged by vindictive women' (Gruber, 2009, p. 598). Such reporting exonerates the perpetrator and discredits the individual victim-survivor. More generally, such reporting conveys how men's sexual violence against women should be considered (as not real) or how consent should be deduced (for example, from kissing). Thus, the responsibility is placed on women to take responsibility for avoiding sexual violence. Moore (2014) also noted that media reporting on rape has used rape myths to create cautionary tales aimed at women, outlining appropriate and inappropriate behaviour (a form of moral regulation). This, she argued, has been a reaction to increased female emancipation and is the reason why so many myths focus on the intoxicated and/or flirtatious women or women having informal relationships (Moore, 2014). In other words, rape myths are used to maintain the status quo in relation to gender norms, just as gender norms are used to maintain and scaffold rape myths.

Stranger Rape.   One way the media perpetuates rape myths is by the exclusion of some stories and the focus on others. A disproportionate amount of attention is given to stranger-perpetrated rape or 'unusual cases' (Kitzinger, 2009), which has the impact of drawing attention away from the realities of sexual violence in everyday life and making cases (and victim-survivors) of rape perpetrated by a partner or former partner almost invisible (i.e., 'symbolic expulsion'). This seems particularly true in terms of the exclusion of marital rape, allowing individuals to believe that this does not happen or is not a significant problem (Cuklanz, 2000). The stranger attack fits with traditional ideas about the nature of 'newsworthiness'. As Schlesinger and Tumber (1994) advanced, not all stories make the news, and this may mean that more stereotypical rape cases are more likely to be reported on. The search for a random sex-attacker has its own momentum and rationale that may attract intense and prolonged coverage (Kitzinger & Skidmore, 1995). In addition to overshadowing the nature of men's sexual violence, media representations also convey to women the need to self-regulate if they are to avoid being victimised, which reinforces women's fear of public spaces.

Descriptions of Rape Perpetrators and Women Subjected to Rape.   The behaviour of women subjected to rape is placed under intense scrutiny by the media, while the men who have been charged with rape tend to have their actions obscured. It has been noted that journalists often use the passive tense (e.g., 'woman got raped when walking home') as opposed to the active tense ('the man raped the woman as she was walking home') to describe assaults which serves to remove agency from the perpetrator and fails to hold him accountable for his choices and actions (Bohner, 2001). Prominence is also often given to the man's claims of 'miscommunication' (e.g., he misread her verbal and non-verbal communication; he falsely believed she wanted to have sex; he misperceived her refusal as 'token'[2];

---

[2]'Token resistance' is the attitudinal belief that women mean 'yes' when they say 'no'

she failed to say 'no' clearly and effectively), or that he was provoked by the woman's behaviour or his uncontrollable lust (Kitzinger, 2009). Similarly, when the perpetrator does not fit the stereotype of what a rape perpetrator 'should' be, the media is prone to include positive labels and descriptions of the perpetrator such as 'devoted father' or 'nice chap'.[3] Although these descriptions are clearly meant to contextualise and sensationalise the offence, they nonetheless position the perpetrator as 'a nice guy,' which makes invisible the offence and the harm caused to the victim-survivor.

Conversely, while 'regular men' are often referred to using positive descriptions, men who have been found guilty of what the media perceive to be more 'severe' cases of rape can be described as monsters or animals, using terms such as 'beast', 'pervert', and 'freak' (Kitzinger, 2009). This construction works on the idea that the rape is stranger-perpetrated and does, as such, not represent most cases. Such language also serves to 'other' the perpetrator and makes them appear to be sub-human, suggesting that men who perpetrate rape are not like 'ordinary' men (Mason & Monckton-Smith, 2008), and this type of imagery has grown increasingly prevalent over time (Kitzinger, 2009). Clearly, using either of the extremes in the 'nice guy/monster-paradox' to describe perpetrators of rape is problematic, as ultimately this fails to recognise that men who perpetrate rape can, on the surface, rarely be distinguished from those who do not and further enhances stereotypes and misconceptions surrounding the nature of rape perpetration. Similarly, victim-survivors can be presented as virgins attacked by these monstrous 'others' or, contrastingly, as promiscuous women who invited the rape through their actions and are, therefore, to blame (Benedict, 1993). Both presentations are problematic and destructive to women, particularly since the media shape public opinion about sexual violence (Emmers-Sommer, Pauley, Hanzal, & Triplett, 2006) and its perpetrators (Kitzinger, 2009).

The history of media coverage of sexual violence is also a history of racism, the White gaze, and selective 'colour blindness' (Tillman, Bryant-Davis, Smith, & Marks, 2010). In the context of rape, women of colour may receive less media attention, their allegations may be given less credibility, and the fact that their victimisation may have been racist as well as sexist ignored (Meyers, 1996). If the media cast a woman of colour as credible and worthy of 'victim-survivor' status, then this may be achieved by erasing her race (Kitzinger, 2004). For example, Mike Tyson's accuser was a Black beauty queen, and was characterised during his trial as the all-American girl, effectively positioning her as the 'White' virginal woman (Kitzinger, 2004; Moorti, 2002). This honorary Whiteness was precarious, however. After the trial, her privileges were withdrawn and she was recast in the mould of the 'temptress Jezebel' (Moorti, 2002, p. 104). Thus, the media

> rarely show how race and gender work together to shape individual experience of sexual violence … [They] either address rape as

---

to sexual advances from men (Muehlenhard & Hollabaugh, 1988).
[3]Both of these examples were used to describe Wayne Couzens who raped and murdered Sarah Everard, by the *Daily Mail* (Sales, 2021) and *The Telegraph* (Evans, 2021), respectively.

it affects (white women) or as an effect of black masculinity, rarely as a site where gender and racial discourse intersect in problematic ways. (Moorti, 2002, pp. 13–14)

Studies show that race-based myths and stereotypes are common in media reports, particularly when the alleged perpetrator is a man of colour (Moorti, 2002). This suggests that the media have likely played a key role in perpetuating racist rape myths (which we elaborate more generally on in Chapter Two), and it also calls for an intersectional understanding of how rape myths are maintained in the media.

Finally, although most pretrial publicity has been found to typically bias jurors against the defendant, research has shown that the opposite bias occurs in sexual assault cases (e.g., Mullin et al., 1996). Franiuk, Seefelt, Cepress, et al. (2008) suggested that exposure to rape myths in articles surrounding sexual assault cases may be one explanation of this pro-defendant bias. Thus, by the time a rape case reaches court, the trial has arguable 'already occurred in the popular press' (Waterhouse-Watson, 2013, p. 8). This further emphasises the media as key for perpetrator exoneration, and it also raises important questions about impartial and fair jury implementation under these conditions.

Women Secretly Want to be Raped.   The pornography industry and other sexually explicit forms of media are arguably the most visible perpetuators of the myth that women enjoy rape, and research suggests that violent and non-consensual content is very common in mainstream pornography (Vera-Gray, McGlynn, Kureshi, & Butterby, 2021). A meta-analysis of non-experimental studies found a significant and positive association between men's consumption of violent pornography and attitudes supporting violence towards women ($r = 0.24$; Hald, Malamuth, & Yuen, 2010), and this appears to be particularly true among men already predisposed to engage in sexual violence (Malamuth, Hald, & Koss, 2012). Another study (Stanley et al., 2018) of young people in five European countries found that, among boys, watching online pornography was associated with the perpetration of sexual coercion and abuse, and that boys who regularly watched online pornography held more negative gender attitudes. Other studies have found positive correlations between pornography consumption and gendered attitudes (Brown & L'Engle, 2009), non-sexual gendered behaviour (Mulac, Jansma, & Linz, 2002), and sexually aggressive behaviour (Wright, Tokunaga, & Kraus, 2016). In a recent meta-analysis on the relationship between pornography and sexual aggression, Ferguson and Hartley (2022) argued that there was no relationship between non-violent pornography and sexual aggression, a weak relationship between violent pornography (arguably the most common type) and sexual aggression, and an absence of long-term effects. However, this research has been criticized by researcher Max Waltman (Waltman, 2021)[4] on the basis of post-treatment bias. Here, post-treatment bias refers to situations where the variables controlled for in the statistical analysis are affected by the casual variable (in this case pornography). This can hide the true effect of a relationship between two variables. Specifically, Waltman argues that Ferguson and Hartley (2022) controlled for variables thought to be impacted by pornography (including hostile masculinity), which resulted in a smaller, less accurate estimation of effects.

---

[4]Please note, the Ferguson and Hartley (2022) research was available online in 2020.

According to Wright's (2011) sexual script acquisition, activation, application model of sexual media socialization ($_3$AM), exposure to pornography can lead to the learning of novel sexual scripts (sexual script acquisition), the priming of already acquired sexual scripts (sexual script activation), and the use of sexual scripts to guide one's own behaviour or judgements about other people's behaviour (sexual script application). Consequently, pornography can provide consumers with cues about what is sexually normative, appropriate, and desirable. Therefore, although pornography may not itself be the sole causative factor for aggressive tendencies or RMA (as indicated by some of the mixed findings above), it can serve to bring these to the surface and reinforce such already held misogynistic beliefs. Swedish criminologist and feminist Nina Rung has long advocated that broader society needs to recognise the violence and degradation of women inherent in much mainstream pornography, as well as the link between men's sexual violence and their pornography consumption (e.g., Rung, 2021). As such, the above suggests that a renewed feminist attention to pornography and the maintenance of rape myths is urgently needed.

Improving Prevention Campaigns and Media Portrayals of Sexual Assault

As outlined above, journalists and other media professionals have the potential to play a crucial role in raising awareness of rape as well as in countering myths and outdated attitudes about victim-survivors and perpetrators. What journalists write matters: it can shape the narratives around violence against women; it can help those experiencing violence realise what is happening to them – and where they can seek help; and it can serve as a reminder to society in general that the blame for violence only ever lies with those who perpetrate it. Only through responsible reporting can the media begin to address the wider societal context such as RMA that contributes to the perpetration of rape. Below are some suggestions for journalists and other media professionals to guide the safe and ethical reporting of rape:

1. **Be Mindful of Context**. Writing about a victim-survivor's history, her sexual practices, and what she was wearing should consistently be avoided, as including this can (and does) imply victim-survivor culpability for the assault. Other contextual factors such as what she was doing, who she was with, where she was, or what time of the day the rape occurred may also not be relevant to the reporting of an offence and should only be included if it is justifiably relevant. Where context is reported, it is crucial to consider how this may be interpreted by the reader in the context of rape myths. Relatedly, the ethnicity of the victim-survivor should not be reported, unless justifiably relevant.
2. **Avoid Passive Coverage**. Headlines such as, 'woman raped' imply that violence is something that 'just happens' to women, when there was in fact a perpetrator who chose to assault someone. The framing of a rape as a 'tragedy' should also be avoided, as this makes it seem as though the rape was unavoidable, instead of a conscious action from the man who perpetrated the offence.
3. **Avoid the 'Nice-Guy/Monster Paradox' When Describing the Perpetrator**. Instead, use objectively verifiable descriptors such as 'man' or 'perpetrator'. Men who commit rape are 'ordinary' men; if the perpetrator is positioned

as a devious monster, for instance, rape becomes a random act of violence rather than a societal problem. Likewise, care should be taken to avoid using language that may generate sympathy for the perpetrator (e.g., great dad, good guy, respected professional/community leader/esteemed coach), as this may imply that there is a 'reason' for their 'out of character' behaviour. No form of violence against women should be presented as 'normal'. The ethnicity of the perpetrator should not be reported, unless justifiably relevant.

4. **Name the Crime.** Use 'rape' rather than phrases that imply consent or minimise and sensationalise the crime (i.e., do not use sex, sex scandal, etc.).

5. **Motivation/Cause.** Do not report rape as a crime of sexual desire or passion (e.g., 'he could not resist her'). This suggests that men do not have control over their own actions. Violence is always a choice, and rape is a crime of violence, abuse, and degradation.

6. **Use Statistics.** Do not write about instances of violence as though they are separated isolated events. This reinforces the idea that the violence was an isolated pathology or deviance (especially when the perpetrator is described according to the 'nice guy/monster-paradox') and denies the social roots of violence against women and absolves larger society of any obligation to end it. Instead, situate incidents using statistics. Illustrate the strikingly high prevalence of rape (individual stories are part of a much larger problem), and that rape can affect any woman, anywhere; women of all ages, sexualities, and racial, cultural, and economic backgrounds are affected.

7. **Do Not Blame the Victim-Survivor.** Make the perpetrator the subject of the sentence and assign the verb to them, i.e., 'The perpetrator forced the victim-survivor to …' Never suggest that the rape occurred because of what a woman was wearing, what she had to drink, if she had cheated, or any other reason. Perpetrators are responsible for their actions.

8. **Do Not Sensationalise Stories.** Stories should not be sensationalised with graphic details of the crime; rape is an act of violence and there is no need for salacious details. Lexical choices made by journalists or editors can obscure the realities of violence against women.

9. **Use Myth-Busting.** If covering an incident of stranger rape, inform readers that this is a rarity – 90% of rapes are committed by someone known to the victim-survivor. It is highly uncommon for women to make false reports of rape, and there are no more false reports of rape than any other crime.

10. **Use Appropriate Images, Footage, and Photographs.** Do not use images that contribute to harmful stereotypes or objectify women. Where possible, images should be used to illustrate a general situation, rather than a specific incident. If photographs are used, it is important to obtain consent from the victim-survivor and review and select images carefully. If stock images are used, they should be selected with care. Images of White, able-bodied, young women reinforce myths that rape does not affect women of colour, older women, or disabled women.

11. **Do Not Focus on Safety Campaigns.** Messages informing women about strategies to avoid being a victim of male violence can inadvertently work to construct avoidance of violence as the responsibility of women, as opposed to perpetrators. Ultimately, this may unwittingly perpetuate victim-survivor-blaming attitudes.

12. **Choose Your Words Carefully.** Great attention should be paid to ensuring that language does not inadvertently contribute to women being ascribed responsibility or blame. Journalists can inadvertently compound such misconceptions through their attitudes and language. Describing victim-survivors as 'risk-taking', for example, places responsibility on the victim-survivor; describing perpetrators as 'lads' underplays threat. The use of euphemisms and ambivalent language can allow risk to go undetected. For example, journalists should not describe a 12-year-old girl as 'sexually active' or a 35-year-old male as a 14-year-old's 'boyfriend' as opposed to an abuser (Beckett, 2011).

Summary. Although journalists continue to employ rape myths in their writing their *reasons* for doing so are often unclear. It could be that economic and time pressures push journalists to sensationalise a story. Alternatively, their inclusion may reflect that author's internalisation of cultural beliefs about men's sexual violence against women, and journalists may believe that they are simply presenting reasonable alternatives to a sexual assault allegation (Franiuk, Seefelt, Cepress, et al., 2008). As Best (2008) argues,

> news workers want to assemble coverage that seems sensible to themselves, and that will also seem sensible to their audiences. Their stories, then, incorporate the culture they take for granted – values, symbols, worldviews, and so on. (p. 142)

In either case, the use of stereotypes hinders discussions about the true nature, and real causes, of sexual violence, which ultimately prevents a reduction in rape myth endorsement.

The Functions of Rape Myths: Why Do People Endorse Them?

As explored in Chapter Two of this book, RMA may be conceived as a general schema, which guides how information about a rape case is processed, interpreted, and organised (Bohner et al., 2009; Temkin & Krahé, 2008). Feminist researchers have long argued that RMA may serve multiple and multilayered psychological functions (Bohner et al., 1998; Brownmiller, 1975/1993; Burt, 1980; Lonsway & Fitzgerald, 1994). This section provides an overview on these complex functions, examining both functions that appear typically only relevant to men or women (i.e., gender-related) and general societal functions.

Individual Functions

Functions for Men: Neutralisation and Rationalisation of Aggressive Tendencies. One prominent approach to explaining juvenile delinquency (Sykes & Matza, 1957) and other socially deviant behaviours, including gang involvement, tax fraud, and identify theft, is through Neutralisation Theory. According to this theory, juvenile delinquents do not generally deny societal norms but instead use various 'techniques' (denial of the victim (e.g., 'they deserved it'), denial of injury (e.g., 'nobody was really hurt'), and denial of responsibility (e.g., 'I was provoked', 'it was not my fault')) to justify norm violation under certain circumstances[5]. By endorsing these beliefs, an individual may avoid perceiving their own acts as 'norm violations'.

Early feminist writers have noted the rationalising functions of rape myths (Brownmiller, 1975/1993; Burt, 1980) and the links between Neutralisation Theory and RMA were further explored by Bohner et al. (1998). Burt, for instance, argued that rape myths may be used as 'psychological releasers or neutralizers, allowing potential rapists to turn off social prohibitions against injuring or using others when they want to commit an assault' (1978, p. 282). Related to this, she went on to outline four victim-related myths that she labelled 'nothing happened', 'no harm was done', 'she wanted or liked it', and 'she asked for or deserved it' (p. 28), as well as two assailant-related myths, namely 'that only crazy men rape' and 'that men cannot control their sexuality' (Burt, 1991, p. 32). This is also considered in Scully's (1990) study on men who had been convicted of rape. Scully suggested that myths about rape allow men to exonerate themselves for being perpetrators of rape, particularly through positioning themselves as victims of circumstances (e.g., intoxication) or of women (e.g., through false allegations or general exaggerations). As such, rape myth beliefs are directly applicable to the functions inherent in rationalisation and neutralisation, where rape myths can be used by men to justify their own inclinations towards sexual violence and to neutralise opposing norms (see also, Bohner et al., 1998).

In line with the suggestion that rape myths may be mechanisms that neutralise or trivialise rape and sexual violence, several studies have shown that high levels of RMA are associated with measures of rape proclivity (RP) – one's likelihood or tendency to choose to rape if you could be assured of not being caught and punished (e.g., Chapleau & Oswald, 2010; Chiroro et al., 2004; Edwards & Vogel, 2015; Persson & Dhingra, 2021). Information about how RP is conceptualised and measured can be found in Chapter Three. For example, Malamuth (1981) asked men to report the likelihood 'that they personally would rape if they could be assured of not being caught and punished' (p. 140) and assessed these men's RMA using Burt's (1980) measure (Rape Myth Acceptance Scale (RMAS)) of RMA. Results showed a strong ($r = 0.60$) correlation between RP and RMA. In a meta-analysis of 11 studies, the mean correlation between Burt's RMA scale and Malamuth's (1981) RP measure was found to be $r = 0.26$, which is considered small (Murnen, Wright, & Kaluzny, 2002). Going beyond correlational research, there is also substantial evidence that RMA may play a causal role in RP. Specifically, several studies have demonstrated that men whose own level of RMA has been made accessible to them (by the initial completion of an RMA scale) show a higher correlation between RMA and RP compared to men who completed the RMA scale only after the RP measure (Bohner et al., 1998; Bohner, Jarvis, Eyssel, & Siebler 2005). Moreover,

---

[5]A similar psychosocial mechanism by which people selectively disengage their moral self-sanctions from their harmful conduct was proposed by Bandura (2006).

findings by Bohner, Siebler, and Schmelcher (2006) suggest that when other men's rape myth beliefs are believed to be high, individual men's levels of RP are subsequently elevated. Rape supportive attitudes present in the media, as detailed above, are, therefore, a cause for concern, as they not only promote rape myths but may work to make salient attitudes that increase men's propensity to engage in sexual violence as they may signal to men that society's RMA levels are high.

Although findings such as those above support the suggestion that rape myths may increase RP by neutralising in advance norms that oppose sexual violence, there is another potential interpretation of this association: high RP may lead to the endorsement of rape myths as a post hoc justification for behavioural tendencies (and even past behaviour). This alterative viewpoint is consistent with the 'social justification' of stereotypes (Tajfel, 1981). Moreover, research indicates that RMA predicts judgements of both victim blame and RP within the same sample of men, suggesting that the justification of sexual violence may coincide with a certain readiness to commit such violence against women (e.g., Abrams, Viki, Masser, & Bohner, 2003). Finally, it is possible that no direct causal link exists between RMA and RP, but rather that some third variable (e.g., aggressively sexist attitudes) influences both kinds of beliefs in the same direction. In other words, RMA and RP can be statistically related not because RMA causes RP or because RP causes RMA, but because some third variable, such as aggressively sexist attitudes, causes both RMA and RP.

Research into RMA and self-reported instances of sexual aggression (as opposed to a theoretical inclination to sexually aggress) suggests that rape myths may reduce the expectation of negative outcomes or consequences in sexual offenders (Chapleau & Oswald, 2010). One study found evidence for a chronically high accessibility of RMA in men who had previously been sexually coercive (Bohner et al., 2005). Generally, these men showed a strong correlation between RMA and RP and were faster in responding to RMA items than were men who had not previously been sexually coercive. This suggests that sexually coercive men may use rape myths to rationalise and justify acts of sexual violence (Bohner et al., 1998; Burt, 1980), and that these myths may become more cognitively accessible to them in future situations, including future sexual encounters. Correlational research has shown associations between RMA and self-reported sexual aggression (Locke & Mahalik, 2005), and experimental research has shown a causal association between RMA and (non-sexual) aggression towards women (but not men, e.g., Donnerstein & Malamuth, 1997).

There is evidence of convicted perpetrators of rape using myths to rationalise their behaviours (Chiroro et al., 2004). A systematic review of eight studies (Johnson & Beech, 2017) found that convicted perpetrators of rape[6] can be distinguished from other non-sexual offenders and from community non-offending males on measures of RMA, particularly on the sex-role stereotyping subscales of the RMAS (Burt, 1980), which reflect the respondent's endorsement of stereotyped

---

[6]Here, it is important to bear in mind that the studies included samples that are not representative of most perpetrators of rape, since most men are never convicted of their offences.

sex roles for men and women. RMA was not, however, a significant predictor of sexual recidivism. Recent research (Hales & Gannon, 2021) on male students in the UK found that men who had been sexually coercive or perpetrated sexual violence against women endorsed rape myths to a greater degree than men who had not engaged in these acts. Consequently, the evidence reviewed here suggests that, among men, RMA as a cognitive schema may facilitate sexual aggression (Bohner et al., 2005).

Finally, there are many men who endorse rape myths but do not perpetrate sexual violence against women. Here, it is possible that, for men who are not perpetrators of sexual aggression, rape myths could still function as a way to neutralise these men's *collective* responsibility in preventing and combating sexual assault, as these beliefs ultimately position women as the cause of rape. As such, these attitudes allow men to refrain from collective action. Rape myth endorsement may also allow men to distance themselves from the 'monstrous' men who perpetrate 'real' rape. In this way, their own sexual coercion may become invisible, and it allows these men to believe that they could not be culpable of sexual violence against women (Lonsway & Fitzgerald, 1995).

Functions for Women: Anxiety Buffer and Self-Esteem Protection.   While it could be tempting to assume that rape myths are only endorsed by men, this is not the case; women accept rape myths, albeit to a lesser degree than men.[7] Apart from having lower (but still detectable) levels of RMA than men, it appears that women may endorse RMA for different reasons than men do (Bohner et al., 2009; Lonsway & Fitzgerald, 1994).

For women, accepting rape myths (which ultimately position women as the cause of rape) may allow for a reduction in perceived subjective vulnerability to sexual assault and thus protect self-esteem. This is because women who endorse rape myths may be more inclined to believe that rape only happens to a *certain type of woman* (e.g., those who provoke rape through their appearance or behaviour), whom they perceive as dissimilar from themselves (Bohner et al., 1998; Bohner, Weisbrod, Raymond, Barzvi, & Schwarz, 1993). By contrast, women who reject rape myths would be more likely construe rape as a potential threat to *all women*, including themselves, which is, understandably, anxiety-provoking. Thus, RMA allows some women to maintain an illusion of control over the threat of rape, so long as they perceive themselves as dissimilar to women who have been raped. Supporting this proposition, RMA in women has been found to be positively correlated with belief in a just world (BJW; Bohner et al., 1998; Lerner, 1977, 1980; see page 100 of this book) and negatively correlated with feelings of vulnerability to rape (Bohner et al., 1998). Further, several studies have found that women low in RMA who were exposed to situations in which rape was salient (e.g., after reading a rape report) subsequently reported lower

---

[7]For example, we found a significant difference in RMA (using the AMMSA; Gerger et al., 2007) between women and men among a sample of 565 Prolific participants (data collected in October 2021).

self-esteem (e.g., agreeing with the statement, 'I often wish I were someone else') and more negative emotions, whereas women high in RMA who were exposed to the same situations remained largely unaffected (Bohner et al., 1993, 1999; Bohner & Lampridis, 2004). However, in recently collected data of ours,[8] we did not find any statistically significant relationship between women's rape myth endorsement (as measured on the Acceptance of Modern Myths about Sexual Aggression (AMMSA); Gerger et al., 2007) and their self-reported self-esteem. However, we did not manipulate salience of rape as part of this study, which may explain the lack of significant association.

By contrast, in the same sample of women, there was a significant negative relationship of small magnitude between rape myth endorsement and fear of crime victimisation: where rape myth endorsement increased, fear of crime victimisation[9] decreased. This raises the possibility of rape myth endorsement potentially protecting against fear of crime victimisation, possibly through positioning victim-survivors of crime as being blameworthy, thus rendering other people able to protect themselves. Similarly, we also found a negative relationship, of small magnitude, between RMA and perceived likelihood of being sexually assaulted,[10] again suggesting a possibility of rape myth beliefs protecting feelings of personal safety (as it may make women feel that they can protect themselves if they make the 'correct' choices). Further research is needed to examine the underlying mechanisms behind these effects.

Although, theoretically, men may accept rape myths to prevent anxiety about the extent of sexual assault (particularly in the context of women known to them as being potentially at risk of being victimised), it is likely that rape myths as a psychological/anxiety buffer is mostly relevant to women, who are themselves at greater risk of being subjected to rape (e.g., Rape Crisis England and Wales, 2021). Consequently, it is likely that accepting rape myths is a tempting option for women, particularly as it also aligns with current models of gender oppression. Specifically, by accepting rape myths, the status quo is not called into question, and these beliefs also find support in much contemporary culture and media (as further detailed in the sections above). However, by reducing anxiety about the threat of sexual violence, women may also ultimately prevent collective action against the true causes of rape.

---

[8]These (not previously published) data were collected through Prolific on a sample of 282 women, in October 2021. Self-esteem was measured using Rosenberg's (1979) self-esteem scale (10 items).

[9]Fear of crime victimisation was measured using 10 items adapted from Cops and Pleysier (2011).

[10]Fear of being sexually assaulted was measured using one item; 'How likely do you think it is that you personally could be sexually assaulted?' answered on a 7-point Likert-type scale. Future research would benefit from devising a multi-item scale, rather than using one item only.

Societal Functions

Denial of the Scope of the Problem.   Rape myths further serve to protect broader society from facing the severity and scope of rape. Around one in five women are subjected to rape or sexual assault in their lifetime but fewer than 1% obtain justice in the form of a perpetrator conviction (a figure that is, currently, decreasing further; Ministry of Justice and Home Office, 2021). These figures paint a bleak picture of society and cast doubt about whether criminal justice systems internationally can adequately protect women against being subjected to rape. If these figures can be construed as false (i.e., through myths around false rape allegations), or as being the consequence of women's own reckless behaviour (e.g., through positioning women as the cause of rape), the status quo is justi-fied, and costly state involvement to alter the situation is avoided. Conversely, if the figures on the low levels of justice for victim-survivors of rape were accepted and disseminated for what they truly are (without underlying rape myth-related explanations) across societal institutions, it would warrant a comprehensive re-organisation of society, and considerable political intervention, beyond anything currently on the horizon.

In this sense, the reasons why people persistently believe in rape myths are perhaps similar to why some people are reluctant to identify as feminists. As dis-cussed above, one reason why people may believe in rape myths is because these beliefs deny and obscure the personal vulnerability of *all* women in the context of sexual assault, which is a frightening and daunting premise to accept. Simi-larly, a potential reason for not identifying with feminism, or for not accepting sexism as prevalent, is because accepting these basic premises would be to accept that, to certain degree, *all* women share a level of personal vulnerability in soci-ety, independent of personal identities (although, of course, personal identities can and do amplify these risks; Chapter Two; Chapter Four). In this sense, the acceptance of rape myths and the denial of sexism fit well into contemporary neoliberalism, where each individual is regarded as being mostly in charge of their personal destiny. Here, rape and discrimination can be positioned to occur *not* because of structural inequalities but rather because of personal failings on behalf of the woman involved, who failed to make the 'correct' choices to avoid rape or sexist treatment. This would, therefore, suggest that so long as neolib-eralism and individualism remain dominant ideologies, rape myths are likely to prevail. This again highlights the complex ways in which the rape myth belief system is scaffolded.

The World as Just.   Blaming the victim-survivor and exonerating the per-petrator of rape could be conceived as part of a more encompassing cognitive motive, the 'belief in a just world' (BJW; Lerner, 1977, 1980). BJW describes a tendency for people to perceive the world as a fair place, where people generally get what they deserve (positive and negative) and where bad things only happen to 'bad people' due to their actions/behaviour (Lerner, 1980). BJW, therefore, offers reassurance to people that if all necessary precautions are taken, and if people are 'good' (i.e., live a good life and do nothing to 'invite' victimisation), nothing bad will happen to them. In other words, BJW provides a psychological buffer against the reality that bad things can happen to anyone, at any given time, without reason or logic (Furnham, 2003). This psychological buffer allows people to feel less personally vulnerable and have a lower perception of risk, as they have done nothing to 'deserve' negative outcomes (Lodewijkx, Wildschut, Nijstad, Savenije, & Smit, 2001). This, in turn, makes the world around them predictable, manageable, and safe (Lodewijkx et al., 2001).

People are reluctant to give up BJW, as this belief serves an important adaptive function for the individual and for society. If this belief is challenged, for example, by encountering information that a 'good' or 'innocent' person has been raped, one way of restoring cognitive consistency (Festinger, 1962) is to deny, neutralise, or nullify the injustice, such as concluding the victim-survivor did something to deserve or prompt what happened (i.e., they blame the victim-survivor; Hafer, 2000). Responsibility for the rape is, therefore, attributed to the victim-survivor's behaviour and/or character, to make what happened appear ordered, fair, and just. Importantly, Lerner (1977) posited that people will automatically reason backwards when they learn a woman has been raped and will then make guesses about her behaviour or character to provide reasons for why she was subjected to rape. The theoretical links between BJW and RMA are, therefore, evident, and this would suggest that these attitudes are relevant to consider together.

Research has shown that greater BJW endorsement is positively associated with RMA (e.g., Bohner et al., 1998; Hayes, Lorenz, & Bell, 2013; Lonsway & Fitzgerald, 1994; Sleath & Woodhams, 2014), negative attitudes towards rape victim-survivors, support for more lenient sentences for perpetrators of rape, and greater victim-survivor blaming, thus placing less blame on the perpetrator (Kleinke & Meyer, 1990; Sakalli-Ugurlu, Yalcin, & Glick, 2007; Strömwall, Alfredsson, & Landström, 2013b). Thus, by interpreting incidents of rape in a way that is consistent with rape myths (and, therefore, also with more general BJW), individuals consequently generate 'evidence' that seemingly supports their own myths. Importantly, however, the association between BJW and victim-survivor blaming appears to differ according to relationship type. In their assessment of the impact of BJW on victim attributions across varying relationship types, Strömwall et al. (2013a) found BJW to only be meaningfully related to assessments of stranger rape. Specifically, women high in BJW were significantly more likely to blame the victim of stranger rape than were women low in BJW. Consistent with this, there is little empirical support for the association between BJW and victim blaming in acquaintance rape cases (Hammond, Berry, & Rodriguez, 2011; Pedersen & Strömwall, 2013; Strömwall et al., 2013a), but for an exception, see Landström, Strömwall, and Alfredsson (2016). Finally, Montada (1998) suggested the BJW may motivate efforts to correct injustice rather than lead to victim-survivor blaming, depending on the perceived costs, responsibilities, and attitudes to the victim-survivor. Further, BJW is not the only motivation for victim-survivor blaming; the need for control, prejudice, or pure self-interest may all play a role (Montada, 1998).

A similar self-perpetuating principle may operate at the societal level in which stereotypical thinking about rape (influenced by rape myths) and jury verdicts influence each other. Sinclair and Bourne (1998) proposed a 'cycle-of-blame' principle that suggests that the same rape myths that lead to attrition and limit convictions may in turn be strengthened by case acquittals. In another words, a self-perpetuating feedback loop exists. On the one hand, jury member rape myth endorsement may lead to more restrictive rape definitions (i.e., what qualifies as rape) and fewer convictions. On the other hand, acquittals may reinforce those very myths that have contributed to the verdicts in the first place.

This 'vicious cycle' was tested by Sinclair and Bourne (1998) by presenting identical case summaries to participants but telling them either that the jury's verdict was 'guilty' or that it was 'not guilty'. Participants' RMA was assessed later, as a dependent variable.[11] The 'cycle of blame' hypothesis was supported for male participants, with results indicating that their RMA scores were higher after a not-guilty verdict and lower after a guilty verdict. Interestingly, for women, the opposite effect was found: a not-guilty verdict lowered RMA and a guilty verdict increased RMA. The researchers suggest that women's discrepancy is the result of a tendency to invoke the just-world hypothesis. This is, because the fear (and threat) of victimisation is greater for women than men, they may endorse rape myths ('If it *was* rape, the woman must have contributed to it happening') in order to deny their personal vulnerability, as discussed in more detail in previous sections. In other words, to feel safe and restore their faith in a just world, women may need to blame the victim-survivor and can do so by accepting victim blaming myths. This proposition is consistent with the results of Seta and Seta (1993), who noted that when an individual is presented with information that runs counter to their strongly held beliefs, he or she will hyper-compensate.

The belief that false rape accusations are commonplace further taps into a central societal function of rape myths: these beliefs allow people to consider rape a morally abhorrent crime but still allow for an exoneration of individual men (i.e., known men, or those who are generally liked). This is likely influenced by the perceived cost(s) of believing a man (who may be known and loved) to have committed rape, as weighted against the perceived likelihood of the rape having taken place. As an example, there would be a higher social and personal cost involved in believing a close friend or partner has committed a rape than a relative stranger. This is supported by research suggesting a negative relationship between a confidant's closeness to the perpetrator and their advising a victim-survivor to report a rape (Puthillam, Parekh, & Kapoor, 2022).

Functions in Court.   Research shows that rape myths may be purposefully used by defence counsel, to distance cases from the 'real rape' stereotype and undermine the credibility of the victim-survivor (Smith, 2018). We explore rape myths in a court context in Chapter Four.

---

[11]As we note in Chapter Three, conceptualising RMA as a dependent variable is, however, problematic.

Conclusion

This chapter has examined the perpetuation of rape myths in society, with a particular focus on the complex ways in which institutions who would – on the surface – disagree with rape myths, often maintain them, with the intent to protect women. We also critically discussed some of the ways in which the media portray rape, since such portrayals have been shown to increase victim-survivor blaming and influence the ways in which victim-survivors are perceived. Within this section, we advanced an outline of changes that could be made to improve prevention campaigns and media portrayals of sexual assault committed against women and girls. Finally, we noted that the perpetuation of rape myths is interlinked with the functions of rape myths, and explored *why* individuals and institutions appear reluctant to completely abandon these ideas. We conclude that the power of rape myths lies in their utility to protect individuals from uncomfortable truths about victim-survivors and perpetrators of sexual assault.

Chapter Six

Rape Myth Acceptance and Other '-Isms'

Chapter Overview

Rape myths do not exist in a vacuum. This was acknowledged by Burt's (1980) original work, which not only formalised the definition and measurement of RMA but also considered its correlation with several other variables (e.g., sex role stereotyping and adversarial sexual beliefs). As Burt (1980) correctly observed, attitudes that blame the victim-survivor and exonerate the perpetrator of rape are maintained in the context of broader societal prejudices. Any consideration of RMA must, therefore, consider how these beliefs relate to other forms of prejudice and stereotyping. This chapter will consider sexism, racism, and classism as relevant constructs (although this list is of course not exhaustive) and, in doing so, highlight that rape prevention programmes, interventions, and policy need to address these other oppressive beliefs ('-isms') if they are to be successful.

Sexism

Sexism and sex role stereotyping have long been noted as important for the maintenance of rape myths (Burt, 1980; Lonsway & Fitzgerald, 1994). This makes sense given the theoretical grounding of RMA in feminism, which acknowledges that these beliefs serve to maintain women's oppression in wider society (Brownmiller, 1975/1993). Sexism and sex role stereotyping do, however, take many forms, and the sections below will consider some of the important theorising on sexism as impacting the maintenance of the rape myth belief system. It will focus specifically on ambivalent sexism (AS) (Glick & Fiske, 1996) as a key construct related to RMA and, as such, note the multifaceted nature of sexism as existing in both overt and covert varieties. It will further consider the increasingly important 'scientific sexism' (the re-selling of stereotypes and regressive arguments as scientific facts) as lending scientific credibility of some of these attitudes.

Rape Myths: Understanding, Assessing, and Preventing, 105–117
Copyright © 2022 by Sofia Persson and Katie Dhingra
Published under exclusive licence by Emerald Publishing Limited
doi:10.1108/978-1-80071-152-520220006

Ambivalent Sexism

Glick and Fiske (1996) conceptualised AS as comprising two distinct but closely related dimensions: hostile sexism (HS) and benevolent sexism (BS). HS reflects antipathy towards women, in particular those who assert their rights and thereby challenge the gender status quo. Thus, HS captures the most 'classic' form of sexism and is, as such, also known as old-fashioned sexism or traditional sexism. BS, by contrast, reflects a paternalistic view of women who gratify men's needs by accepting traditional gender roles (e.g., wife, mother); it characterises women as creatures that should be protected, adored, and supported, and whose love is necessary to complete a man. Hostile and benevolent sexism correlate strongly and positively with each other (Glick & Fiske, 2001).

Firmly rooted in social psychological theory of stereotypes, AS proposes that while prejudice against women generally positions women as inferior to men, it cannot be wholly adversarial, as men depend on women for intimacy and sexual access. This, therefore, creates a need to avoid alienating women entirely, but also entrenches a further level of animosity towards women, as women are regarded as using men's dependence on them to their advantage. As such, AS captures a largely antagonistic view of heterosexual relationships, where relationship and intimacy satisfaction is a zero-sum game[1] between women and men. One reason for the development of AS was as a response to the evolving nature of sexism. Previous investigations into sexism addressed mainly negative evaluations of women; these not only underestimated the general prevalence of sexism but also did not reflect women's actual experience of sexism (Glick & Fiske, 1996). Again, this stresses the need for psychological theory to fully capture the lived experience of women to remain relevant. Earlier investigations also failed to acknowledge the ambivalent and interrelated nature of hostility and benevolence towards women, which seems to be a key aspect of how these beliefs are maintained.

Even before the wider dissemination of AS theory, similar constructs had been noted as important for understanding the contexts around RMA. Lonsway and Fitzgerald's (1994) review stressed 'adversarial sexual beliefs' as a construct that correlated with RMA. Adversarial sexual beliefs are similar to AS (and especially HS) in that they assume an ultimately antagonistic relationship between women and men (e.g., an expectation that the other in a relationship is manipulative, exploitative, sly, and not to be trusted; Burt, 1980), particularly in heterosexual relationships, which are viewed as a 'battle of the sexes'. Hostility towards women is a component of this construct and it shares many conceptual similarities with HS. BS is perhaps more like 'attitudes towards women and social roles' (as largely concerned with sex role stereotyping as opposed to outright negative views of women's abilities), which has also been noted as important for understanding RMA (Lonsway & Fitzgerald, 1994).

AS is measured through the Ambivalent Sexism Inventory (ASI; Glick & Fiske, 1996), although there are other scales that meaure related constructs, such as The Attitudes towards Women Scale (AWS; Spence & Helmreich, 1972) or the Modern

---

[1]Gender-based zero-sum thinking reflects beliefs that women's status gains correspond directly with men's status losses.

Sexsim Scale (MS; Swim et al., 1995). The ASI has been used cross-culturally and continues to exhibit good reliability across varying samples (Glick & Fiske, 2011). Its continued relevance despite being relatively dated is likely because central tenets of sexism have, despite some cultural and time-dependent variation, remained largely the same (e.g., feminists as being adversarial to men, women as being untrustworthy, women as being more morally refined than men, and so on). The ASI has also mostly avoided colloquialism, which has likely contributed to its continued usage. Below, we outline the direct relationship between RMA and benevolent and hostile sexism.

BS and RMA.   BS encapsulates attitudes that may, on the surface, seem beneficial to women and appear to place women on a moral pedestal (i.e., women being pure and innocent and in need of protection from men). The often subtle and ostensibly 'positive' nature of these stereotypes means that they can be difficult to detect and as such challenge (Becker & Wright, 2011; Dardenne et al., 2007). Glick and Fiske (1996) proposed three subcomponents of these attitudes: (a) protective paternalism (example ASI item: 'Women should be cherished and protected by men'), (b) complementary gender differentiation (example ASI item: 'Women, compared to men, tend to have a superior moral sensibility'), and (c) intimate heterosexuality (example ASI item: 'No matter how accomplished he is, a man is not truly complete as a person unless he has the love of a woman'). Broadly, these components tap into men as protectors of women (and ultimately, women as needing protection), women and men as occupying distinct and different social roles (e.g., women as the wife/ mother), and women and men as only being fully 'complete' when in heterosexual relationships. Ultimately, these attitudes are strongly tied to gender roles and the heterosexual norm; they serve to create a set of rules for women, where women who comply with these rules (i.e., through occupying traditional female roles and behaving in traditional feminine ways) are ostensibly rewarded (seen as 'good'), and women who do not comply (i.e., through challenging gender stereotypes) are punished (e.g., by no longer being considered worthy of protection).

It can be argued that measures of benevolently sexist attitudes are better than measures of direct (or hostile) sexism in capturing the lived experiences of women in the context of discrimination and stereotyping, which links with the reason AS was developed in the first place (i.e., to capture sexist attitudes beyond those that are directly derogatory). As such, it addresses an important aim of feminist research more generally, i.e., to go beyond data measurement from a male perspective (which, in this context, may be focused on more direct instances of sexism), towards accurately capturing women's actual experiences of living in a sexist society. In other words, BS as a construct seems to be informative for the 'compounded' experience of sexism, as lived by women, where the daily and more subtle instances of stereotyping and minimisation blend together (Becker & Wright, 2011; Dardenne, Dumont, & Bollier, 2007). BS is prevalent across different cultures, and generally, women tend to reject BS less than HS, likely because isolated incidents of BS are more difficult to detect, or because women may be more prone to agree with BS as opposed to HS (Glick et al., 2000; Dardenne et al., 2007). That women subscribe to benevolently sexist attitudes is perhaps unsurprising, given that they present a kind of reward in an overall sexist society (Becker & Wright, 2011). As argued by Glick and Fiske (1997) and Chapleau et al. (2007), BS may be the 'carrot' in the overall 'stick and carrot' system, which keeps women within the patriarchal order, as it justifies male domination while ostensibly rewarding women who comply with its rules. Without reward, it is unlikely women would be motivated to comply with sexist systems. While the above would suggest that some women can thrive within the context of benevolently sexist attitudes, the rules are arbitrary, and women who are raped can be construed as 'bad' and ultimately culpable (Sakalli-Ugurlu et al., 2007).

Past research (e.g., Abrams et al., 2003) indicates that BS has a positive relationship with RMA (albeit to a lesser extent than HS; as further outlined below). We found similar patterns in our meta-analysis, where BS generally correlated positively with RMA (Persson & Dhingra 2020), as well as in some of our primary research (Persson & Dhingra, 2021), where BS correlated positively with RMA in a mixed-gender as well as an all-male sample.[2] In other words, higher levels of BS are associated with higher levels of RMA. Theoretically, the subcomponent of 'gender differentiation' is perhaps most relevant for RMA, as it captures the differentiation of women and men's social and sexual roles, which is central to many measures of RMA (e.g., the Acceptance of Modern Myths about Sexual Aggression (AMMSA) by Gerger et al., 2007). Through viewing women as more moral than men, these attitudes ultimately emphasise women's responsibility to serve as 'gatekeepers' of male sexuality (which is, in turn, viewed as 'dangerous' and 'uncontrollable'). When women fail to account for men's sexuality through, for instance, being alone with men, drinking with men, taking drugs with men, etc., they are viewed as having behaved recklessly and thus as having precipitated the rape. These attitudes therefore link with central components of RMA (particularly the domains of 'blame the victim', and 'only certain types of women are raped') in how they categorise women as being deserving or undeserving (of rape or male protection) as based on their behaviour (Viki & Abrams, 2002). Therefore, those who score highly on BS may extend a level of protection to women who are raped in certain circumstances, particularly if the perpetrator can be viewed as having violated prescribed gender roles, and the woman can be viewed as having followed them. A relevant example of such a scenario would be what MacKinnon (1989/1991) termed 'the legally perfect rape', i.e., a rape with obvious and evidenced physical violence (beyond the violence of the rape itself) perpetrated by a stranger, against a sober, White, middle class woman, who seeks medical and legal assistance immediately following the assault. In the context of rape, therefore, BS (and AS more broadly) is perhaps best understood as a schema, where information about a rape case is re-construed and imagined detail is added to fit with these attitudes. It also links more broadly with the belief in a just world (Lerner, 1977; as outlined in Chapter Five), as women (and to a lesser extent men) are prescribed certain behaviours and presumed to deserve negative outcomes if they act outside these.

---

[2]The correlations were $r = 0.65$ in our mixed-gender sample of 252 participants, and $r = 0.50$ in our all-male sample of 182 participants. Further data collected from 565 mixed-gender participants in October 2021 confirm a medium-sized correlation of $r = 0.44$ for RMA and BS.

HS and RMA. HS is the overt form of sexism, which encompasses negative attitudes towards women and their capabilities, such as women being inferior to men and deceitful and untrustworthy (Glick & Fiske, 1996; Lee, Fiske, Glick, & Chen, 2010). Example HS items from the ASI include 'Women are too easily offended' and 'Women seek to gain power by getting control over men'. HS as a construct was originally composed of three subcomponents, mirroring those of BS (dominative paternalism, competitive gender differentiation, and heterosexual hostility), but as little support has been found for these through empirical research, HS is more commonly considered a unitary construct (Glick & Fiske, 1996). It is not implausible, however, that future research may consider new and improved subcategories, as some aspects of overt sexism become obsolete. HS supports the overall adversarial nature of AS, where women and men are regarded as dependent on each other, but that positive outcomes are a zero-sum game, with one gender 'winning' at the expense of the other. Because of the negative evaluations present in HS, it is perhaps not surprising that women, as compared to men, are more likely to reject HS (Glick et al., 2000).

HS may have a more straightforward relationship with RMA than BS does, and these beliefs generally seem to correlate across studies and contexts (Persson & Dhingra, 2020, 2021).[3] In other words, higher levels of HS are consistently associated with higher levels of RMA. This relationship appears to be stronger and more consistent than the relationship between RMA and BS. This is perhaps unsurprising, given that HS and RMA primarily tap into aggressively sexist attitudes and negative views about women and their capabilities. Importantly, they have considerable overlapping content in the context of heterosexual intimacy, where women are seen to utilise various sexual strategies (e.g., 'leading a man on') to gain an advantage. This stands in contrast with benevolently sexist attitudes, where women and men are regarded as different but complementary. Importantly, HS views women as deceitful and able to lie to gain advantage, which bears direct relevance to the belief that false rape accusations are commonplace. Moreover, by casting women as less intellectually able than men, it further implies that women may overstate or exaggerate instances of sexual violence. Although HS does not directly address rape, it does so indirectly through the casting of doubt on women's abilities to correctly identify sexual violence and it also questions women's general truthfulness (e.g., 'Most women interpret innocent remarks or acts as being sexist'; Glick & Fiske, 1996). This implies that all women have the potential to exaggerate or misunderstand sexual violence and to fabricate rape accusations, particularly in a context where this can be construed as giving women an advantage over men (e.g., in custody disagreements or relationship fallouts). As the belief that false rape allegations are commonplace seems to emerge as a key aspect of RMA, it is

---

[3]We found a positive correlation of $r = 0.84$ in a mixed-gender sample of 252 participants, and a positive correlation of $r = 0.77$ in an all-male sample of 182 participants. Recently collected data (from October 2021) on 565 mixed-gender participants confirm a strong positive correlation of $r = 0.81$ between RMA and HS.

likely that HS will continue to be of relevance for understanding perceived victim-survivor blame in rape cases.

Unlike BS, clear instances of obvious HS have become increasingly rare, at least in the physical world. The emergence of the men's rights movement (particularly in the context of an increased digitalisation of the political discourse) has, however, seen a renewal of instances of overt and direct aggressive misogyny directed towards women (Bates, 2020; Ging, 2019). Both the online and offline aspects of men's right activism lean more towards hostile than benevolent sexism and have highlighted false rape accusations and false accusations of domestic violence as key priorities, particularly in the context of father's rights and political strategy (Gotell & Dutton, 2016; Messner, 2016). It is therefore likely that as HS becomes increasingly unacceptable in the physical world, these attitudes may become more vitriolic through online platforms (e.g., Twitter and Reddit; Ging, 2019; Jane, 2018).

Scientific Sexism and Gender Essentialism

Another relevant form of sexism is the renewal of what has, by researchers and feminist scholars, been termed 'scientific sexism' (e.g., Fine, 2010; Ruti, 2015). Scientific sexism refers to neuropsychological and evolutionary investigations into biological explanations for observed gender differences in behaviour and aptitudes, often with an underlying sexist agenda. The positioning of biological differences as the main cause of gendered behaviour also falls under the wider umbrella of 'biological essentialism'. While biological explanations for gender differences have a long and thorny history (see Rippon, 2019, for an overview of this topic), rather than dissipating over time, the belief that men and women are wired differently[4] has seen a recent renewal (Persson & Pownall, 2021) possibly due to a growing public interest in science communications as reflected in media reporting on the topic (Cassidy, 2005; O'Connor & Joffe, 2014). Historically, these theories have focused on women's physical and intellectual inferiority (as more obviously offensive to women), as opposed to more modern theories, which tend to focus on *difference* rather than hierarchies (Rippon, 2019). Although it is difficult to state with certainty that women and men's brains are similar, most research stating brain differences fail to replicate across contexts (Eliot, Ahmed, Khan, & Patel, 2021) and findings should also be considered in the context of an overall tendency in the sciences to report on (and as such, publish) findings of difference, rather than similarity (Chambers, 2017; Rippon, 2019).

Evolutionary psychology's (EP) sex-selection theory (SST) has been positioned as key within 'scientific sexism'. Originating from Darwin's evolutionary theory (ET), EP is a branch of psychology concerned with evolutionary adaptation and its impact on human psychology and behaviour. It focuses specifically on the natural selection for adaptive traits and how this has influenced a wide array of human behaviour, psychology, and abilities (Buss & Schmitt, 2011; Confer

---

[4]This is sometimes referred to as 'hardwired' brain sex differences, where the female brain is cast as empathiser and the male brain as systemiser.

et al., 2010). A prominent argument within the SST is that females and males of all species (including humans) have evolved gender-specific traits in the areas where they have faced differential problems throughout evolution, especially regarding mating and sexuality (Buss & Schmitt, 2011; Lippa, 2007). According to the SST, men have evolved a desire for mating with as many *different* women as possible (Brown et al., 2009; Buss, 1995). Conversely, the SST would suggest that women's greater parental investment (in terms of the relative scarcity of eggs as opposed to sperm, as well as in pregnancy) has resulted in women being choosy regarding sexual relations (Archer, 2019; Buss, 1995).

Scientific Sexism and RMA. There are several ways in which 'scientifically sexist' theories have implications for rape myth endorsement. First, past research has found that biological explanations for gender differences can increase both negative and 'positive' gender stereotyping (Brescoll & LaFrance, 2004), which lends scientific credibility to benevolently (and to a lesser extent) hostile sexist attitudes. Moreover, biological essentialism and ETs propose what is ultimately an adversarial nature of sexual relationships, where women and men's sexual goals are largely incompatible (i.e., women want to mate with fewer, high-quality men, and men want to mate with as many women as possible). As such, hetero-sexual intimacy is construed as a zero-sum game, with both sexes employing a variety of strategies to advance their interest (Buss, 2021), which mirrors many ambivalently sexist attitudes (Glick & Fiske, 1996).

Second, and perhaps most importantly, biologically-based theories of sexual behaviour have the potential for considerable perpetrator exoneration. Some ETs suggest that rape can be explained as a conditional mating strategy, employed by *some* men under *certain* conditions where non-coercive strategies would not be successful (e.g., McKibbin et al., 2008; Thornhill & Palmer, 2000). While the suggestion that men may be biologically predestined to rape under certain conditions exists on the extreme end of the spectrum, biological and evolutionary under-standings of the causes, consequences, and preventions for rape do nonetheless contribute to a meta-narrative about the reasons (and excuses) for perpetration. This point was supported by Chiroro et al. (2004), who suggested that ETs may be particularly important for how laypeople understand the motivations for rape in the context of rape myths. As such, the emphasis on biological and genetic causes for sexual aggression links strongly with tenets of both HS and RMA, in that men's sexuality is positioned as fundamentally dangerous and unpredict-able. Empirical research on this topic is, however, scarce. A study by Dar-Nimrod, Heine, Cheung, and Schaller (2011) indicated that an evolutionary explanation for a sexual crime did not impact recommended perpetrator punishment com-pared to a control condition, but that a social explanation led to harsher recom-mended perpetrator punishment. However, this study used only a single item to measure recommended punishment and crucially did not consider RMA. It is therefore clear that this area needs more empirical research and an incorporation of how RMA may interact with biological or essentialist explanations for gender differences to potentially impact perceptions of perpetrators.

Finally, some EP researchers (e.g., Thornhill & Palmer, 2011) have suggested that men's natural propensity to sexually aggress should be taken into consideration in rape prevention strategies, where women should be advised to be mindful of the way in which they dress and behave to prevent rape. As such, even if not overtly supportive of blaming the victim-survivor of rape, suggestions such as these do nonetheless position women as a cause of rape, as they are advised to modify their behaviour according to men's innate tendencies. We expanded further on how victim-survivor-centred rape prevention strategies may contribute to rape myths in Chapter Five. Empirical investigations on biological theories and victim-survivor blame are still relatively scarce, and it would be worthwhile to conduct more research in this area.

Sexism and the Maintenance of RMA

The sections above have outlined the direct relationship between sexist attitudes and RMA, but it is also important to consider how a sexist belief system indirectly scaffolds a broader environment where rape myths are maintained. The sections below detail two potentially relevant aspects of how sexism maintains rape myth beliefs in a societal context.

General Acceptance of Gender Differentiations. Stereotypes about women and men in terms of their nature, aptitude, and capabilities (Glick & Fiske, 1996) are central to most forms of sexism. Although some of these stereotypes can ostensibly be perceived as 'positive' (e.g., women as needing protection), we argue that this 'softer' type of sexism creates an environment that makes the more extreme and aggressive versions of sexism possible. This is further evidenced through the wealth of research indicating correlations between BS and HS (Glick & Fiske, 1996, 2011; Persson & Dhingra, 2020, 2021). As stated above, some of these attitudes may not seem ostensibly offensive to women, as they are implemented in a 'positive' way (e.g., encouraging women's participation in science with pink branding) or because they stress women's moral superiority. In doing this, however, they mark women as fundamentally different to men, which is, ultimately, highly important for rape myth beliefs, e.g., men as having uncontrollable sexual urges and women as being natural gatekeepers of sexual activity (Burt, 1980; Gerger et al., 2007). Relatedly, if, as we have argued in Chapter Two, RMA is best conceptualised as a schema (e.g., Krahé et al., 2008; Süssenbach et al., 2012), these 'softer' stereotypes of women can also elicit the more negative ones that are core to RMA.

Importantly, these stereotypes (especially if considered as having a biological basis) often set unattainably high standards for women's behaviour (e.g., moral superiority, sexual modesty) and a comparatively low standard for men's behaviour (e.g., as having an inherently aggressive and uncontrollable sexuality and loose morals). The high behavioural standard for women ultimately labels women according to whether they live up to this standard (Glick & Fiske, 1996, 2011), which is especially problematic given that no woman can consistently behave according to the plethora of arbitrary rules. Ultimately, this categorisation of women is also at the core of RMA, especially in the domains 'only certain types of women are raped' and 'blame the victim' (Bohner et al., 2009). For men, this gender differentiation serves to entrench what is ultimately a highly pessimistic view of men's moral capabilities, which, while obviously insulting to men, also implicitly serves to promote an environment that holds men to lower sexual moral standards than women, including for sexual aggression. Ultimately, this is highly important for societal perpetrator exoneration but, as noted previously in the context of the functions of rape myths (Chapter Five), it may also mean that men hold themselves to lower standards in their sexual conduct towards women.

In this context, the effect of gender stereotyping and differentiation may be particularly insidious, as women (and, to a lesser degree men) may struggle to recognise, and as such challenge, subtler forms of sexism, particularly if paternal and ostensibly 'helpful' in nature (Becker & Wright, 2011). This may, in turn, have the unintended consequence of signalling that this gender stereotyping is appropriate, despite its negative consequences on gender equality. This may be particularly problematic, as the 'giver' of sexism that is ostensibly 'positive' may not see any issue with these attitudes, thus drawing on one of the initial reasons for the conceptualisation of AS in the first place (i.e., to measure sexism among groups of people who do not *seem* sexist; Glick & Fiske, 1996). While men should ultimately feel insulted to be considered of lesser moral capabilities than women, these beliefs may also be partially convenient, as it allows men a certain amount of discretion in their behaviours towards women; this may explain why men have not collectively engaged against these beliefs on any substantial level. It does, however, signpost that feminist interventions to reduce any form of sexism will need involvement from men as well as women (Persson & Hostler, 2021).

The Backlash against Feminism.   Sexism may also maintain RMA through the backlash against feminism, which has seen a renewal of aggressive (or hostile) forms of sexism (Persson & Hostler, 2021). Feminist scholars have recognised this backlash as intermittently dormant and resurgent since the 1980s (Faludi, 1993), and there appears to be a current revival of this backlash. It has been suggested that aggressively misogynist and anti-feminist attitudes have experienced a resurgence through the digitalisation of the political discourse, particularly in the context of the alt-right and men's rights activism (Bates, 2020; Ging, 2019). Van Valkenburgh (2021) has noted the importance of 'scientific sexism' in supporting claims made about women and men in online extreme men's rights groups. Much of this hostile behaviour towards women takes place online, which has the added effect of being disinhibitory[5] and empathy-reducing. As such, the ease with which messages can be disseminated through online platforms has increased the scope of hostile forms of sexism, and as such scaffolded a climate conducive to rape myths as well.

A useful example here is the belief that false rape allegations are commonplace, which we argue has emerged as important for the maintenance of Western RMA today. False rape allegations as commonplace is an important tactic employed within the backlash against feminism more generally, as this backlash

---

[5]This has been referred to as the 'online disinhibition effect', which recognises that people often say or do things in the online space that they would not ordinarily say and do in the offline world (Suler, 2004).

is often centred on 'protecting' men from these allegations (Gotell & Dutton, 2016). In particular, false rape allegations as commonplace are important for how some extreme men's rights groups understand heterosexual relationships, i.e., that women employ various (sexual) strategies to exert interpersonal power over men (Van Valkenburgh, 2021). It is likely that this has been a particularly successful rhetoric, as evidence suggests that the public misjudge the prevalence of false rape allegations and conflate false allegations with those that lack sufficient evidence to investigate/prosecute (Huntington et al., 2022). These beliefs further appear to be reproduced in both public and less public cases of rape, where women are frequently portrayed as levelling false accusations against men to gain personal or political leverage (Banet-Weiser, 2021; Huntington et al., 2022). This suggests that anti-feminist discourse is not limited to extreme groups (even if many of these ideas originate there), but rather that diluted versions of these messages are reproduced in more mainstream settings. While public discourse rarely states that women (as a group) want to take advantage of men, the justifications for disbelieving individual women usually draw on themes surrounding adversarial sexual relationships (i.e., that a woman has an ulterior motive for a rape allegation). Here, various strategies are employed to cast doubt on individual women's testimony (many of these are outlined in previous sections of this book), highlighting how the backlash against feminism creates an environment that can also perpetuate RMA.

Racism, Classism, and Ableism

Black feminist scholars have long advocated for an intersectional understanding of how sexism and racism interact (e.g., Collins, 1990/2009; Crenshaw, 1989; Lorde, 1984/2007; and as further elaborated on in Chapter Two). Past empirical research has noted the relationship between racism and sexism (Nicol & Rounding, 2013) and suggested that racist beliefs follow similar patterns in existing as both 'old-fashioned' (i.e., overt) and more modern (and subtle) forms of prejudice (Swim, Aikin, Hall, & Hunter, 1995). Less research has, however, empirically investigated the relationship between RMA and racism. The research that is available does indicate a relationship between racism and RMA, which makes sense given how rape myths can reinforce racist beliefs about victim-survivors and perpetrators (as outlined further in Chapter Two). Specifically, Suarez and Gadalla's (2010) review found a strong relationship between combined racism[6] and endorsement of rape myths among three studies. One of these studies was by Aosved and Long (2006), who investigated the co-occurrence of RMA, sexism, racism, and classism (alongside other prejudice such as homophobia) in a mixed-gender student sample. Sexism (modern and old-fashioned, as being relatively like HS and BS), racism (modern and old-fashioned), and classism all predicted RMA, with sexism showing the strongest effect. The authors suggest that the overlap between racism

---

[6]Combined racism included old racism, modern racism, and general racism.

and sexism is of particular importance and points to an underlying intolerant belief system as connecting all these constructs (as further detailed below).

Further, scholars such as Crenshaw (1989) and Davis (1981/2019) have posited that classism is an important correlate of racism and sexism, and that these constructs interact to produce specific forms of prejudice directed at working class women and women of colour. As with racism and sexism, classism is concerned with the enforcement of group-bases hierarchies. Empirical research in this area has, however, been relatively recent, something that can perhaps be best understood in the context of the limited attention mainstream feminist theorists have paid to the specific pressures faced by minority and working class women (as further outlined in Chapter Two). Davis (1981/2019) noted that Black women and working class women face similar biases in the context of rape. These biases tend to involve beliefs about fecklessness, sexual promiscuity, and a general immorality (Jones, 2011).

Importantly, classism also links and interacts more specifically with the different rape myth domains. In the context of rape myths, many of the central characteristics of the 'certain' types of women who are perceived as being the 'type' to be assaulted (in accordance with RMA) align with stereotypes about working class women, e.g., in terms of perceived carelessness and promiscuity (Spencer, 2016). As per intersectionality theory, these beliefs create a distinct set of stereotypes when applied to working class women (as opposed to middle class women) within the context of rape. Here, research suggests that a rape victim-survivor of lower perceived social class is blamed for the assault to a greater degree and viewed as more promiscuous than a victim-survivor of higher perceived social class (Spencer, 2016). Ultimately, this minimises the perceived severity and impact of rape occurring within women of lower perceived social class and positions them as being partly responsible for any assault committed against them.

Finally, we note the theoretical links between RMA and ableism, where many of the strategies used to blame the victim-survivor link with already existing stereotypes about disabled women (e.g., women as childlike and unreliable witnesses) much like with racist and classist rape myths. Past research on victim-survivor disability status and sexual assault attributions suggests negligible differences in blame attributions between physically disabled and non-disabled victim-survivors (Dalton et al., 2021; Hughes, Skoda, Parsons, Brown, & Pedersen, 2020), but this does not account for any potential relationship with rape myths. In her court observations, Smith (2018) noted that in cases where the victim-survivor had any kind of disability, this was often indirectly addressed in the perpetrator's defence along the line of rape myths. Specifically, disabled women were often cast as being untrustworthy witnesses, and misremembering the incident, meaning that the perpetrator could be exonerated. The indirectness of this stereotyping (and especially when interacting with rape myths) may be particularly difficult to directly measure (as few legal professionals would admit to ableist attitudes), which could explain the scant scientific evidence on this topic. We note, therefore, that disabled women may be uniquely vulnerable to being stereotyped within rape myth beliefs, but unfortunately, research on the specific links between ableism and RMA remains scarce.

Social Dominance

The theoretical links between RMA and the prejudices outlined in this book can perhaps be best understood in the context of social dominance, which underpins all these constructs. White et al. (1998) noted social domination as important in the context of racism and RMA and this seems to extend to other forms of prejudice as well (Nicol & Rounding, 2013). Social Dominance Theory (Sidanius & Pratto, 1999) seeks to explain how group hierarchies are maintained and reproduced and includes a consideration of legitimising myths as one strategy for how this is achieved. As such, this theory is directly applicable to the functions of RMA (i.e., as enforcing gender inequality and legitimising men's sexual violence against women) and applies to the other forms of prejudice discussed in this chapter. Support for social dominance, in this case, would indicate a support for in-group hierarchies (whatever these may be) as well as an intolerant belief system. Empirical research in the context of RMA seems to support this notion, where endorsement of various social hierarchies correlates across the literature (e.g., Suarez & Gadalla, 2010). Hockett, Saucier, Hoffman, Smith, and Craig (2009) examined social dominance specifically and explored the relationship between general social dominance (using a variety of measures) and RMA among 161 student participants. They found that both general social dominance scores and AS (operationalised in this study as part of a wider assessment of 'sex-based oppression') predicted RMA. Research such as the above underscores the importance of prioritizing a feminist understanding of rape (for an overview of this, see Chapter Two), in how dominance and group-based oppressions are important for understanding the perpetration of, and responses to, rape in society (e.g., Brownmiller, 1975/1993). It also supports contentions by researchers such as White et al. (1998) that an ahistorical and acontextual approach to understanding RMA is likely to be theoretically impoverished.

Conclusion

The literature outlined in this chapter suggests that research into rape myths often fails to pay sufficient attention to the broader environment in which these myths are perpetuated, despite Burt's (1980) original theorising centring correlates of these beliefs. In this chapter, we have highlighted several relevant correlates of RMA, and out of these, sexism emerges as the most prominent one. Benevolently sexist attitudes entrench gender differentiations and HS maintains the extreme misogyny stemming from the feminist backlash; these attitudes support several of the central assumptions underlying rape myths, both in terms of victim-survivors and perpetrators. Concerningly, these ideas are lent scientific credibility by biological theories that stress the innate differences between women and men's sexuality. Sexism further interacts with other oppressive structures in society such as racism and classism, all broadly linking with beliefs about social domination and group hierarchies more generally. While the current chapter has outlined sexism, racism, classism, and ableism as relevant theoretical considerations in the context of rape myths, this list is not exhaustive, and future investigations in this area may well wish to incorporate a wider array of other prejudices. Incorporating a diverse range of prejudices in RMA theorising and considering their impact on victim-survivors in the context of intersectionality will be crucial, as ignoring the multiple and diverse layers of oppression only serves to protect current hierarchies, which ultimately pits disadvantaged groups against each other (Crenshaw, 1989). Because of this, the most effective theorising on rape will incorporate multiple types of prejudice and ensure collective rather than individualised action. It is, therefore, likely that one of the main reasons why interventions to target RMA have only been moderately successful (Wright, Zounlome, & Whiston, 2020) is their failure to consider social domination more generally. We will explore interventions to target RMA further in the next and final chapter.

Chapter Seven

Ways Forward in Addressing Sexual Violence

Chapter Overview

The final chapter of this book will draw on the evidence presented in previous chapters and examine how sexual violence can be addressed and rape myths prevented. In addition, it seeks to explore whether pre-existing rape myth endorsement among individuals can be altered. We will outline some of the previous attempts at designing sexual violence and rape myth prevention programmes and, drawing on meta-analytical findings in this area, comment on the short- and long-term effectiveness of these programmes. Placing these programmes within the context of theories of attitudinal change (e.g., Rosenberg, 1956) and attitude-change programmes more generally, we will consider some of the issues involved in using these strategies to impact deep-seated beliefs regarding the nature of rape, victim-survivors, and perpetrators. We will argue that short-term interventions to lessen attitudes such as RMA are not a panacea, considering how pervasive these myths are and their schematic nature. We further posit that so long as more benevolently sexist attitudes remain socially acceptable, interventions to reduce rape myths will have little effect. Here, we therefore conclude that a wider discussion around sexism, as underpinned by feminist understandings of social dominance and gender inequality, is necessary. Finally, we propose ways in which research in this area can move forward to facilitate this discussion, drawing the lessons learned from the history of RMA research.

Interventions to Address Sexual Violence

There exists a plethora of educational programmes aimed at addressing sexual violence, but there has traditionally been a lack of clarity about what behaviours and attitudes these interventions are targeting and who the target audience is. As such, this chapter takes a wider focus than that of the rest of this book and seeks to examine interventions and programmes aimed at addressing sexual violence in its broadest sense, both in terms of attitudes and cognitions surrounding sexual

Rape Myths: Understanding, Assessing, and Preventing, 119–137
Copyright © 2022 by Sofia Persson and Katie Dhingra
Published under exclusive licence by Emerald Publishing Limited
doi:10.1108/978-1-80071-152-520220007

violence (including those relating to rape myths), as well as behaviours relating to sexual violence, both in terms of potential bystander intervention and perpetration. These interventions have mostly been delivered to the general population (and overwhelmingly at university/college campuses), but we also review evidence relating to specific groups such as men imprisoned for rape. Intervention efficacy has typically been evidenced through a change in the targeted attitude/behaviour from pre- to post-intervention. However, when considering the efficacy of these programmes, it is worth noting that these interventions often vary considerably, making it difficult to directly compare them. Moreover, such variation in the design of interventions makes it challenging to identify what works (or may work) for whom and under what circumstances. Variation between programmes usually stems from factors such as:

- Content (e.g., rape myth information, materials promoting empathy towards victim-survivors, bystander intervention strategies)
- Format (e.g., video/film/audio clips, web-based format, face to face (typically supplemented by PowerPoint slides and discussions), information booklet, improvisational theatre)
- Duration (e.g., one session of 90 minutes or less or several sessions)
- Trainers (e.g., peer educators, graduate students, 'experts')
- Type of population that received the intervention (e.g., fraternity members, police officers, college students)
- Type of attendance (optional or forced/mandated)
- Outcomes measured (e.g., attitudes, cognitions, RMA, behavioural intentions)
- Theoretical foundations

Theoretical Foundations

Although numerous researchers have emphasised the importance of using a theoretical framework to determine the content and format of an intervention (e.g., Heppner, Humphrey, Hillenbrand-Gunn, & DeBord, 1995; Yeater & O'Donohue, 1999), there currently appears to be few rape myth prevention programmes that offer a clear theoretical foundation (Bohner et al., 2005; Mujal, Taylor, Fry, Gochez-Kerr, & Weaver, 2021). Consequently, it will be important for future research to further examine the effects of theoretically driven interventions (especially when compared to non-theoretically driven ones), as progress in this area may help to delineate components of effective programming. Below we briefly articulate the main theories that underpin some of the programmes that have been developed to address sexual violence.

    The Elaboration Likelihood Model (ELM; Petty & Cacioppo, 1986). The ELM is a theory of persuasion that proposes two routes to attitudinal change, each associated with a distinct processing style; the 'peripheral route', linked with heuristic processing, and the 'central route', associated with systematic, thoughtful processing. The ELM posits that long-term attitude change, which is predictive of an individual's subsequent behaviour, is more likely to occur via the central route. Further, the model advances that the greater the motivation to attend to a message, the more likely an individual is to systematically process, engage with, and evaluate it. An individual's motivation can be affected by a variety of factors, including whether the message has personal relevance, the degree of need for cognition, the source of the message argument, and whether the advocated position is pro- or counter-attitudinal.

Because of its potential to promote systematic processing, the ELM should be well suited to address RMA. As the schematic nature of RMA means that facts about rape are mostly processed heuristically, strategies relying on the ELM could, in theory, produce deeper and more thoughtful reasoning. Therefore, interventions designed to change rape-supportive attitudes should use well-argued messages (e.g., based on clear and indisputable facts), establish the personal relevance of these messages to their target audience[1] (e.g., police officers, college students, fraternity group members), and be delivered by a trainer best suited to the target audience (e.g., someone the group can view as relatable or an expert or authority on the topic). Applying the ELM to rape prevention has shown signs of success (Foubert, 2000; Foubert & La Voy, 2000; Heppner et al., 1995).

Belief Systems Theory (BST; Grube, Mayton, & Ball-Rokeach, 1994). BST suggests that interventions must maintain participants' existing self-conceptions to produce lasting attitudinal change. In other words, when incorporating this theory, programmes should appeal to the way men perceive themselves (i.e., as potential helpers rather than potential perpetrators), thereby avoiding defensive responses and encouraging co-operation. Promoting a positive self-image in a gender equality context has been successfully used to promote feminist solidarity among men (Wiley, Srinivasan, Finke, Firnhaber, & Shilinsky, 2012), and applying the BST to rape prevention has shown signs of success (e.g., Foubert & Masin, 2012).

Cognitive Dissonance Theory (CDT; Festinger, 1962). CDT advances that an individual experiences cognitive dissonance when they hold two contradictory beliefs or when they are aware that their current behaviour is not in line with their pre-existing beliefs. Here, it is suggested that because cognitive dissonance is psychologically uncomfortable, its presence can lead to either a change in beliefs or a change in behaviour, to reduce dissonance. The greater the magnitude of the dissonance, the greater is the pressure to reduce dissonance. Applying the CDT to rape prevention (through asking male participants to write arguments against raping women) has shown some signs of success (e.g., Stephens & George, 2009), although the CDT was here also combined with the ELM.

Situational Model of Bystander Intervention (Latane & Darley, 1968). This model is often used to predict the likelihood that an individual will engage in prosocial intervention behaviour. This would, in the context of rape, involve behaviours

---

[1]One of the issues faced in efforts to engage men in prevention is whether to instigate voluntary or compulsory attendance. Voluntary programmes have been shown to be relatively unlikely to be attended by many men who need to hear the message (i.e., strategically avoided; Rich, Utley, Janke, & Moldoveanu, 2010). Equally, mandatory attendance may result in resistance.

intended to prevent sexual assault from happening, such as challenging a man who is attempting to isolate a woman who is too intoxicated to consent or who seems scared or uncomfortable. The model has five stages bystanders must undergo to intervene: (a) notice the event (or its warning signs, e.g., a man attempting to isolate an intoxicated woman); (b) interpret the event as warranting action/intervention; (c) take intervention responsibility (i.e., feel a sense of personal duty to act); (d) know how to intervene or provide help (e.g., approach the man, or alert the police or security staff); and (e) implement intervention decisions. Situational barriers at any of these steps halt the bystander intervention process. Therefore, if incorporating this theory, interventions designed to change rape-supportive attitudes should consider how RMA may act as a barrier to bystander intervention. Individuals high in RMA may observe warning signs ahead of, or ongoing, sexually aggressive behaviour (i.e., Stage 1), but their inaccurate or false beliefs about rape and perpetrators of rape may distort their perceptions, preventing them from interpreting the situation as warranting action/intervention (i.e., Stage 2; LeMaire, Oswald, & Russell, 2016). Further, the endorsement of rape myths may prevent individuals from empathising with women who at risk of being victimised (Leone, Oyler, & Parrot, 2021). If a bystander believes a woman is 'asking for it' by wearing certain clothing, for example, a bystander may not appraise her of meriting intervention. Those high in RMA may also fail to take responsibility for intervening (Yule et al., 2022). In other words, RMA may be a barrier to intervention, as potential bystanders attribute less worthiness to the potential victim and thereby feel less responsibility to intervene (Banyard, 2008; Burn, 2009; McMahon, 2010). We discuss bystander interventions in more detail below, including some of the issues involved in their implementation.

Other Theoretical Underpinnings. Other rape prevention programmes (e.g., Anderson & Whiston, 2005; Mujal et al., 2021; O'Donohue, Yeater, & Fanetti, 2003) have drawn on theoretical models that are widely used in the aetiology of child sexual abuse or adult sexual assault, as well as several cognitive and information processing models. Two examples here are Finkelhor's (1984) four-pre-conditions model and Bandura's (1977) social learning model of aggression. According to these theories, aggressive behaviour (e.g., rape) is the product of cognitions (e.g., rape myths) that make reprehensible conduct ethically acceptable, minimise the consequences of that behaviour, and devalue or blame the victim-survivor (O'Donohue et al., 2003). As previously stated, a major issue here is that multiple theories are often combined, meaning that it can be hard to determine which theory contains the more effective component(s).

Outcomes Assessed

We briefly note here the considerable between-study differences in outcomes used to index intervention efficacy. These include (a) sexually violent behaviour including reported rates of perpetration and/or victimisation (at the individual or community level, i.e., university/college campus); (b) rape proclivity (self-reported likelihood of future sexual perpetration); (c) attitudes about gender roles, sexual violence, sexual behaviour, or bystander intervention; (d) knowledge about sexual violence rates, definitions, and laws; (e) bystander behaviour related to sexual violence, such as intervening or providing help; (f) bystander intentions or self-reported likelihood of intervening in a hypothetical scenario; (g) relevant skills related to communication, relationships, or bystander behaviour; and (h) affect/arousal to violence including victim-related empathy and sexual attraction to violence. We emphasise the wide range of outcomes assessed to draw attention to the difficulty in determining *what*, if anything, works in sexual violence prevention strategies.

Specific Strategies to Address Sexual Violence

Broadly, most strategies aimed at addressing sexual violence seek to provide participants with educational information about the nature of, and context to, sexual violence and its perpetrators, as well as on its impact on victim-survivors. These strategies largely seek to bust myths around rape and provide participants with a more accurate understanding of the realities of sexual assault. Anderson and Whiston (2005) identified four primary types of content in North American college student sexual assault prevention education programmes: (a) informative (provision of factual information and statistics; reviewing myths and facts; consideration of the consequences of rape; and identification of characteristics of rape scenarios); (b) empathy-focused (helping participants understand and share the feelings of rape victim-survivors); (c) socialisation-focused (examining gender-role stereotyping and societal messages that influence rape); and (d) risk-reducing (teaching specific strategies to reduce one's personal vulnerability to rape). Their meta-analysis ($n = 69$ studies) found statistically significant effect sizes for rape knowledge, behavioural intention, rape-related attitudes, and incidence of sexual assault. However, only rape knowledge reached the criteria for a moderate effect size ($d = 0.57$); the other three only had small effect sizes (0.14, 0.12, and 0.10, respectively), suggesting that the changes may have very little clinical or real-world significance. They concluded that sexual assault education programmes are somewhat effective in changing attitudes towards rape and increasing rape knowledge, but 'if effectiveness is defined solely as a decrease in sexual assault, then there is little support available from the current pool of studies' (p. 381). This is concerning, as interventions to address sexual violence rest upon the assumption that attitudes and behaviours are related.

Anderson and Whiston (2005) also noted that the effect sizes of certain outcome constructs (e.g., rape attitudes) were, apart from being directly impacted by characteristics of the intervention (e.g., status of the facilitator, length of programme, content of the programme), also likely influenced by other variables such as participants (e.g., all-female, women from a mixed-gender group, all-male, men from a mixed-gender group, women and men combined), and research methodology (e.g., sample size, random assignment, and time of follow-up measure) and call for additional controlled studies that examine factors that impact the effectiveness of sexual assault education programming. The sections below review the available evidence on some of the specific approaches to, and formats taken of, strategies used to prevent and address sexual violence, focusing specifically on poster campaigns, bystander interventions, victim-empathy training, social norms, and gender socialisation.

Poster Campaigns. There is some evidence that poster campaigns, as a type of anti-rape intervention, can be effective (Potter, 2012; Potter, Moynihan, Stapleton, & Banyard, 2009; Potter & Stapleton, 2012). As noted in Chapter Five, the findings of an evaluation into Rape Crisis Scotland's campaign, 'This is not an invitation to rape me' were promising. Research suggests that well-planned (e.g., through focus group consultation) and best practice (e.g., those that are centred on the behaviour of the bystander or potential perpetrator, rather than the victim-survivor) poster interventions can decrease individuals' RMA, attraction to sexual aggression, and hostile attitudes towards women (Baker et al., 2013; Flood, 2015). Underlying the implementation of poster campaigns, however, is the assumption that there is potential for the target audience to be repeatedly exposed to these posters (i.e., by regularly frequenting the areas where the posters are displayed). Because of this, these types of interventions may be best suited to contexts such as university/college campuses or train/tube stations with a high footfall. As participants are typically exposed to posters in a naturalistic setting (i.e., by walking past them during their daily activities), it is incredibly difficult to state with any certainty that a poster intervention is the specific driver of any observed behavioural or attitudinal change.

Bystander Interventions. Sexual violence prevention interventions have also targeted bystanders. In this context, bystanders are third-party witnesses to situations where there is high risk of sexual violence and who by their presence can do nothing, make the situation worse (i.e., by supporting or ignoring perpetrator actions), or make the situation better by intervening in pro-social ways. Bystander interventions approach participants (both men and women) as 'empowered' individuals who can proactively confront sexist and abusive behaviour among their peers and establish intolerance of violence as the norm.

Unlike many other programmes, the bystander approach does not identify men as potential perpetrators or focus on women as victims, as these are messages that may promote defensiveness among men (Foubert, 2000; Schwartz, DeKeseredy, Tait, & Alvi, 2001). As Howe (2008) observed, to name violence against women as men's violence incites a strong backlash. Exclamations are made that 'not all men are violent', 'women are violent too',[2] and 'men can also be victims of violence'. The bystander approach, therefore, shifts the focus of prevention efforts away from potential victim-survivors and perpetrators onto peers and community members (McMahon, Postmus, & Koenick, 2011; Potter et al., 2009). The approach aligns with calls for more ecological approaches to sexual violence prevention that move beyond changing individuals to changing peer and community interactions, social norms, and behaviours (e.g., Moynihan,

---

[2]Shifting the argument to say, 'women are violent too', creates a false parallel between women and men where it is assumed that women and men are already equal in social life and male privilege and women's oppression do not exist (Johnson, 2005). We would agree that that not all men are violent towards women. However, it is important to acknowledge the benefits that men receive from a society that tolerates men's violence (Hearn, 1998).

Banyard, Arnold, Eckstein, & Stapleton, 2011). In theory, this should create an environment less conducive to sexual violence perpetration. Berkowitz (2003), for instance, claims that men who engage in violence – both physical and verbal – incorrectly assume that other men's silence is indicative of approval, thus feeling emboldened to express and act violently towards women. Accordingly, teaching male peers to 'speak out' will serve to inhibit violence by other men. The following are examples of preventative bystander intervention actions men and women could take, according to bystander interventions:

• Remind a male friend that consent is required in all sexual interactions or that a woman he is targeting is too intoxicated or underage to provide consent
• Prevent a man from taking an intoxicated woman to a private location
• Tell a man trying to take sexual advantage of another person he must leave a party
• Call or locate an authority (e.g., police)

Several studies on bystander intervention programmes have reported significant decreases in RMA from pre- to post- intervention (Foubert, 2000; Foubert & Newberry, 2006; Stephens & George, 2004, 2009). However, while there is a growing consensus about the value of addressing the social structures that underpin the perpetration of sexual violence, most studies evaluating the effectiveness of bystander interventions on sexual assault perpetration only report on changed attitudes or self-reported willingness to intervene as a bystander (Langhinrichsen-Rohling, Foubert, Brasfield, Hill, & Shelley-Tremblay, 2011), rather than changes in *behaviour*. It is also unclear whether a theoretical willingness to intervene translates to practical action, should the situation arise. Moreover, although some studies have included multi-month follow-up assessment, long-term follow-up (i.e., over several years) is lacking. A recent meta-analysis (Mujal et al., 2021) noted that not a single study has assessed bystander intervention effectiveness beyond 12 months post-course completion. Consequently, the permanency of bystander intervention outcomes (e.g., changes in attitudes, knowledge, confidence in intervening, and behaviours) is uncertain. It is possible that such interventions may require one or several follow-up session(s) to maintain effectiveness. Recent research (Jouriles, Krauss, Vu, Banyard, & McDonald, 2018) supports this possibility, finding that programme effects diminished over time (although meaningful changes did persist for at least three months). One possible explanation for the attenuated effects of the programme is that the external environment was not supportive enough of participants' newly formed positive social norms or behaviour, which we also suggest in Chapter Five as a possible reason for a lack of effectiveness in addressing police officers' RMA. An ecological model of violence prevention (Banyard, Plante, & Moynihan, 2004; Heise, 1998) requires change in social norms at the community level, which is not the target of this intervention.

Further, given ethnic differences in bystander behaviour (e.g., Black people reporting more bystander behaviours than White people; Brown, Banyard, & Moynihan, 2014) and cross-cultural differences in empathy (Cassels et al., 2010), it is not clear whether promising findings related to bystander interventions would generalise to all college populations and/or non-college samples. Relatedly, findings by Katz, Merrilees, Hoxmeier, and Motisi (2017) indicate that White women are less likely to report intentions to intervene in a hypothetical sexual assault when the name of the potential victim-survivor is distinctively Black (as opposed to a non-distinct control name). This suggests that findings of bystander intervention programmes may not be universally applicable to all types of victim-survivors (and potential bystanders), and that interventions should also consider and address ethnicity. Future programme development and evaluation research efforts should examine the extent to which interventions with culturally specific approaches result in increased cultural relevance, recruitment, retention, and impact on preventing sexual violence.

It also appears that the efficacy of bystander interventions may be less prominent for men who are at higher risk of sexual assault perpetration, which is concerning. Elias-Lambert and Black (2016) conducted a study on the effectiveness of a bystander intervention programme for low- and high-risk (of sexual violence perpetration) fraternity members ($n = 142$). Men who had engaged in sexually aggressive or coercive behaviour in the past and who were, therefore, likely to be less receptive to anti-rape content were classified as 'high-risk', and the remaining men were categorised as 'low-risk'. The findings showed significant improvements in attitudes and future behavioural intentions for the low-risk group but not the high-risk group. Here, it was suggested that high-risk men may have internalised misogynistic norms and beliefs, so they are much less receptive to anti-rape content compared to their non-coercive counterparts. As such, high-risk males may require a different type of prevention programme to low-risk males or a 'higher dose' of programme participation to see attitudinal and behavioural changes. This is in line with suggestions that longer, more intensive interventions are required to see changes in attitudes related to sexual violence among high-risk males (Mujal et al., 2021). Additionally, while Elias-Lambert and Black (2016) found a statistically significant decrease in the full group's self-reported sexually coercive behaviour at five-week follow-up, they cautioned that the follow-up period was short, which means the opportunity to initiate sexually coercive behaviour was substantially reduced.

Finally, we note several limitations and ideological issues with bystander intervention programmes. Most bystander programmes tend to focus on sexual assault on college campuses, which may mean that the findings do not generalise or apply to other contexts (Flood & Howson, 2015). Moreover, it is evident that these strategies fail to account for the realities of rape, e.g., in how it is much more typical that sexual assault will occur by isolating the victim away from potential bystander detection (as opposed to it taking place in front of bystanders; Clark & Quadara, 2010). Further, in positioning sexual violence as occurring in the vicinity of bystanders, these strategies also contribute little to tackling acquaintance rape and rape within relationships, which are overwhelmingly more common (Rape Crisis England and Wales, 2021). Because of this, these types of interventions may also misrepresent the realities of rape, which is concerning. Moreover, if a situation did occur where a bystander managed to prevent a man from isolating an intoxicated woman (a typical example of a bystander action), it is likely that the potential perpetrator would just target another woman instead, as the intervention has failed to address the true cause of sexual assault (i.e., the perpetrator). Further, by placing the responsibility for preventing sexual assault onto bystanders, these interventions can fail to hold perpetrators of sexual violence fully accountable and can, as such, place unnecessary blame on friends of a victim-survivor, if an assault did occur. Finally, as bystander interventions target both women and men, these strategies can render the gendered nature of sexual violence invisible. This is a serious limitation, as we argue that gender inequality underpins the causes and perpetuation of sexual violence. This is particularly true given the sexist nature of rape myths, which are firmly anchored in hostile attitudes towards women and general sexism. As such, bystander interventions may have limited effectiveness in targeting rape myths, and these beliefs are likely best addressed through strategies anchored in a feminist understanding of sexual violence. Bystander interventions may, therefore, be best suited to address some, highly specific, patterns of sexual violence (e.g., in public spaces such as bars or clubs), and we recommend that these implementations bear the above caveats in mind.

Victim-Empathy Training. The association between empathy (i.e., the capacity to be affected by the emotional or cognitive states of others) and prosocial behaviour and cooperative/socially competent behaviour is well established (Davis, 2015; Eisenberg & Miller, 1987). These findings are consistent with broader theories of the relationship between empathy and prosocial behaviour. For instance, the Empathy-Altruism Hypothesis (EAH) posits that empathy evokes an altruistic motive, the goal of which is to protect or promote the welfare of the person for whom empathy is felt (Batson & Shaw, 1991). Furthermore, empirical research demonstrates that feelings of empathy are associated with concerns about others' outcomes (i.e., altruism) to the exclusion of concerns about one's own outcomes (Van Lange, 2008). In the context of sexual violence, therefore, empathy training could have the potential to promote welfare concerns for potential victim-survivors, both among potential perpetrators and among bystanders. When used with potential perpetrators, victim-empathy induction approaches are designed to prevent men from engaging in sexually aggressive behaviour by helping them identify with victim-survivors of sexual assault. When used with potential bystanders, victim-empathy training and information about rape myths seek to enhance participants' motivation to become active bystanders and intervene before sexual assault takes place. It is, of course, not always possible to neatly distinguish between those interventions aimed at potential perpetrators and those aimed at potential bystanders, which again emphasises the overall difficulties involved in assessing the effectiveness of interventions to address sexual violence.

Overall, the assessment of interventions that contain victim-empathy components produces mixed findings regarding their impact on RMA. O'Donohue et al. (2003) assessed one such intervention among male undergraduates ($n = 102$), which also provided participants with rape myth debunking information, and reported that thus intervention was effective in reducing RMA. Again, the inclusion of multiple intervention components (i.e., victim-empathy *and* rape myth debunking information) complicates determining which component is the most effective. Conversely, Schewe and O'Donohue (1996) found that although an intervention containing an empathy component led to increases in empathy, it did not impact RMA levels, whereas an intervention that focused on rape myth information did. Here, it was expected that participants would acquire rape myth information by inference through increased empathy (resulting from the empathy component intervention), which did not occur. Consequently, although victim-empathy training may be an important component of wider rape prevention programmes, it may not directly impact RMA levels unless combined with rape myth information as well.

Consistent with the above, Leone et al. (2000) found that although victim-empathy was related to stronger intentions to intervene in cases of potential sexual assault, this was only among individuals who tended not to endorse rape myths. This would suggest that empathy interventions may only be effective when RMA levels have already been reduced (again emphasising that empathy training may need to be combined with rape myth information). Further, strong RMA endorsement appears to act as a barrier to intervention among individuals who are generally empathic by lowering their ability to perceive benefits of preventing a sexual assault. Interpreted within the context of Latane and Darley's (1968) decision-making model, empathy may provide motivation for a bystander to take responsibility to intervene (i.e., Stage 3) or implement intervention actions (i.e., Stage 5). However, individuals high in RMA may fail to notice a sexually aggressive situation (or its warning signs) because they do not consider the witnessed behaviour as problematic (Stage 1). Consequently, they may fail to perceive high-risk situations as dangerous (Stage 2), which limits their experience of empathy in such situations. In other words, adherence to rape myths may prevent empathetic individuals from moving past Step 2 of the decision-making model. It is also important to note that empathy training delivered without other components (e.g., RMA information) may have unintended negative consequences (Berg, Lonsway, & Fitzgerald, 1999). Specifically, Berg et al. found *higher* levels of reported intentions to engage in future sexual aggression among the empathy-promoting intervention group, as compared to the control group. Together, these findings suggest that in programmes comprising both victim-empathy training and rape myth information, the rape myth component may have been instrumental in producing observed RMA reductions. More research is, however, needed to understand why these interventions are not working as intended with their target populations. Moreover, in the absence of additional research, training providers may wish to select other interventions without evidence of potentially unintended negative consequences.

Social Norms Strategies.   Social norms have been defined as 'rules and standards that are understood by members of a group, and that guide and/or constrain behavior' (Cialdini & Trost, 1998, p. 152). In other words, social norms are the way in which the environment tells people what is acceptable and what is not acceptable and are conceptualised as predictors of behaviour in several theoretical approaches (for a review, see Cialdini & Trost, 1998). Most men are not perpetrators of sexual violence,[3] and, therefore, sexual violence is not considered 'normal behaviour' in terms of perpetration. However, the prevalence of victim-survivors of rape (as well as how a majority of women have been subjected to forms of sexual violence as per the 'continuum' of sexual violence; Kelly, 1987), would, unfortunately, suggest a norm for women being subjected to sexual violence. Moreover, the societal norms (e.g., in terms of a 'rape culture'; as further outlined in Chapter Two) that exist surrounding sexual violence imply a level of acceptance and a sense of complacency regarding the issue, especially when considered in the context of the lack of legal repercussions for men who perpetrate rape (Molina & Poppleton, 2020). This creates an environment where men's sexual violence against women can take place and inhibits appropriate action while condoning inappropriate inaction. The social scaffolding around the norms of sexual violence has been central to most feminist theorising on rape and sexual violence, which suggests that these approaches may be important in understanding rape myth endorsement and prevention. Social norms may be especially important in addressing sexual violence given that past research suggests that men report higher rape proclivity when thinking that other men's RMA is high (e.g., Bohner et al., 2006).

An example of a programme that used social norms to impact sexual violence beliefs is the 'Mentors in Violence Project' (MVP; Katz, 1995). It encouraged male students (n = 635) to become leaders in delegitimising 'rape-supportive' and 'battering-supportive' attitudes. Injunctive normative information ('what people *should* do' norms) was used to emphasise that peers believe bystander intervention is appropriate. Evaluations of this programme suggest positive effects on several self-reported bystander intention measures, but findings have not been peer-reviewed (Culture of Respect, 2018). Social norms theory suggests that providing men with accurate statistics about their male peers' attitudes and behaviours related to sexual assault may help men avoid overestimating their peers' sexually aggressive behaviour and, in turn, decrease the pressure on men to engage in sexually aggressive behaviour themselves (Gidycz, Orchowski, & Berkowitz, 2011). Gidycz et al. evaluated a combined bystander prevention and social norms–focused intervention and found that men in the treatment group were significantly more likely to believe that men would intervene to prevent sexual assault from occurring if they witnessed inappropriate behaviour compared to the control group. Importantly, the men themselves did not indicate a greater tendency to intervene as a function of programme participation, suggesting that these types of interventions may only work to increase knowledge about sexual violence and not impact behaviours.

Gender-Socialisation-Focused Interventions.   Finally, research assessing gender-socialisation interventions has produced mixed findings. Typically, these types of interventions stress the link between sex role socialisation/oppressive masculine

---

[3]It should, however, be noted that recent research does suggest that a significant minority (around one in nine) of men report having engaged in sexually coercive or violent conduct towards women (Hales & Gannon, 2021).

gender roles and sexual aggression and seek to deconstruct gendered stereotypes about sexual behaviour and consent (Choate, 2003; Davis & Liddell, 2002).
Some of these interventions (e.g., Choate, 2003) are delivered alongside myth-
busting information about rape. Some authors reported that such interventions
reduced RMA (e.g., Davis & Liddell, 2002; Salazar, Vivolo-Kantor, Hardin, &
Berkowitz, 2014), whereas others (Heppner et al., 1995) did not. Again, as
these types of strategies can vary according to a number of different variables
(e.g., presenting of sexual violence statistics; inclusion/exclusion of rape myth
information; information about media influences on socialisation, etc.), it is
difficult to determine which components are driving any observed effects.

Addressing Sexual Violence in Specific Groups

The following section will consider the effectiveness of RMA prevention and
intervention approaches in specific groups. See Chapter Four for strategies
to mitigate the impact of RMA within the criminal justice system (CJS)
(i.e., policing and courts).

Convicted Perpetrators of Rape. Researchers and clinicians hypothesise
that sexual offenders hold offence-supportive beliefs or cognitive distortions
(e.g., RMA) that require restructuring for successful rehabilitation. Despite this,
limited attention has been allocated to the treatment of RMA in sexual offenders. The four studies included in Johnson and Beech's (2017) meta-analysis do,
however, suggest that RMA can be altered as part of sex offender treatment programmes. Beech, Oliver, Fisher, and Beckett (2006) found that treatment did not
significantly impact RMA in samples of sexual murderers (i.e., murders in which
there was a sexual element to the crime; $n = 58$) and perpetrators of rape ($n = 112$)
overall. However, when the rape perpetrators and sexual murderers were classified
into three groups according to the main motivation for their offending (Knight
& Prentky, 1990), important differences emerged. The three groups were (a) sexually motivated (opportunistic and sexual non-sadistic), (b) grievance motivated
(pervasively angry and vindictive), and (c) sadistically motivated (calculated pain
infliction). Analysis revealed that following treatment, levels of rape-supportive
beliefs and victim blaming attitudes decreased significantly among grievance
motivated offenders. Among the sexually motivated and sadistically motivated
offenders, stereotypical views about women, and attitudes about the acceptance
of violence against women, did not change. This suggests that the identification
of sub-types within a sample may be important to help to elucidate treatment
gains (by individuals or groups of individuals), which may be masked by variance
in treatment responsivity between groups.

Olver, Nicholaichuk, and Wong (2014) reported a significant decrease
($d = 0.68$) in rape myth endorsement within a sample of 267 Canadian federal sex
offenders (from pre- to post-treatment), which suggests treatment has the capacity
to effect positive change. It is important to note, however, that the mean (average)
RMA score in the sample was significantly lower than would be expected, and
lower than the average scores reported elsewhere for other offenders and non-
offenders (see Burt, 1980) both pre- and post-treatment. Accordingly, it is

possible that participants were 'faking good' (i.e., deliberately hiding their beliefs or 'giving the right answer').

Similar to Olver et al. (2014), Pithers (1994) reported a significant treatment effect (a reduction in RMA) after treatment completion in a sample of 20 offenders (10 paedophiles and 10 rape perpetrators with adult victims). Webster et al.'s (2004) study also found that both Black and White sexual offenders evidenced significant post-treatment reductions in RMA. However, it is important to note that the study looked at a combined sample of child molesters and rape perpetrators, and that the overall reduction in RMA appeared to be largely driven by child molesters who had a significant, positive change in their RMA post-treatment, as compared to the rape perpetrators who exhibited very little/no change at all. Additionally, an interaction seemed to be apparent here whereby the White rape perpetrators experienced a positive change in rape myths post-treatment, whereas Black rape perpetrators did not. As this was not the main study focus, this possible interaction was not explored statistically.

Although lower post-treatment endorsements of RMA may reflect treatment gains (i.e., are genuine responses), and treatment may act to make men more open and self-reflective, it may be naive to assume that convicted sex offenders will not fake good following treatment. It could well be that the intervention only teaches convicted rape perpetrators to pretend their RMA levels have reduced (i.e., 'hold yet hide'). A compelling argument can be made that post-treatment, convicted sex offenders have even more incentive to fake good than they did previously, because they want to be good programme graduates or to please a therapist or expect prison-related advantages, such as more positive evaluations, earlier parole, and/or positioning in less controlled settings. Further, the empirical demonstration that an intervention does reduce RMA (as compared to no intervention) does not imply that content intended to reduce RMA has caused the effect. To demonstrate the effectiveness of an RMA intervention in sexual offenders, it would be necessary to show that the intervention reduces RMA as compared to a control condition, and that the reduction of RMA leads to the reduction of recidivism (i.e., being convicted by a court of another offence post-treatment) and/or unofficial records or self-reports (e.g., offence-related behaviours).

Randomised control trials (RCTs) are considered the 'gold standard' for intervention evaluation across disciplines. However, in practice, it has proven difficult to implement RCTs for ethical and practical reasons, such as concerns regarding withholding treatment and/or providing suboptimal treatment to one or more groups within a trial and the potential for community harm (Marshall, 2020). A more feasible and ethically less problematic alternative would be the use of a dismantling or component-analysis design. In this approach, modular treatment programmes are delivered as usual, but (almost) all participants skip one randomly selected programme module (e.g., a victim-empathy module or a module targeting RMA). Another alternative is a delayed-start design, where initially, participants would receive either a placebo intervention or a RMA-focused intervention for a certain period of time, before the placebo group is also eventually moved onto to the RMA-focused intervention. Thus, more high-quality studies are needed to enable stronger conclusions to be drawn about the wider effect of RMA treatment for convicted sexual offenders. Finally, a major issue in researching men convicted of rape is that most perpetrators of rape are never convicted (or even prosecuted; Crown Prosecution Service, 2020; Kelly et al., 2005; Rape Crisis England and Wales, 2021). As such, it is unlikely that these men can be taken as representative of rape perpetrators more generally, and results on these groups may not be indicative of how these interventions would work on larger, more diverse samples of non-convicted perpetrators of rape.

Individuals Working in the CJS.   Strategies and considerations relevant to the intervention and prevention of RMA in police officers and within the court system are outlined in detail in Chapter Four of this book. However, it is important to note here that studies tend to evaluate individual officers' *attitudes* through surveys rather than examining officers' *behavioural performance* (Lonsway, Welch, & Fitzgerald, 2001). These approaches may therefore not detect implicit attitudes and preclude assessing whether such attitudes affect sexual assault investigations (Shaw et al., 2017).

College and University Students.   A considerable number of educational programmes, particularly in the US, address sexual violence on campuses (for a review, see Wright et al., 2020). However, Wright et al.'s (2020) review found little evidence that suggests that male-targeted sexual assault prevention programmes actually lower the incidence of sexual assault. The lack of programme effectiveness is not surprising, however, given that interventions are often brief (Foubert & Perry, 2007; Gidycz et al., 2011). Further, previous studies have also been limited by non-random assignment of participants to programmes and control groups, small sample sizes, and short follow-up assessment intervals (Gidycz et al., 2002).

Limitations of Existing Intervention Approaches

Clearly, the evidence on the effectiveness of interventions to address sexual violence is mixed. The studies reviewed suggest that these approaches can, in some cases, decrease sexually aggressive behaviour (in some people), increase empathy for victim-survivors, and increase confidence and skills in bystander intervention. However, the research also indicates that many of the observed attitude changes revert to previous levels within months, that men's rape-supportive attitudes sometimes increase post-intervention, and that there may be limited effects on the actual incidence of sexual assault (Breitenbecher, 2000; Rozee & Koss, 2001; Sochting et al., 2004). It is highly likely that some of these mixed findings can be at least partially explained by the considerable limitations present in the current research base, especially when bearing in mind the methodological limitations within RMA research more generally. Below we review a number of these limitations, before signposting recommendations for future directions.

RMA as a Cognitive Schema.   If, as we argue in Chapter Two, RMA is best conceptualised as a cognitive schema (e.g., Bohner et al., 2009), this presents several challenges in attempting to alter these beliefs. Importantly, cognitive schemas are notoriously difficult to change, as they are an integral part of how individuals organise their social reality. As evidence on the schematic nature of RMA suggests that even where information with the potential to alter these beliefs is presented, this information may merely be assimilated into existing (rape myth endorsing) knowledge structures (e.g., Krahé et al., 2007). This would, therefore, call into question whether providing educational myth-busting information about rape can genuinely work to alter these schemas and would as such potentially render most strategies for addressing sexual violence ineffective. Moreover, it is possible that any discussion around rape myths has the potential to activate related schematic beliefs about rape or hostile attitudes towards women (e.g., Süssenbach et al., 2012), and that participants in the interventions reviewed above may have filled in gaps in the information provided with rape myth endorsing information (Eyssel & Bohner, 2010).

Unintended Consequences.   Some studies have also found that interventions may have the opposite effect to that intended and lead to poorer outcomes (i.e., a potential increase, rather than decrease, in violence against women). As stated by Hilton (2000, p. 221), 'trying to persuade people to change their attitudes in one direction can lead instead to people taking more extreme versions of their existing attitudes'. This has also been referred to as the 'backfire effect' (Lewandowsky, Ecker, Seifert, Schwarz, & Cook, 2012). One study (Winkel & de Kleuver, 1997), for instance, found an increase in boys' self-reported RMA, coerced sex, and macho behaviour after a video presentation of sexual assault showing undesirable consequences for the male perpetrator. In another study (Berg, Lonsway, & Fitzgerald, 1999), male undergraduates reported an increase in the likelihood of engaging in rape-supportive behaviours after listening to the account of a female rape victim-survivor. The presentation of information pertaining to descriptive norms (such as the high rate of sexual assault among university students) may also lead to an increased perception among some men that sexual assault is normative behaviour among university students (Paul & Gray, 2011). This contention finds further support in research demonstrating that other's men's high RMA can work to increase individual men's inclination to sexually aggress (e.g., Bohner et al., 2006). Consequently, further research is needed to determine what, if anything, can be added to interventions or taken away from them, in order to reduce the potential for such unintended consequences.

Measurement Difficulties.   As further elaborated on in Chapter Three, rape myth research does, in general, suffer considerable methodological difficulties. These difficulties mean that aside from the issues involved in assessing RMA more generally, it is also challenging to measure changes in RMA following intervention. One prominent challenge is the social desirability of the target groups, where an intervention may make rape myth beliefs even less socially desirable than they were prior to intervention and thus even harder to accurately measure. This may seemingly produce an intervention effect where none really exists. Moreover, we have also signposted the many RMA scales used to assess rape myth endorsement (Persson & Dhingra, 2020; Suarez & Gadalla, 2010); the scale chosen has the potential to impact the assessment of RMA following an intervention, and some of these scales may also not be culturally sensitive enough to be used cross-culturally which is problematic. Of particular importance here is the lack of validated scales to use specifically as outcome measures of RMA; because of this, there would likely be value in developing specific measures for this very purpose.

Effectiveness Duration.   The reported effects of many interventions appear to often be relatively short-term (e.g., Foubert & McEwen, 1998), and we lack information on the long-term effectiveness of interventions (e.g., Johnson & Beech, 2017; Parratt & Pina, 2017; Wright et al., 2020). Moreover, a systematic evaluation of some of the specific programmes reviewed above has not yet been undertaken, thus making the assessment of success of such programmes very difficult (Lonsway & Kothari, 2000). Despite this, it appears that the effects of several programmes attenuate over time (Anderson & Whiston, 2005; Paul & Gray, 2011).

Outcomes.   A review of 140 outcome evaluations of sexual assault prevention programmes (DeGue et al., 2014) found that an overwhelming majority of the studies did not administer behavioural outcome measures (e.g., perpetration of sexual violence, bystander intervention, etc.) to participants. This lack of empirical evidence surrounding behavioural outcomes is a substantial limitation of the available literature surrounding the effectiveness of programmes aimed at addressing sexual violence. As previously noted, intervention studies also often use a plethora of outcome measures. This makes comparison between studies difficult, and it may also inflate the perceived positive findings of the interventions, as significant measures can be selected and reported post hoc, especially when combined with a lack of transparency (e.g., Chambers, 2017).

Intervention Focus.   It is important to underscore that interventions to address sexual violence are predominantly based on psychological models that are focused on attitudinal and behavioural change in individuals, rather than structural changes (Gavey, 2018a, 2018b). We argue that explanations of men's violence against women must not be solely grounded in individually held attitudes or even in social and cultural norms on a micro-level. To do so is at the cost of potential changes in broader structural relations and social practices (Pease & Flood, 2008). Howe (2008), for instance, argues that men's violence against women is inextricably part of a gendered social order and is, as such, not a sign of breakdown of this order. This is in line with feminist considerations of sexual violence more generally, which position rape firmly within existing patriarchal structures (for an overview of this, see Chapter Two). Because of how sexual violence is both maintained by, and maintains, gender inequality, it is likely not possible to eliminate men's sexual violence against women while unequal gender power relations remain intact, something that many of the interventions reviewed above neglect. When we focus on specific sexist and violent behaviours without locating them within their social context and power structure, we ignore the social system that constructs them. We, therefore, argue that as feminist theory has consistently located men's sexual violence within an overall structure of gender inequality, the feminist background to RMA is crucial not only for understanding these beliefs but ultimately for reducing them. As elaborated on further in Chapter Six, the more legitimate forms of societal sexism (e.g., benevolently sexist attitudes and scientific sexism) are likely key for scaffolding 'harsher' sexism towards women through the legitimisation of gender differentiations and the backlash against feminism. These attitudes are often overlooked by interventions addressing sexual violence.

Moreover, these interventions fail to consider the intersectional nature of sexual violence victimisation and rape myths (e.g., Collins, 1990/2009; Katz et al., 2017). This means that findings may fail to be applicable across contexts, and it also makes invisible the relationships between RMA and other forms of prejudice, including racism, classism, and ableism. Finally, many other sexual violence risk factors – well grounded in theory – have been overlooked in the interventions reviewed above. For example, childhood exposure to violence, aggression, and early sexual behaviour have consistent empirical support but are rarely addressed in sexual violence prevention efforts (Tharp et al., 2013).

Ways Forward

The sections above have considered many issues involved in preventing and impacting sexual violence behaviours and cognitions. Below, we draw on these considerations as well on the previous chapters in this book, to propose ways forward, in terms of what types of interventions have the potential to work, and what researchers and practitioners should consider when implementing them.

- As most programmes have taken an approach consisting of multiple components, it is not possible to determine which factors are responsible for observed changes in RMA, with regard to content, format, and duration (Paul & Gray, 2011; Pinzone-Glover, Gidycz, & Jacobs, 1998; Schewe & O'Donohue, 1996). While this is not a problem unique to the area of sexual violence (i.e., as it is an issue throughout applied psychology in general), it is nonetheless important to address. Disentangling the impact of specific intervention components will require relatively complex evaluations (such as dismantling designs) which are capable of identifying the essential components of RMA interventions (O'Donohue et al., 2003). We recommend that researchers implement these types of complex designs, and that they are also clear on the theoretical foundations of any intervention. Here, research transparency and international collaboration will be key (as further discussed in Chapter Three).
- As it is not currently possible to state with certainty what works and what does not work in terms of strategies to reduce sexual violence (e.g., Wright et al., 2020), we strongly recommend that any intervention does, at the very minimum, avoid the potential to reinforce myths and misconceptions surrounding rape. This is achieved by consistently avoiding any content that is victim-survivor centred (Mardorossian, 2002; Stern Review, 2010), and blame and responsibility for sexual assault should be consistently placed with the perpetrator. In particular, care needs to be taken with bystander interventions, so that these do not unnecessarily shift the responsibility for preventing sexual assault onto everyone but the perpetrator.
- As previously discussed (e.g., Chapter Three), the expression of rape myths is not globally homogeneous (e.g., Bergenfeld et al., 2022), and as such, barriers and enablers to successful sexual violence prevention programmes may be

different in other parts of the world based on the specific culture of gender violence. Therefore, further research is warranted to determine which approaches may best suited cross-culturally, and here, researchers will need to pay particular attention to how these attitudes are conceptualised and assessed. Likewise, future researchers will need to bear in mind that there may be group differences in how sexual violence prevention strategies are received (Brown et al., 2014), and that not all potential victim-survivors are treated the same in terms of bystanderism (Katz, Merrilees, LaRose, & Edgington, 2018). As such, an intersectional approach to addressing sexual violence will need to be considered, and prevention strategies broadened to also address other oppressive beliefs concurrent with RMA (Hockett et al., 2009).

- Future research would benefit from addressing the functions of rape myth beliefs in attempting to prevent them, as this may have the potential to get to the root cause of *why* people may be reluctant to completely abandon these ideas. Specifically, these beliefs appear to justify sexually aggressive behaviour/a lack of collective effort for social change among men (Bohner et al., 1998; Burt, 1980) and reduce feelings of personal vulnerability among women (Bohner & Lampridis, 2004). Future strategies to address sexual violence will, therefore, likely benefit from incorporating information that can target these specific functions, as otherwise, participants may be unlikely to fully engage with an intervention.
- Finally, and most importantly, so long as gender inequality remains, interventions to address sexual violence will remain unsuccessful. As we have argued throughout this book, rape myths do not exist in a vacuum, but rather, they are the logical result of a patriarchal society that shames women for straying outside prescribed gender norms. Because of this, broader political interventions to prioritise a feminist approach to gender inequality are urgently needed. These interventions should include an effort to eradicate gender differentiations on all levels, and a consistent effort to accurately name and situate sexual violence against women as part of an overall system of gender inequality. On a micro-level, individual institutions and interventions should, alongside addressing rape myths, also include broader approaches to address sexism and racism.

Conclusion

This chapter has brought together the information reviewed throughout this book and sought to determine if current sexual violence prevention strategies can produce changes in attitudes and behaviour and how this may be done. Here, we have outlined the main theoretical approaches underpinning *some* of these strategies and provided an overview of the various forms these types of interventions can take. We have reviewed the evidence on the effectiveness of these strategies among different groups, including the general population (as often represented by college/university students) as well as the smaller body of evidence on convicted sex offenders. In doing this, it can be concluded that interventions to address sexual violence are incredibly varied, and that, generally, the different components thought to elicit change are poorly defined and conceptualised. We note that prevention approaches have often taken a 'shotgun' approach to intervention and have been developed with insufficient attention to the theory behind programming and behaviour change. The studies examining the effectiveness of these strategies have also used an abundance of outcome measures (e.g., attitudinal, cognitive, behavioural, behavioural intentions etc.), making the comparison and synthesis of findings problematic. As such, the measurement of intervention effects in the context of RMA and sexual violence suffers similar methodological difficulties as research into sexual violence attributions more generally, and clearer and improved transparent methodologies are urgently needed. From the literature reviewed, it is apparent that the current state of the literature offers few definitive answers as to how targeted interventions can prevent men's sexual violence against women.

Importantly, many of the interventions reviewed failed to locate sexual violence within an overall structure of gender inequality present on all levels in society. In doing this, interventions of this kind have the potential to make invisible how RMA and rape perpetration are scaffolded and maintained by more legitimate forms of sexism in society, which ultimately renders these interventions less effective than they ought to be. Drawing on the considerations in this book, we, therefore, strongly recommend that policymakers, practitioners, and researchers name men's sexual violence against women for what it is and situate it within pervasive societal gender inequality. In this, we further recommend to link RMA consistently and clearly to sexism as this has the potential to address the root causes of these deeply held misconceptions about rape on a substantial level. We further stress the need for a feminist and intersectional understanding of these beliefs, to ensure that prevention strategies are effective in reducing the incidence and impact of sexual violence among all women.

References

Abrams, D., Viki, G. T., Masser, B., & Bohner, G. (2003). Perceptions of stranger and acquaintance rape: The role of benevolent and hostile sexism in victim blame and rape proclivity. *Journal of Personality and Social Psychology*, *84*(1), 111–125.

Adler, Z. (1987). *Rape on trial*. Routledge.

Ahmad, F., Driver, N., McNally, M. J., & Stewart, D. E. (2009). "Why doesn't she seek help for partner abuse?" An exploratory study with South Asian immigrant women. *Social Science & Medicine*, *69*(4), 613–622.

Ahrens, C., & Campbell, R. (2020). Assisting rape victims as they recover from rape: The impact on friends. *Journal of Interpersonal Violence*, *15*(9), 959–986.

Åklagarmyndigheten. (2021). *Oaktsam våldtäkt*. https://www.aklagare.se/ordlista/o/oaktsam-valdtakt/

Alderden, M. A., & Ullman, S. E. (2012). Creating a more complete and current picture: Examining police and prosecutor decision-making when processing sexual assault cases. *Violence Against Women*, *18*(5), 525–551.

Alvidrez, J. (1999). Ethnic variations in mental health attitudes and service use among low-income African American, Latina, and European American young women. *Community Mental Health Journal*, *35*(6), 515–530.

Amnesty International. (2005). *Sexual assault research: Summary report*. https://www.amnesty.org.uk/press-releases?NewsID=16618#

Anderson, L. A., & Whiston, S. C. (2005). Sexual assault education programs: A meta-analytic examination of their effectiveness. *Psychology of Women Quarterly*, *29*(4), 374–388.

Angel, K. (2021). *Tomorrow sex will be good again*. Verso Books.

Angiolini, E. (2015). *Report of the independent review into the investigation and prosecution of rape in London*. London Metropolitan Police Service and Crown Prosecution Service. https://www.cps.gov.uk/publication/report-independent-review-investigation-and-prosecution-rape-london-rt-hon-dame-elish

Anitha, S., & Dhaliwal, S. (2019). South Asian feminisms in Britain. *Economic and Political Weekly*, *54*(17), 7–8.

Antaki, C., Richardson, E., Stokoe, E., & Willott, S. (2015). Can people with intellectual disability resist implications of fault when police question their allegations of sexual assault and rape? *Intellectual and Developmental Disabilities*, *53*(5), 346–357.

Aosved, A. C., & Long, P. J. (2006). Co-occurrence of rape myth acceptance, sexism, racism, homphobia, ageism, classism, and religious intolerance. *Sex Roles*, *55*(7), 481–492.

Archer, J. (2019). The reality and evolutionary significance of human psychological sex differences. *Biological Reviews*, *94*(4), 1381–1415.

Areh, I., Mesko, G., & Umek, P. (2009). Attribution of personal characteristics to victims of rape – Police officers' perspectives. *Studia Psychologica*, *51*(1), 85–100.

Ask, K., & Landström, S. (2010). Why emotions matter: Expectancy violation and affective response mediate the emotional victim effect. *Law and Human Behavior*, *34*(5), 392–401.

Baker, C. K., Gleason, K., Naai, R., Mitchell, J., & Trecker, C. (2013). Increasing knowledge of sexual abuse: A study with elementary school children in Hawaii. *Research on Social Work Practice*, *23*(2), 167–178.

Bandura, A. (1977). *Social learning theory*. Prentice-Hall.

Bandura, A. (2016). *Moral disengagement: How people do harm and live with themselves*. Worth Publishers.

Banet-Weiser, S. (2021). 'Ruined' lives: Mediated white male victimhood. *European Journal of Cultural Studies*, *24*(1), 60–80.

Banyard, V. L. (2008). Measurement and correlates of prosocial bystander behavior: The case of interpersonal violence. *Violence and Victims*, *23*(1), 83–97.

Banyard, V. L., Plante, E. G., & Moynihan, M. M. (2004). Bystander education: Bringing a broader community perspective to sexual violence prevention. *Journal of Community Psychology*, *32*(1), 61–79.

Bass, A. (2017). Legal prostitution zones reduce incidents of rape and sexual abuse. *Huffington Post*. https://www.huffpost.com/entry/legal-prostitution-zones-reduce-incidents-of-rape-and_b_58c83be1e4b01d0d473bce8a

Batchelder, J., Koski, D., & Byxby, F. (2004). Women's hostility toward women in rape trials: Testing the intra-female gender hostility thesis. *American Journal of Criminal Justice*, *28*, 181–200.

Bates, L. (2020). *Men who hate women: From incels to pickup artists, the truth about extreme misogyny and how it affects us all*. Simon & Schuster UK.

Batson, C. D., & Shaw, L. L. (1991). Evidence for altruism: Toward a pluralism of prosocial motives. *Psychological Inquiry*, *2*(2), 107–122.

Becker, J. C., & Wright, S. C. (2011). Yet another dark side of chivalry: Benevolent sexism undermines and hostile sexism motivates collective action for social change. *Journal of Personality and Social Psychology*, *101*(1), 62–77.

Beckett, H. (2011). *Not a world away: the sexual exploitation of children and young people in Northern Ireland*. Barnado's Northern Ireland.

Beech, A., Oliver, C., Fisher, R., & Beckett, R. (2006). *STEP 4: The sex offender treatment programme in prison: Addressing the needs of rapists and sexual murderers*. University of Birmingham. Prepared for HMPS (Her Majesty's Prison Service). https://research.birmingham.ac.uk/portal/en/publications/step-4-the-sex-offender-treatment-programme-in-prison-addressing-the-needs-of-rapists-and-sexual-murderers(0075e349-8ecb-49ad-af47-66881e1f1da9).html

Beichner, D., & Spohn, C. (2012). Modeling the effects of victim behavior and moral character on prosecutors' charging decisions in sexual assault cases. *Violence and Victims*, *27*(1), 3–24.

Belknap, J. (2010). Rape: Too hard to report and too easy to discredit victims. *Violence Against Women*, *16*(12), 1335–1344.

Benedict, H. (1993). *Virgin or vamp: How the press covers sex crimes*. Oxford University Press.

Berg, D. R., Lonsway, K. A., & Fitzgerald, L. F. (1999). Rape prevention education for men: The effectiveness of empathy-induction techniques. *Journal of College Student Development*, *40*(3), 219–234.

Beshers, S., & DiVita, M. (2021). Changes in rape myth acceptance among undergraduates: 2010 to 2017. *Journal of Interpersonal Violence*, *36*(19–20), 9371–9392.

Bergenfeld, I., Lanzas, G., Trang, Q. T., Sales, J., & Yount, K. M. (2022). Rape myths among university men and women in Vietnam: A qualitative study. *Journal of Interpersonal Violence*, *37*(3–4), NP1401-NP1431.

Berkowitz, L. (2003). Affect, aggression, and antisocial behavior. In R. J. Davidson, K. R. Scherer, & H. H. Goldsmith (Eds.), *Handbook of Affective Sciences* (pp. 804–823). New York, NY: Oxford University Press.

Bindel, J. (2019). *The pimping of prostitution: Abolishing the sex work myth* (2nd ed.). Palgrave Macmillan UK.

Boeschen, L. E., Sales, B. D., & Koss, M. P. (1998). Rape trauma experts in the courtroom. *Psychology, Public Policy, and Law*, *4*(1–2), 414–432.

Bohner, G. (2001). Writing about rape: Use of the passive voice and other distancing text features as an expression of perceived responsibility of the victim. *British Journal of Social Psychology*, *40*, 515–529.

Bohner, G., Eyssel, F., Pina, A., Siebler, F., Viki, G. T. (2009). Rape myth acceptance: Cognitive, affective and behavioural effects of beliefs that blame the victim and exonerate the perpetrator. In M. A. H. Horvath & J. M. Brown (Eds.), *Rape: Challenging contemporary thinking* (pp. 17–45). Willan

Bohner, G., Jarvis, C. I., Eyssel, F., & Siebler, F. (2005). The causal impact of rape myth acceptance on men's rape proclivity: Comparing sexually coercive and noncoercive men. *European Journal of Social Psychology, 35*(6), 819–828.

Bohner, G., & Lampridis, E. (2004). Expecting to meet a rape victim affects women's self-esteem: The moderating role of rape myth acceptance. *Group Processes & Intergroup Relations, 7*(1), 77–87.

Bohner, G., Reinhard, M. A., Rutz, S., Sturm, S., Kerschbaum, B., & Effler, D. (1998). Rape myths as neutralizing cognitions: Evidence for a causal impact of anti-victim attitudes on men's self-reported likelihood of raping. *European Journal of Social Psychology, 28*(2), 257–268.

Bohner, G., Siebler, F., & Schmelcher, J. (2006). Social norms and the likelihood of raping: Perceived rape myth acceptance of others affects men's rape proclivity. *Personality and Social Psychology Bulletin, 32*(3), 286–297.

Bohner, G., Weisbrod, C., Raymond, P., Barzvi, A., & Schwarz, N. (1993). Salience of rape affects self-esteem: The moderating role of gender and rape myth acceptance. *European Journal of Social Psychology, 23*(6), 561–579.

Bollingmo, G. C., Wessel, E. O., Eilertsen, D. E., & Magnussen, S. (2008). Credibility of the emotional witness: A study of ratings by police investigators. *Psychology, Crime & Law, 14*(1), 29–40.

Bongiorno, R., McKimmie, B. M., & Masser, B. (2016). The selective use of rape-victim stereotypes to protect culturally similar perpetrators. *Psychology of Women Quarterly, 40*(3), 398–413.

Bornstein, B. H. (1999). The ecological validity of jury simulations: Is the jury still out? *Law and Human Behavior, 23*(1), 75–91.

Bornstein, B. H., Golding, J. M., Neuschatz, J., Kimbrough, C., Reed, K., Magyarics, C., & Luecht, K. (2017). Mock juror sampling issues in jury simulation research: A meta-analysis. *Law and Human Behavior, 41*(1), 13–28.

Botta, R., & Pingree, S. (1997). Interpersonal communication and rape: Women acknowledge their assaults. *Journal of Health Communication, 2*(3), 197–212.

Bows, H., & Westmarland, N. (2017). Rape of older people in the United Kingdom: Challenging the 'real-rape' stereotype. *The British Journal of Criminology, 57*(1), 1–17.

Branscombe, N. R., Owen, S., Garstka, T. A., & Coleman, J. (1996). Rape and accident counterfactuals: Who might have done otherwise and would it have changed the outcome? *Journal of Applied Social Psychology, 26*(12), 1042–1067.

Branscombe, N. R., Wohl, M. J. A., Owen, S., Allison, J. A., & N'gbala, A. (2003). Counterfactual thinking, blame assignment, and well-being in rape victims. *Basic and Applied Social Psychology, 25*(4), 265–273.

Breitenbecher, K. H. (2000). Sexual assault on college campuses: Is an ounce of prevention enough? *Applied and Preventive Psychology, 9*(1), 23–52.

Bremh, J. (1966). *A theory of psychological reactance*. Academic Press.

Brescoll, V., & LaFrance, M. (2004). The correlates and consequences of newspaper reports of research on sex differences. *Psychological Science, 15*(8), 515–520.

Brooks, O. (2011). 'Guys! Stop Doing It!': Young women's adoption and rejection of safety advice when socializing in bars, pubs and clubs. *The British Journal of Criminology, 51*(4), 635–651.

Brown, A. L., Banyard, V. L., & Moynihan, M. M. (2014). College students as helpful bystanders against sexual violence: Gender, race, and year in college moderate the impact of perceived peer norms. *Psychology of Women Quarterly, 38*(3), 350–362.

Brown, G. R., Laland, K. N., & Mulder, M. B. (2009). Bateman's principles and human sex roles. *Trends in Ecology & Evolution, 24*(6), 297–304.

Brown, J. D., & L'Engle, K. L. (2009). X-rated: Sexual attitudes and behaviors associated with U.S. early adolescents' exposure to sexually explicit media. *Communication Research, 36*(1), 129–151.

Brown, J. M., & Horvath, M. A. H. (2009). Do you believe her and is it real rape? M. A. H. Horvath & J. M. Brown (Eds.), *Rape: Challenging contemporary thinking* (pp. 325–341). Willan.

Brownmiller, S. (1993). *Against our will: Men, women, and rape.* Fawcett. (Original work published 1975)

Buchwald, E., Fletcher, P., & Roth, M. (1993). *Transforming a rape culture.* Milkweed Editions.

Buntins, M., Buntins, K., & Eggert, F. (2017). Clarifying the concept of validity: From measurement to everyday language. *Theory & Psychology, 27*(5), 703–710.

Burn, S. (2009). A situational model of sexual assault prevention through bystander intervention. *Sex Roles, 60*, 779–792.

Burrowes, N. (2013). *Responding to the challenge of rape myths in court: A guide for prosecutors.* NB Research.

Burt, M. R. (1980). Cultural myths and supports for rape. *Journal of Personality and Social Psychology, 38*(2), 217–230.

Burt, M. R. (1991). Rape myths and acquaintance rape. *Acquaintance rape: The hidden crime.* John Wiley & Sons.

Burton, M., Evans, R., & Sanders, A. (2006). *Are special measures for vulnerable and intimidated witnesses working? Evidence from the criminal justice agencies.* Home Office.

Buss, D. M. (1995). Psychological sex differences: Origins through sexual selection. *American Psychologist, 50*(3), 164–168.

Buss, D. M. (2021). *Bad men: The hidden roots of sexual deception, harassment, and assault.* Hachette UK.

Buss, D. M., & Schmitt, D. P. (2011). Evolutionary Psychology and Feminism. *Sex Roles, 64*(9), 768.

Cameron, B., & Murphy, L. (2009). *This is not an invitation to rape me: Campaign evaluation.* Progressive. https://www.rapecrisisscotland.org.uk/publications/TINAITRM-Testing-Report.pdf

Campbell, A. (2005). Keeping the 'lady' safe: The regulation of femininity through crime prevention literature. *Critical Criminology, 13*(2), 119–140.

Campbell, B. A., Menaker, T. A., & King, W. R. (2015). The determination of victim credibility by adult and juvenile sexual assault investigators. *Journal of Criminal Justice, 43*(1), 29–39.

Campbell, R. (1998). The community response to rape: Victims' experiences with the legal, medical, and mental health systems. *American Journal of Community Psychology, 26*(3), 355–379.

Campbell, R. (2006). Rape survivors' experiences with the legal and medical systems: Do rape victim advocates make a difference? *Violence Against Women, 12*(1), 30–45.

Campbell, R. (2008). The psychological impact of rape victims. *American Psychologist, 63*(8), 702–717.

Campbell, R., Ahrens, C. E., Sefl, T., Wasco, S. M., & Barnes, H. E. (2001). Social reactions to rape victims: Healing and hurtful effects on psychological and physical health outcomes. *Violence and Victims, 16*(3), 287–302.

Campbell, R., & Johnson, C. (1997). Police officers' perceptions of rape: Is there consistency between state law and individual beliefs? *Journal of Interpersonal Violence, 12*(2), 255–274.

Campbell, R., & Raja, S. (1999). Secondary victimization of rape victims: Insights from mental health professionals who treat survivors of violence. *Violence and Victims*, *14*(3), 261–275.

Campbell, R., & Raja, S. (2005). The sexual assault and secondary victimization of female veterans: Help-seeking experiences with military and civilian social systems. *Psychology of Women Quarterly*, *29*(1), 97–106.

Campbell, R., Sefl, T., Barnes, H. E., Ahrens, C. E., Wasco, S. M., & Zaragoza-Diesfeld, Y. (1999). Community services for rape survivors: Enhancing psychological well-being or increasing trauma? *Journal of Consulting and Clinical Psychology*, *67*(6), 847–858.

Capers, B. (2012). Real women, real rape. *UCLA Law Review*, *60*(4), 826–883.

Carline, A., & Gunby, C. (2011). "How an ordinary jury makes sense of it is a mystery": Barristers' perspectives on rape, consent and the sexual offences act 2003. *Liverpool Law Review*, *32*, 237–250.

Carmody, M. (2003). Sexual ethics and violence prevention. *Social & Legal Studies*, *12*(2), 199–216.

Cassels, T. G., Chan, S., Chung, W., Birch, S. A. J. (2010). The role of culture in affective empathy: Cultural and bicultural differences. *Journal of Cognition and Culture*, *10*, 309–326.

Cassidy, A. (2005). Popular evolutionary psychology in the UK: An unusual case of science in the media? *Public Understanding of Science*, *14*(2), 115–141.

Castelli, L., Vanzetto, K., Sherman, S. J., & Arcuri, L. (2001). The explicit and implicit perception of in-group members who use stereotypes: Blatant rejection but subtle conformity. *Journal of Experimental Social Psychology*, *37*(5), 419–426.

Centre for Women's Justice, End Violence Against Women Coalition, & Rape Crisis England & Wales. (2020). *The decriminalisation of rape: Rape Crisis England & Wales*. https://rapecrisis.org.uk/get-informed/reports/reports-archive/the-decriminalisation-of-rape/

Chalmers, J., Leverick, F., & Munro, V. E. (2021). The provenance of what is proven: Exploring (mock) jury deliberation in Scottish rape trials. *Journal of Law and Society*, *48*(2), 226–249.

Chambers, C. (2017). *The 7 deadly sins of psychology: A manifesto for reforming the culture of scientific practice*. Princeton University Press.

Chan, J. B. L., Devery, C., & Doran, S. (2016). *Fair cop*. University of Toronto Press.

Chapleau, K. M., & Oswald, D. L. (2010). Power, sex, and rape myth acceptance: Testing two models of rape proclivity. *The Journal of Sex Research*, *47*(1), 66–78.

Chapleau, K. M., Oswald, D. L., & Russell, B. L. (2007). How ambivalent sexism toward women and men support rape myth acceptance. *Sex Roles*, *57*(1-2), 131–136.

Chiroro, P., Bohner, G., Viki, G. T., & Jarvis, C. I. (2004). Rape myth acceptance and rape proclivity: Expected dominance versus expected arousal as mediators in acquaintance-rape situations. *Journal of Interpersonal Violence*, *19*(4), 427–442.

Choate, L. H. (2003). Sexual assault prevention programs for college men: An exploratory evaluation of the men against violence model. *Journal of College Counseling*, *6*(2), 166–176.

Cialdini, R. B., & Trost, M. R. (1998). Social influence: Social norms, conformity and compliance. In *The handbook of Social Psychology* (Vols. 1–2, 4th ed., pp. 151–192). McGraw-Hill.

Clark, H., Quadara, A. (2010). *Insights into sexual assault perpetration: Giving voice to victim/survivors' knowledge* (Research Report No. 18). Melbourne: Australian Institute of Family Studies.

Cocca, C. (2004). *Jailbait: The politics of statutory rape laws in the United States*. SUNY Press.

Cockbain, E. (2013). Grooming and the 'Asian sex gang predator': The construction of a racial crime threat. *Race & Class*, *54*(4), 22–32.

Cockcroft, T. (2020). *Police culture: Research and practice*. Policy Press.

Collins, P. H. (2009). *Black feminist thought: Knowledge, consciousness, and the politics of empowerment*. Routledge. (Original work published 1990)

Confer, J. C., Easton, J. A., Fleischman, D. S., Goetz, C. D., Lewis, D. M. G., Perilloux, C., & Buss, D. M. (2010). Evolutionary psychology: Controversies, questions, prospects, and limitations. *American Psychologist, 65*(2), 110–126.

Cook, D., Burton, M., Robinson, A., & Vallely, C. (2004). *Evaluation of specialist domestic violence courts/fast track systems*. https://wlv.openrepository.com/handle/2436/22612

Cops, D., & Pleysier, S. (2011). 'Doing gender' in fear of crime: The impact of gender identity on reported levels of fear of crime in adolescents and young adults. *British Journal of Criminology, 51*(1), 58–74.

Costin, F. (1985). Beliefs about rape and women's social roles. *Archives of Sexual Behavior, 14*(4), 319–325.

Crank, J. P. (2003). Institutional theory of police: A review of the state of the art. *Policing: An International Journal of Police Strategies & Management, 26*(2), 186–207.

Crenshaw, K. W. (1989). Demarginalizing the intersection of race and sex: A black feminist critique of antidiscrimination doctrine, feminist theory and antiracist politics. *University of Chicago Legal Forum, 1989*(1), 31.

Crenshaw, K. W. (1993). Beyond racism and misogyny: Black feminism and 2 live crew. In M. J. Matsuda, C. R. Lawrence, R. Delgado, K. W. Crenshaw (Eds.), *Words that wound: Critical race theory, assaultive speech, and the first amendment* (1st ed). Routledge. (pp. 111–123).

Crown Prosecution Service. (2017). *Rape and sexual offences – Chapter 3: Consent*. https://www.cps.gov.uk/legal-guidance/rape-and-sexual-offences-chapter-3-consent

Crown Prosecution Service. (2020). *CPS data summary Quarter 4 2019-2020*. https://www.cps.gov.uk/publication/cps-data-summary-quarter-4-2019-2020

Crown Prosecution Service. (2021). *Prosecution statistics published for 2020-21*. https://www.cps.gov.uk/cps/news/prosecution-statistics-published-2020-21

Cuklanz, L. M. (2000). *Rape on prime time: Television, masculinity, and sexual violence*. University of Pennsylvania Press.

Culture of Respect. (2018). *Mentors in violence prevention (MVP)*. https://cultureofrespect.org/program/mentors-in-violence-prevention-mvp/

Dalton, A., Henry, D., Blackstone, S., Passuth, J., Birchfield, H., & Peterson, B. (2021). Does the presence of a physical disability affect classification of sexual assault? *Journal of Interpersonal Violence*, 0886260521997951.

Daly, E., Smith, O., Bows, H., Brown, J., Chalmers, J., Cowan, S., ... & Willmott, D. (2021). Myths about myths? A commentary on Thomas (2020) and the question of jury rape myth acceptance. *Journal of Gender-Based Violence*.

Dardenne, B., Dumont, M., & Bollier, T. (2007). Insidious dangers of benevolent sexism: Consequences for women's performance. *Journal of Personality and Social Psychology, 93*(5), 764–779.

Dar-Nimrod, I., Heine, S. J., Cheung, B. Y., & Schaller, M. (2011). Do scientific theories affect men's evaluations of sex crimes? *Aggressive Behavior, 37*(5), 440–449.

Darwinkel, E., Powell, M., & Tidmarsh, P. (2013). Improving police officers' perceptions of sexual offending through intensive training. *Criminal Justice and Behavior, 40*(8), 895–908.

Davis, A. Y. (2019). *Women, race & class*. Penguin. (Original work published 1981)

Davis, M. H. (2015). Empathy and prosocial behavior. In D. A. Schroeder & W. G. Graziano (Eds.), *The Oxford handbook of prosocial behavior* (pp. 282–306). Oxford University Press.

Davis, T. L., & Liddell, D. L. (2002). Getting inside the house: The effectiveness of a rape prevention program for college fraternity men. *Journal of College Student Development, 43*(1), 35–50.

DeGue, S., Valle, L. A., Holt, M. K., Massetti, G. M., Matjasko, J. L., & Tharp, A. T. (2014). A systematic review of primary prevention strategies for sexual violence perpetration. *Aggression and Violent Behavior, 19*(4), 346–362.

Devine, D. J., Buddenbaum, J., Houp, S., Studebaker, N., & Stolle, D. P. (2009). Strength of evidence, extraevidentiary influence, and the liberation hypothesis: Data from the field. *Law and Human Behavior, 33*(2), 136–148.

Dewald, S., & Lorenz, K. (2021). Lying about sexual assault: A qualitative study of detective perspectives on false reporting. *Policing and Society, 0*(0), 1–21.

Diamond, S. S., & Rose, M. R. (2005). Real juries. *Annual Review of Law and Social Science, 1*(1), 255–284.

D'Ignazio, C., & Klein, L. (2020). *Data feminism*. The MIT Press.

Donat, P. L., & D'Emilio, J. (1992). A feminist redefinition of rape and sexual assault: Historical foundations and change. *Journal of Social Issues, 48*(1), 9–22.

Donnerstein, E., & Malamuth, N. M. (1997). Pornography: Its consequences on the observer. In L. B. Schlesinger, & E. Revitch (Eds.) *Sexual dynamics of anti-social behavior* (pp. 30–49) Charles C. Thomas Publisher, Ltd.

Dripps, D. (2008). After rape law: Will the turn to consent normalize the prosecution of sexual assault. *Akron Law Review, 41*(4), 957–980.

Dussich, J. P. J. (2001). Decisions not to report sexual assault: A comparative study among women living in Japan who are Japanese, Korean, Chinese, and English-speaking. *International Journal of Offender Therapy and Comparative Criminology, 45*(3), 278–301.

Dworkin, A. (1993). Prostitution and male supremacy. *Michigan Journal of Gender & Law, 1*(1), 1–12.

Dworkin, A. (2006). *Intercourse*. Basic Books. (Original work published 1987)

Dworkin, E. R., Brill, C. D., & Ullman, S. E. (2019). Social reactions to disclosure of interpersonal violence and psychopathology: A systematic review and meta-analysis. *Clinical Psychology Review, 72*, 101750.

Edwards, K. M., Turchik, J. A., Dardis, C. M., Reynolds, N., & Gidycz, C. A. (2011). Rape myths: History, individual and institutional-level presence, and implications for change. *Sex Roles, 65*(11), 761–773.

Edwards, S. R., & Vogel, D. L. (2015). Young men's likelihood ratings to be sexually aggressive as a function of norms and perceived sexual interest. *Psychology of Men & Masculinity, 16*(1), 88–96.

Eisenberg, N., & Miller, P. A. (1987). The relation of empathy to prosocial and related behaviors. *Psychological Bulletin, 101*(1), 91–119.

Ekis Ekman, K. (2011). *Varat och varan*. Leopard Förlag.

Elias-Lambert, N., & Black, B. M. (2016). Bystander sexual violence prevention program: Outcomes for high- and low-risk university men. *Journal of Interpersonal Violence, 31*(19), 3211–3235.

Eliot, L., Ahmed, A., Khan, H., & Patel, J. (2021). Dump the "dimorphism": Comprehensive synthesis of human brain studies reveals few male-female differences beyond size. *Neuroscience and biobehavioral reviews, 125*, 667–697.

Ellison, L. (2001). *The adversarial process and the vulnerable witness*. Oxford University Press.

Ellison, L. (2009). The use and abuse of psychiatric evidence in rape trials. *The International Journal of Evidence & Proof, 13*(1), 28–49.

Ellison, L., & Munro, V. E. (2009a). Reacting to rape: Exploring mock jurors' assessments of complainant credibility. *The British Journal of Criminology, 49*(2), 202–219.

Ellison, L., & Munro, V. E. (2009b). Turning mirrors into windows? Assessing the impact of (mock) juror education in rape trials. *The British Journal of Criminology, 49*(3), 363–383.

Ellison, L., & Munro, V. E. (2010). Getting to (not) guilty: Examining jurors' deliberative processes in, and beyond, the context of a mock rape trial. *Legal Studies, 30*(1), 74–97.

Ellison, L., & Munro, V. E. (2013). Better the devil you know? 'Real rape' stereotypes and the relevance of a previous relationship in (mock) juror deliberations. *The International Journal of Evidence & Proof, 17*(4), 299–322.

Ellison, L., Munro, V. E., Hohl, K., & Wallang, P. (2015). Challenging criminal justice? Psychosocial disability and rape victimization. *Criminology & Criminal Justice, 15*(2), 225–244.

Emmers-Sommer, T. M., Pauley, P., Hanzal, A., & Triplett, L. (2006). Love, suspense, sex, and violence: Men's and women's film predilections, exposure to sexually violent media, and their relationship to rape myth acceptance. *Sex Roles, 55*(5), 311–320.

Equality and Human Rights Commission (EHRC). (2010). *How fair is Britain: Findings and challenges.* Equality and Human Rights Commission. https://www.equalityhumanrights.com/en/publication-download/how-fair-britain

Estrich, S. (1987). *Real rape.* Harvard University Press.

Evans, M. (2021). Wayne Couzens: The former met officer who hid dark secrets behind family-man facade. *The Telegraph.* https://www.telegraph.co.uk/news/2021/09/29/wayne-couzens-former-met-officer-hid-dark-secrets-behind-facade/

Eyssel, F., & Bohner, G. (2010). Schema effects of rape myth acceptance on judgments of guilt and blame in rape cases: The role of perceived entitlement to judge. *Journal of Interpersonal Violence, 26*(8), 1579–1605.

Eyssel, F., Bohner, G., & Siebler, F. (2006). Perceived rape myth acceptance of others predicts rape proclivity: Social norm or judgmental anchoring? *Swiss Journal of Social Psychology, 65*(2), 93–99.

Fakunmoju, S. B., Abrefa-Gyan, T., Maphosa, N., & Gutura, P. (2021). Rape myth acceptance: Gender and cross-national comparisons across the United States, South Africa, Ghana, and Nigeria. *Sexuality & Culture, 25*(1), 18–38.

Faludi, S. (1993). *Backlash: The undeclared war against women.* Penguin.

Feild, H. S. (1978). Attitudes toward rape: A comparative analysis of police, rapists, crisis counselors, and citizens. *Journal of Personality and Social Psychology, 36*(2), 156–179.

Felson, R. B., & Pare, P.-P. (2008). Gender and the victim's experience with the criminal justice system. *Social Science Research, 37*(1), 202–219.

Ferguson, C. J., & Hartley, R. D. (2022). Pornography and sexual aggression: Can meta-analysis find a link?. Trauma, *Violence, & Abuse, 23*(1), 278–287.

Festinger, L. (1962). *A theory of cognitive dissonance.* Stanford University Press.

Finch, E., & Munro, V. E. (2005). Juror stereotypes and blame attribution in rape cases involving intoxicants: The findings of a pilot study. *The British Journal of Criminology, 45*(1), 25–38.

Fine, C. (2010). *Delusions of gender.* W. W. Norton and Company.

Finkelhor, D. (1984). *Child sexual abuse.* New York.

Finkelson, L., & Oswalt, R. (1995). College date rape: Incidence and reporting. *Psychological Reports, 77*(2), 526–526.

Finn, J., McDonald, E., & Tinsley, Y. (2011) Introduction to this special issue. *Canterbury Law Review, 17,* 1–7.

Finn, J., McDonald, E., & Tinsley, Y. (2011). Identifying and qualifying the decision-maker: The case for specialisation. In *From "Real Rape" to Real Justice: Prosecuting Rape in New Zealand.* Victoria University Press.

Fisher, B. S., Daigle, L. E., Cullen, F. T., & Turner, M. G. (2003). Reporting sexual victimization to the police and others: Results from a national-level study of college women. *Criminal Justice and Behavior, 30*(1), 6–38.

Flood, M., & Howson, R. (2015). *Engaging men in building gender equality.* Cambridge Scholars Publishing.

Flores, S. A., & Hartlaub, M. G. (1998). Reducing rape-myth acceptance in male college students: A meta-analysis of intervention studies. *Journal of College Student Development, 39*(5), 438–448.

Foubert, J. D. (2000). The longitudinal effects of a rape-prevention program on fraternity men's attitudes, behavioral intent, and behavior. *Journal of American College Health, 48*(4), 158–163.

Foubert, J. D., & La Voy, S. A. (2000). A qualitative assessment of 'the men's program': The impact of a rape prevention program on fraternity men. *NASPA Journal, 38*(1), 18–30.

Foubert, J. D., & Masin, R. C. (2012). Effects of the men's program on U.S. army soldiers' intentions to commit and willingness to intervene to prevent rape: A pretest posttest study. *Violence and Victims, 27*(6), 911–921.

Foubert, J. D., & McEwen, M. k. (1998). An all-male rape prevention peer education program: Decreasing fraternity men's behavioral intent to rape. *Journal of College Student Development, 39*(6), 548–556.

Foubert, J. D., & Newberry, J. T. (2006). Effects of two versions of an empathy-based rape prevention program on fraternity men's survivor empathy, attitudes, and behavioral intent to commit rape or sexual assault. *Journal of College Student Development, 47*(2), 133–148.

Foubert, J. D., & Perry, B. C. (2007). Creating lasting attitude and behavior change in fraternity members and male student athletes: The qualitative impact of an empathy-based rape prevention program. *Violence Against Women, 13*(1), 70–86.

Franiuk, R., Seefelt, J. L., Cepress, S. L., & Vandello, J. A. (2008). Prevalence and effects of rape myths in print journalism: The Kobe Bryant case. *Violence Against Women, 14*(3), 287–309.

Franiuk, R., Seefelt, J. L., & Vandello, J. A. (2008). Prevalence of rape myths in headlines and their effects on attitudes toward rape. *Sex Roles, 58*(11), 790–801.

Frazier, P. A. (2003). Perceived control and distress following sexual assault: A longitudinal test of a new model. *Journal of Personality and Social Psychology, 84*(6), 1257–1269.

Frazier, P., Valtinson, G., & Candell, S. (1994). Evaluation of a coeducational interactive rape prevention program. *Journal of Counseling & Development, 73*(2), 153–158.

Furnham, A. (2003). Belief in a just world: Research progress over the past decade. *Personality and Individual Differences, 34*(5), 795–817.

Garza, A. D., & Franklin, C. A. (2021). The effect of rape myth endorsement on police response to sexual assault survivors. *Violence Against Women, 27*(3–4), 552–573.

Gavey, N. (2018a). *The gender of rape culture: Revisiting the cultural scaffolding of rape* (2nd ed.). Routledge.

Gavey, N. (2018b). *Just sex? The cultural scaffolding of rape* (2nd ed.). Routledge.

Gbahabo, D. D., & Duma, S. E. (2021). 'I just became like a log of wood … I was paralyzed all over my body': Women's lived experiences of tonic immobility following rape. *Heliyon, 7*(7), e07471.

George, R., & Ferguson, S. (2021). *Review into the Criminal Justice System response to adult rape and serious sexual offences across England and Wales Research Report.* https://assets.publishing.service.gov.uk/government/uploads/system/uploads/attachment_data/file/994817/rape-review-research-report.pdf

Gerger, H., Kley, H., Bohner, G., & Siebler, F. (2007). The acceptance of modern myths about sexual aggression scale: Development and validation in German and English. *Aggressive Behavior, 33*(5), 422–440.

Ghavami, N., & Peplau, L. A. (2013). An intersectional analysis of gender and ethnic stereotypes: Testing three hypotheses. *Psychology of Women Quarterly, 37*(1), 113–127.

Gidycz, C. A., Orchowski, L. M., & Berkowitz, A. D. (2011). Preventing sexual aggression among college men: An evaluation of a social norms and bystander intervention program. *Violence Against Women, 17*(6), 720–742.

Gidycz, C. A., Rich, C. L., Marioni, N. L. (2002). Interventions to prevent rape and sexual assault. In J. Petrak & B. Hedge (Eds.), The trauma of adult sexual assault: Treatment, prevention, and policy (pp. 235–259). Wiley.

Gill, A. K. (2009). Narratives of survival: South Asian women's experience of rape. In M. A. H. Horvath & J. M. Brown (Eds.), *Rape: Challenging contemporary thinking.* (pp. 161–183). Willan.

Gill, A. K., & Harrison, K. (2019). 'I am talking about it because I want to stop it': Child sexual abuse and sexual violence against women in British South Asian communities. *The British Journal of Criminology, 59*(3), 511–529.

Ging, D. (2019). Alphas, betas, and incels: Theorizing the masculinities of the manosphere. *Men and Masculinities, 22*(4), 638–657.

Gleibs, I. H. (2017). Are all "research fields" equal? Rethinking practice for the use of data from crowdsourcing market places. *Behavior Research Methods, 49*(4), 1333–1342.

Glick, P., & Fiske, S. T. (1996). The ambivalent sexism inventory: Differentiating hostile and benevolent sexism. *Journal of Personality and Social Psychology, 70*(3), 491–512.

Glick, P., & Fiske, S. (1997). Hostile and benevolent sexism: Measuring ambivalent sexist attitudes toward women. *Psychology of Women Quarterly, 21*, 119–136

Glick, P., & Fiske, S. T. (2011). Ambivalent sexism revisited. *Psychology of Women Quarterly, 35*(3), 530–535.

Glick, P., Fiske, S. T., Mladinic, A., Saiz, J. L., Abrams, D., Masser, B., Adetoun, B., Osagie, J. E., Akande, A., Alao, A., Annetje, B., Willemsen, T. M., Chipeta, K., Dardenne, B., Dijksterhuis, A., Wigboldus, D., Eckes, T., Six-Materna, I., Expósito, F., ... López, W. L. (2000). Beyond prejudice as simple antipathy: Hostile and benevolent sexism across cultures. *Journal of Personality and Social Psychology, 79*(5), 763–775.

Goodman-Delahunty, J., & Graham, K. (2011). The influence of victim intoxication and victim attire on police responses to sexual assault. *Journal of Investigative Psychology and Offender Profiling, 8*(1), 22–40.

Gotell, L., & Dutton, E. (2016). Sexual violence in the 'manosphere': Antifeminist men's rights discourses on rape. *International Journal for Crime, Justice and Social Democracy, 5*(2), 65–80.

Gravelin, C. R., Biernat, M., & Bucher, C. E. (2018). Blaming the victim of acquaintance rape: Individual, situational, and sociocultural factors. *Frontiers in Psychology, 9*, 2422.

Greenwald, A. G., McGhee, D. E., & Schwartz, J. L. (1998). Measuring individual differences in implicit cognition: The implicit association test. *Journal of Personality and Social Psychology, 74*(6), 1464–1480.

Grubb, A., & Turner, E. (2012). Attribution of blame in rape cases: A review of the impact of rape myth acceptance, gender role conformity and substance use on victim blaming. *Aggression and Violent Behavior, 17*(5), 443–452.

Grube, J. W., Mayton II, D. M., & Ball-Rokeach, S. J. (1994). Inducing change in values, attitudes, and behaviors: Belief system theory and the method of value self-confrontation. *Journal of Social Issues, 50*(4), 153–173.

Gruber, A. (2009). Rape, feminism, and the war on crime. *Washington Law Review, 84*(4), 581–660.

Gylys, J. A., & McNamara, J. R. (1996). Acceptance of rape myths among prosecuting attorneys. *Psychological Reports, 79*(1), 15–18.

Haddad, R. I. (2005). Shield or sieve – People v. Bryant and the rape shield law in high-profile cases. *Columbia Journal of Law and Social Problems, 39*(2), 185–222.

Hafer, C. L. (2000). Do innocent victims threaten the belief in a just world? Evidence from a modified Stroop task. *Journal of Personality and Social Psychology, 79*(2), 165–173.

Hald, G. M., Malamuth, N. M., & Yuen, C. (2010). Pornography and attitudes supporting violence against women: Revisiting the relationship in nonexperimental studies. *Aggressive Behavior, 36*(1), 14–20.

Hales, S. T., & Gannon, T. A. (2021). Understanding sexual aggression in UK male university students: an empirical assessment of prevalence and psychological risk factors. *Sexual Abuse: a Journal of Research and Treatment*, 10790632211051682. Advance online publication.

Hammond, E. M., Berry, M. A., & Rodriguez, D. N. (2011). The influence of rape myth acceptance, sexual attitudes, and belief in a just world on attributions of responsibility in a date rape scenario. *Legal and Criminological Psychology*, *16*(2), 242–252.

Hans, V., & Jehle, A. (2003). Avoid bald men and people with green socks-other ways to improve the voir dire process in jury selection. *Chicago-Kent Law Review*, *78*, 1179.

Harding, S. (2004). *The feminist standpoint theory reader*. Routledge.

Hardwicke, T. E., & Ioannidis, J. P. A. (2018). Mapping the universe of registered reports. *Nature Human Behaviour*, *2*(11), 793–796.

Hart, C. M., Ritchie, T. D., Hepper, E. G., & Gebauer, J. E. (2015). The balanced inventory of desirable responding short form (BIDR-16). *SAGE Open*, *5*(4), 2158244015621113.

Hauser, D., Paolacci, G., & Chandler, J. (2019). Common concerns with MTurk as a participant pool: Evidence and solutions. In F. R. Kardes, P. M. Herr, & N. Schwarz (Eds.), *Handbook of research methods in consumer psychology* (pp. 319–337). Routledge/Taylor & Francis Group.

Hayes, R. M., Lorenz, K., & Bell, K. A. (2013). Victim blaming others: Rape myth acceptance and the just world belief. *Feminist Criminology*, *8*(3), 202–220.

Hearn, J. (1998). *The violences of men: How men talk about and how agencies respond to men's violence to women*. SAGE.

Heise, L. L. (1998). Violence against women: An integrated, ecological framework. *Violence Against Women*, *4*(3), 262–290.

Heppner, M. J., Humphrey, C. F., Hillenbrand-Gunn, T. L., & DeBord, K. A. (1995). The differential effects of rape prevention programming on attitudes, behavior, and knowledge. *Journal of Counseling Psychology*, *42*(4), 508–518.

Her Majesty's Crown Prosecution Service Inspectorate [HMCPSI]. (2007). *Without consent: Joint review of the investigation and prosecution of rape offences*. HMCPSI. https://www.justiceinspectorates.gov.uk/cjji/inspections/without-consent-joint-review-of-the-investigation-and-prosecution-of-rape-offences/

Hilton, N. Z. (2000). The role of attitudes and awareness in anti-violence education. *Journal of Aggression, Maltreatment & Trauma*, *3*(1), 221–238.

Hinck, S. S., & Thomas, R. W. (1999). Rape myth acceptance in college students: How far have we come? *Sex Roles: A Journal of Research*, *40*(9–10), 815–832.

Hine, B., & Murphy, A. (2017). The impact of victim-perpetrator relationship, reputation and initial point of resistance on officers' responsibility and authenticity ratings towards hypothetical rape cases. *Journal of Criminal Justice*, *49*, 1–13.

Hlavka, H. R. (2014). Normalizing sexual violence: Young women account for harassment and abuse. *Gender & Society*, *28*(3), 337–358.

Hockett, J. M., & Saucier, D. A. (2015). A systematic literature review of "rape victims" versus "rape survivors": Implications for theory, research, and practice. *Aggression and Violent Behavior*, *25*, 1–14.

Hockett, J. M., Saucier, D. A., Hoffman, B. H., Smith, S. J., & Craig, A. W. (2009). Oppression through acceptance? Predicting rape myth acceptance and attitudes toward rape victims. *Violence Against Women*, *15*(8), 877–897.

Hockett, J. M., Smith, S. J., Klausing, C. D., & Saucier, D. A. (2016). Rape myth consistency and gender differences in perceiving rape victims: A meta-analysis. *Violence Against Women*, *22*(2), 139–167.

Hohl, K., & Stanko, E. A. (2015). Complaints of rape and the criminal justice system: Fresh evidence on the attrition problem in England and Wales. *European Journal of Criminology*, *12*(3), 324–341.

Home Office. (2009). *Results from the Ipsos Mori poll of telephone interviews with people in England and Wales regarding their opinions on violence against women.* Home Office. https://www.ipsos.com/en-uk/violence-against-women-eu-wide-survey

Horvath, M. A. H., Hegarty, P., Tyler, S., & Mansfield, S. (2012). "Lights on at the end of the party": Are lads' mags mainstreaming dangerous sexism? *British Journal of Psychology, 103*(4), 454–471.

Houlder, B. (1997). The importance of preserving the jury system and the right of election for trial. *Criminal Law Review*, 875–881.

Howe, A. (2008). *Sex, violence and crime: Foucault and the 'man' question.* Routledge-Cavendish.

Hughes, S., Skoda, K., Parsons, A., Brown, K., & Pedersen, C. L. (2020). (Dis)abling blame: The influence of disability status on attributions of blame toward victims of sexual assault. *Sexuality Research and Social Policy, 17*(2), 219–228.

Huntington, C., Berkowitz, A. D., & Orchowski, L. (2022). False accusations of sexual assault: Prevalence, misperceptions, and implications for prevention work with men and boys. In L. M. Orchowski & A. D. Berkowitz (Eds.), *Engaging boys and men in sexual assault prevention: Theory, research, and practice* (pp. 379–391). Academic Press

Hust, S. J. T., Rodgers, K. B., Ebreo, S., & Stefani, W. (2019). Rape myth acceptance, efficacy, and heterosexual scripts in men's magazines: Factors associated with intentions to sexually coerce or intervene. *Journal of Interpersonal Violence, 34*(8), 1703–1733.

Ioannidis, J. P. A. (2005). Why most published research findings are false. *PLOS Medicine, 2*(8), e124.

Jane, E. A. (2018). Systemic misogyny exposed: Translating Rapeglish from the manosphere with a random rape threat generator. *International Journal of Cultural Studies, 21*(6), 661–680.

Johnson, A. G. (2005). *The gender knot: Unraveling our patriarchal legacy.* Temple University Press.

Johnson, L. G., & Beech, A. (2017). Rape myth acceptance in convicted rapists: A systematic review of the literature. *Aggression and Violent Behavior, 34*, 20–34.

Jones, M. E., Russell, R. L., & Bryant, F. B. (1998). The structure of rape attitudes for men and woman: A three-factor model. *Journal of Research in Personality, 32*(3), 331–350.

Jones, O. (2011). *Chavs: The demonization of the working class.* Verso Books.

Jordan, J. (2004). *The word of a woman? Police, rape and belief.* Springer.

Jouriles, E. N., Krauss, A., Vu, N. L., Banyard, V. L., & McDonald, R. (2018). Bystander programs addressing sexual violence on college campuses: A systematic review and meta-analysis of program outcomes and delivery methods. *Journal of American College Health, 66*(6), 457–466.

Judicial Studies Board. (2010). *Crown court bench book: Directing the jury.* Ministry of Justice.

Kathawalla, U.-K., Silverstein, P., & Syed, M. (2021). Easing into open science: A guide for graduate students and their advisors. *Collabra: Psychology, 7*(1).

Katz, J. (1995). Reconstructing masculinity in the locker room: The mentors in violence prevention project. *Harvard Educational Review, 65*(2), 163–175.

Katz, J., Merrilees, C., Hoxmeier, J. C., & Motisi, M. (2017). White female bystanders' responses to a black woman at risk for incapacitated sexual assault. *Psychology of Women Quarterly, 41*(2), 273–285.

Katz, J., Merrilees, C., LaRose, J., & Edgington, C. (2018). White female bystanders' responses to a black woman at risk for sexual assault: Associations with attitudes about sexism and racial injustice. *Journal of Aggression Maltreatment & Trauma, 27*(4), 444–459.

Kebbell, M. R., O'Kelly, C. M. E., & Gilchrist, E. L. (2007). Rape victims' experiences of giving evidence in English courts: A survey. *Psychiatry, Psychology and Law, 14*(1), 111–119.

Kelly, L. (1987). The continuum of sexual violence. In J. Hanmer & M. Maynard (Eds.), *Women, violence and social control* (pp. 46–60). Palgrave Macmillan UK.

Kelly, L., Lovett, J. , & Regan, L. (2005). *A gap or chasm? Attrition in reported rape cases* (Home Office Research Study 293). London: Home Office Research, Development and Statistics Directorate.

Kelly, L., Regan, L., & Burton, S. (1992). Defending the indefensible? Quantitative methods and feminist research. H. Hinds, A. Phoenix, & J. Stacey (Eds.), *Working out: New directions in women's studies.* (pp. 149–161). Routledge.

Kelly, L., Temkin, J., & Griffiths, S. (2006). *Section 41: An evaluation of new legislation limiting sexual history evidence in rape trials.* Home Office. https://citeseerx.ist.psu.edu/viewdoc/download?doi=10.1.1.628.3925&rep=rep1&type=pdf

Keogh, A. (2007). Rape trauma syndrome – Time to open the floodgates? *Journal of Forensic and Legal Medicine, 14*(4), 221–224.

Kibble, N. (2008). Uncovering judicial perspectives on questions of relevance and admissibility in sexual offence cases. *Journal of Law and Society, 35*, 91–107.

Kirkwood, M. K., & Cecil, D. K. (2001). Marital rape: A student assessment of rape laws and the marital exemption. *Violence Against Women, 7*(11), 1234–1253.

Kitzinger, J. (2004). Media coverage of sexual violence against women and children. In *Women and media: International perspetives* (pp. 13–38). Blackwell.

Kitzinger, J. (2009). Rape in the media. In M. A. H. Horvath & J. Brown (Eds.), *Rape: Challenging contemporary thinking.* (pp. 74–98). Willan.

Kitzinger, J., & Skidmore, P. (1995). Playing safe: Media coverage of child sexual abuse prevention strategies. *Child Abuse Review, 4*(1), 47–56.

Kleinke, C. L., & Meyer, C. (1990). Evaluation of rape victim by men and women with high and low belief in a just world. *Psychology of Women Quarterly, 14*(3), 343–353.

Knight, R. A., & Prentky, R. A. (1990). Classifying sexual offenders. In W. L. Marshall, D. R. Laws, & H. E. Barbaree (Eds.), *Handbook of sexual assault: Issues, theories, and treatment of the offender* (pp. 23–52). Springer US.

Konradi, A. (2007). *Taking the stand: Rape survivors and the prosecution of rapists.* Praeger.

Koss, M. P. (1985). The hidden rape victim: Personality, attitudinal, and situational characteristics. *Psychology of Women Quarterly, 9*(2), 193–212.

Koss, M. P., Figueredo, A. J., & Prince, R. J. (2002). Cognitive mediation of rape's mental, physical, and social health impact: Tests of four models in cross-sectional data. *Journal of Consulting and Clinical Psychology, 70*(4), 926–941.

Koss, M. P., & Harvey, M. R. (1991). *The rape victim: Clinical and community interventions* (2nd ed., pp. xiv, 313). Sage Publications, Inc.

Kossmeier, M., Tran, U. S., & Voracek, M. (2020). Power-enhanced funnel plots for meta-analysis. *Zeitschrift Für Psychologie, 228*(1), 43–49.

Krahé, B., & Temkin, J. (2009). Addressing the attitude problem in rape trials: Some proposals and methodological considerations. In M. A. H. Horvath & J. M. Brown (Eds.), *Rape: Challenging contemporary thinking.* (pp. 301–321). Willan.

Krahé, B., Temkin, J., & Bieneck, S. (2007). Schema-driven information processing in judgements about rape. *Applied Cognitive Psychology, 21*(5), 601–619.

Krahé, B., Temkin, J., Bieneck, S., & Berger, A. (2008). Prospective lawyers' rape stereotypes and schematic decision making about rape cases. *Psychology, Crime & Law, 14*(5), 461–479.

Kunda, Z. (1999). *Social cognition.* MIT Press.

Landström, S., Strömwall, L. A., & Alfredsson, H. (2016). Blame attributions in sexual crimes: Effects of belief in a just world and victim behavior. *Nordic Psychology*, *68*(1), 2–11.

Langhinrichsen-Rohling, J., Foubert, J. D., Brasfield, H. M., Hill, B., & Shelley-Tremblay, S. (2011). The men's program: Does it impact college men's self-reported bystander efficacy and willingness to intervene? *Violence Against Women*, *17*(6), 743–759.

Larcombe, W. (2002). The 'ideal' victim v successful rape complainants: Not what you might expect. *Feminist Legal Studies*, *10*(2), 131–148.

Latane, B., & Darley, J. M. (1968). Group inhibition of bystander intervention in emergencies. *Journal of Personality and Social Psychology*, *10*(3), 215–221.

Law Commission. (1992). *Criminal law: Rape within marriage*. https://www.gov.uk/government/publications/criminal-law-rape-within-marriage

Lawson, S., & Olle, L. (2006). Dangerous drink spiking archetypes. *Women Against Violence: An Australian Feminist Journal*, *18*, 46–55.

Lee, T. L., Fiske, S. T., Glick, P., & Chen, Z. (2010). Ambivalent sexism in close relationships: (Hostile) power and (benevolent) romance shape relationship ideals. *Sex Roles*, *62*(7–8), 583–601.

Lee, T., & Krogh, C. (2005). Where do you suggest we stand? Subject positions inherent in sexual assault prevention messages. *Social Change in the 21st Century*. https://eprints.qut.edu.au/3507/

Lees, S. (2002). *Carnal knowledge: Rape on trial*. Women's Press.

Legislation.gov.uk. (2003). Sexual Offences Act 2003. Retrieved from http://www.legislation.gov.uk/ukpga/2003/42/section/68

LeMaire, K. L., Oswald, D. L., & Russell, B. L. (2016). Labeling sexual victimization experiences: The role of sexism, rape myth acceptance, and tolerance for sexual harassment. *Violence and Victims*, *31*(2), 332–346.

Leone, R. M., Oyler, K. N., & Parrott, D. J. (2021). Empathy is not enough: The inhibiting effects of rape myth acceptance on the relation between empathy and bystander intervention. *Journal of Interpersonal Violence*, *36*(23–24), 11532–11552.

Lerner, M. J. (1977). The justice motive: Some hypotheses as to its origins and forms. *Journal of Personality*, *45*(1), 1–52.

Lerner, M. J. (1980). The belief in a just world. In M. J. Lerner (Ed.), *The belief in a just world: A fundamental delusion* (pp. 9–30). Springer US.

Leverick, F. (2020). What do we know about rape myths and juror decision making? *The International Journal of Evidence & Proof*, *24*(3), 255–279.

Lewandowsky, S., Ecker, U. K. H., Seifert, C. M., Schwarz, N., & Cook, J. (2012). Misinformation and its correction: Continued influence and successful debiasing. *Psychological Science in the Public Interest*, *13*(3), 106–131.

Lieberman, J. D., & Arndt, J. (2000). Understanding the limits of limiting instructions: Social psychological explanations for the failures of instructions to disregard pretrial publicity and other inadmissible evidence. *Psychology, Public Policy, and Law*, *6*(3), 677–711.

Lippa, R. A. (2009). Sex differences in sex drive, sociosexuality, and height across 53 nations: Testing evolutionary and social structural theories. *Archives of Sexual Behavior*, *38*(5), 631–651.

Lievore, D. (2003). *Non-reporting and hidden recording of sexual assault: An international literature review*. Australian Institute of Criminology. https://www.aic.gov.au/publications/archive/archive-135

Littleton, H. L., Axsom, D., & Grills-Taquechel, A. (2009). Sexual assault victims' acknowledgment status and revictimization risk. *Psychology of Women Quarterly*, *33*(1), 34–42.

Littleton, H. L., Axsom, D., Breitkopf, C. R., & Berenson, A. (2006). Rape acknowledgment and postassault experiences: How acknowledgment status relates to disclosure, coping, worldview, and reactions received from others. *Violence and Victims*, *21*(6), 761–778.

Locke, B. D., & Mahalik, J. R. (2005). Examining masculinity norms, problem drinking, and athletic involvement as predictors of sexual aggression in college men. *Journal of Counseling Psychology*, *52*(3), 279–283.

Lodewijkx, H. F. M., Wildschut, T., Nijstad, B. A., Savenije, W., & Smit, M. (2001). In a violent world a just world makes sense: The case of "senseless violence" in the Netherlands. *Social Justice Research*, *14*(1), 79–94.

Lonsway, K. A. (2005). The use of expert witnesses in cases involving sexual assault. *Violence Against Women Online Resources*, 379–486. Available from: http://www.mincava. umn.edu/documents/commissioned/svandexpertwitnesses/svandexpertwitnesses. pdf.

Lonsway, K. A., & Fitzgerald, L. F. (1994). Rape myths: In review. *Psychology of Women Quarterly*, *18*(2), 133–164.

Lonsway, K. A., & Fitzgerald, L. F. (1995). Attitudinal antecedents of rape myth acceptance: A theoretical and empirical reexamination. *Journal of Personality and Social Psychology*, *68*(4), 704–711.

Lonsway, K. A., & Kothari, C. (2000). First year campus acquaintance rape education Evaluating the Impact of a Mandatory Intervention. *Psychology of Women Quarterly*, *24*(3), 220–232.

Lonsway, K. A., Welch, S., & Fitzgerald, L. F. (2001). Police training in sexual assault response: Process, outcomes, and elements of change. *Criminal Justice and Behavior*, *28*(6), 695–730.

Lorde, A. (2007). *Sister outsider: Essays and speeches*. Crossing Press. (Original work published 1984)

Lorenz, K., & Jacobsen, C. (2021). Sexual violence survivors' experiences with the police and willingness to report future victimization. *Women & Criminal Justice*, 1–23.

Lorenz, K., & Maskaly, J. (2018). The relationship between victim attitudes, training, and behaviors of sexual assault investigators. *Journal of Crime & Justice*, *41*(1), 81–97.

Lovett, J., Uzelac, G., Horvath, M. A. H., & Kelly, L. (2007). *Rape in the 21st century: Old behaviours, new contexts and emerging patterns*. ESRC End of Award Report RES-000-22-1679. Available from: https://cwasu.org/resource/rape-in-the-21st-century-old-behaviours-new-contexts-and-emerging-powers

MacKinnon, C. A. (1991). *Toward a feminist theory of the state*. Harvard University Press. (Original work published 1989)

MacKinnon, C. A. (2007). *Women's lives, men's laws*. Harvard University Press.

Maddox, L., Lee, D., & Barker, C. (2011). Police empathy and victim PTSD as potential factors in rape case attrition. *Journal of Police and Criminal Psychology*, *26*(2), 112–117.

Maier, S. L. (2008). "I have heard horrible stories . . .": Rape victim advocates' perceptions of the revictimization of rape victims by the police and medical system. *Violence Against Women*, *14*(7), 786–808.

Malamuth, N. M. (1981). Rape proclivity among males. *Journal of Social Issues*, *37*(4), 138–157.

Malamuth, N. M., Hald, G. M., & Koss, M. (2012). Pornography, individual differences in risk and men's acceptance of violence against women in a representative sample. *Sex Roles*, *66*(7), 427–439.

Mardorossian, C. M. (2002). Toward a new feminist theory of rape. *Signs: Journal of Women in Culture and Society*, *27*(3), 743–775.

Markusoff, J. (2016). What's at stake in the case of Justice Robin Camp. *Macleans*. https:// www.macleans.ca/news/canada/beyond-one-judge-whats-at-stake-in-the-case-of-justice-robin-camp/

Marshall, L. E. (2020). The utility of treatment for sexual offenders. In *The Wiley handbook of what works with sexual offenders : Contemporary Perspectives in Theory, Assessment, Treatment, and Prevention* (pp. 175–183). John Wiley & Sons, Ltd.

Marx, B. P., Forsyth, J. P., Gallup, G. G., Fusé, T., & Lexington, J. M. (2008). Tonic immobility as an evolved predator defense: Implications for sexual assault survivors. *Clinical Psychology: Science and Practice, 15*(1), 74–90.

Mason, P., & Monckton-Smith, J. (2008). Conflation, collocation and confusion: British press coverage of the sexual murder of women. *Journalism, 9*(6), 691–710.

Mason, W., & Suri, S. (2012). Conducting behavioral research on Amazon's Mechanical Turk. *Behavior Research Methods, 44*(1), 1–23.

Masser, B., Viki, G. T., & Power, C. (2006). Hostile sexism and rape proclivity amongst men. *Sex Roles, 54*(7), 565–574.

Matsick, J. L., Kruk, M., Oswald, F., & Palmer, L. (2021). Bridging feminist psychology and open science: Feminist tools and shared values inform best practices for science reform. *Psychology of Women Quarterly, 45*(4), 412–429.

McCannon, B. C., & Wilson, M. (2019). "A million dollars in free advertising" politics and sex offense prosecution in the wake of Duke lacrosse. *Supreme Court Economic Review, 27*, 167–187.

McConahay, J. B. (1983). Modern racism and modern discrimination: The effects of race, racial attitudes, and context on simulated hiring decisions. *Personality and Social Psychology Bulletin, 9*(4), 551–558.

McEwan, J. (2005). Proving consent in sexual cases: Legislative change and cultural evolution. *The International Journal of Evidence & Proof, 9*(1), 1–28.

McGee, H., O'Higgins, M., Garavan, R., & Conroy, R. (2011). Rape and child sexual abuse: What beliefs persist about motives, perpetrators, and survivors? *Journal of Interpersonal Violence, 26*(17), 3580–3593.

McGlynn, C. (2010). Feminist activism and rape law reform in England and Wales: A Sisyphean struggle? In *Rethinking rape law.* (pp. 155–169) Routledge-Cavendish.

McGlynn, C., & Westmarland, N. (2019). Kaleidoscopic Justice: Sexual violence and victim-survivors' perceptions of justice. *Social & Legal Studies, 28*(2), 179–201.

McGregor, M. J., Wiebe, E., Marion, S. A., & Livingstone, C. (2000). Why don't more women report sexual assault to the police? *Canadian Medical Association Journal, 162*(5), 659–660.

McKibbin, W. F., Shackelford, T. K., Goetz, A. T., & Starratt, V. G. (2008). Why do men rape? An evolutionary psychological perspective. *Review of General Psychology, 12*(1), 86–97.

McMahon, S. (2010). Rape myth beliefs and bystander attitudes among incoming college students. *Journal of American College Health, 59*(1), 3–11.

McMahon, S., & Farmer, G. L. (2011). An updated measure for assessing subtle rape myths. *Social Work Research, 35*(2), 71–81.

McMahon, S., Postmus, J. L., & Koenick, R. A. (2011). Conceptualizing the engaging bystander approach to sexual violence prevention on college campuses. *Journal of College Student Development, 52*(1), 115–130.

McMillan, L. (2018). Police officers' perceptions of false allegations of rape. *Journal of Gender Studies, 27*(1), 9–21.

Mennicke, A., Anderson, D., Oehme, K., & Kennedy, S. (2014). Law enforcement officers' perception of rape and rape victims: A multimethod study. *Violence and Victims, 29*(5), 814–827.

Messner, M. A. (2016). Forks in the Road of men's gender politics: Men's rights vs feminist allies. *International Journal for Crime, Justice and Social Democracy, 5*(2), 6–20.

Meyers, M. (1996). *News coverage of violence against women: Engendering blame.* SAGE Publications.

Middleton, J. (2021). Met Police issues advice to women to 'shout or wave a bus down' if they don't trust a male officer. *The Independent*. https://www.independent.co.uk/news/uk/home-news/met-police-sarah-everard-couzens-b1930331.html

Miller, A. K., Amacker, A. M., & King, A. R. (2011). Sexual victimization history and perceived similarity to a sexual assault victim: A path model of perceiver variables predicting victim culpability attributions. *Sex Roles*, *64*(5–6), 372–381.

Ministry of Justice and Home Office. (2021). *End-to-end rape review report on findings and actions*. GOV.UK. https://www.gov.uk/government/publications/end-to-end-rape-review-report-on-findings-and-actions

Molina, J., & Poppleton, S. (2020). *Rape survivors and the criminal justice system*. https://s3-eu-west-2.amazonaws.com/victcomm2-prod-storage-119w3o4kq2z48/uploads/2020/10/OVC-Rape-Survivors-and-the-Criminal-Justice-System.pdf

Möller, A., Söndergaard, H. P., & Helström, L. (2017). Tonic immobility during sexual assault – A common reaction predicting post-traumatic stress disorder and severe depression. *Acta Obstetricia et Gynecologica Scandinavica*, *96*(8), 932–938.

Montada, L. (1998). Belief in a just world: A hybrid of justice motive and self-interest? In L. Montada & M. J. Lerner (Eds.), *Responses to victimizations and belief in a just world* (pp. 217–246). Springer US.

Moore, S. E. H. (2014). *Crime and the media*. Macmillan International Higher Education.

Moorti, S. (2002). *Color of rape: Gender and race in television's public spheres*. SUNY Press.

Morabito, M. S., Pattavina, A., & Williams, L. M. (2019). It all just piles up: Challenges to victim credibility accumulate to influence sexual assault case processing. *Journal of Interpersonal Violence*, *34*(15), 3151–3170.

Moynihan, M. M., Banyard, V. L., Arnold, J., Eckstein, R., & Stapleton, J. (2011). Sisterhood may be powerful for reducing sexual and intimate partner violence: An evaluation of the bringing in the bystander in-person program with sorority members. *Violence Against Women*, *17*(6), 703–719.

Muehlenhard, C. L., & Hollabaugh, L. C. (1988). Do women sometimes say no when they mean yes? The prevalence and correlates of women's token resistance to sex. *Journal of Personality and Social Psychology*, *54*(5), 872–879.

Mujal, G. N., Taylor, M. E., Fry, J. L., Gochez-Kerr, T. H., & Weaver, N. L. (2021). A systematic review of bystander interventions for the prevention of sexual violence. *Trauma, Violence, & Abuse*, *22*(2), 381–396.

Mulac, A., Jansma, L., & Linz, D. (2002). Men's behavior toward women after viewing sexually-explicit films: Degradation makes a difference. *Communication Monographs*, *69*(4), 311–328.

Mullin, C., Imrich, D. J., & Linz, D. (1996). The impact of acquaintance rape stories and case-specific pretrial publicity on juror decision making. *Communication Research*, *23*(1), 100–135.

Munro, V. E., & Kelly, L. (2009). A vicious cycle? Attrition and conviction patterns in contemporary rape cases in England and Wales. In M. A. H. Horvath & J. M. Brown (Eds.), *Rape: Challenging contemporary thinking*. (pp. 281–300). Willan.

Murnen, S. K., Wright, C., & Kaluzny, G. (2002). If "boys will be boys," then girls will be victims? A meta-analytic review of the research that relates masculine ideology to sexual aggression. *Sex Roles*, *46*(11), 359–375.

Murphy, A., Hine, B., Yesberg, J. A., Wunsch, D., & Charleton, B. (2021). Lessons from London: A contemporary examination of the factors affecting attrition among rape complaints. *Psychology, Crime & Law*, 1–33.

Murphy, M. C., Mejia, A. F., Mejia, J., Yan, X., Cheryan, S., Dasgupta, N., Destin, M., Fryberg, S. A., Garcia, J. A., Haines, E. L., Harackiewicz, J. M., Ledgerwood, A., Moss-Racusin, C. A., Park, L. E., Perry, S. P., Ratliff, K. A., Rattan, A., Sanchez, D. T.,

Savani, K., ... Pestilli, F. (2020). Open science, communal culture, and women's participation in the movement to improve science. *Proceedings of the National Academy of Sciences, 117*(39), 24154–24164.

Nationellt Centrum för Kvinnofrid. (2021). *Sexualbrottslagstiftningen.* https://nck.uu.se/kunskapsbanken/amnesguider/sexuellt-vald/sexualbrottslagstiftningen/

Neville, H. A., Oh, E., Spanierman, L. B., Heppner, M. J., & Clark, M. (2004). General and culturally specific factors influencing black and white rape survivors' self-esteem. *Psychology of Women Quarterly, 28*(1), 83–94.

Nicol, A. A. M., & Rounding, K. (2013). Alienation and empathy as mediators of the relation between social dominance orientation, right-wing authoritarianism and expressions of racism and sexism. *Personality and Individual Differences, 55*(3), 294–299.

Nisbett, R. E., & Wilson, T. D. (1977). Telling more than we can know: Verbal reports on mental processes. *Psychological Review, 84*(3), 231–259.

O'Connor, C., & Joffe, H. (2014). Gender on the brain: A case study of science communication in the new media environment. *PLoS ONE, 9*(10), e110830.

O'Donohue, W., Yeater, E. A., & Fanetti, M. (2003). Rape prevention with college males: The roles of rape myth acceptance, victim empathy, and outcome expectancies. *Journal of Interpersonal Violence, 18*(5), 513–531.

Oh, E., & Neville, H. (2004). Development and validation of the Korean Rape Myth Acceptance Scale. *The Counseling Psychologist, 32*(2), 301–331.

Olive, V. C. (2012). Sexual assault against women of color. *Journal of Student Research, 1*(1), 1–9.

Olver, M. E., Nicholaichuk, T. P., & Wong, S. C. P. (2014). The predictive and convergent validity of a psychometric battery used to assess sexual offenders in a treatment programme: An 18-year follow-up. *Journal of Sexual Aggression, 20*(2), 216–239.

O'Neil, M. (2016). Canadian judge could lose job over shocking comments to alleged rape victim. *News.com.au.* https://www.news.com.au/lifestyle/reallife/news-life/canadian-judge-robin-camp-could-lose-job-over-shocking-commentsto-alleged-rape-victim/news-story/99453728ec49e91285ce809e5c4a2820

O'Neill, R. (2018). *Seduction.* Polity.

ONS. (2019). Sexual Offences in England and Wales. https://www.ons.gov.uk/peoplepopulationandcommunity/crimeandjustice/articles/sexualoffencesinenglandandwales/yearendingmarch2017

Orchowski, L. M., & Gidycz, C. A. (2012). To whom do college women confide following sexual assault? A prospective study of predictors of sexual assault disclosure and social reactions. *Violence Against Women, 18*(3), 264–288.

Orchowski, L. M., & Gidycz, C. A. (2015). Psychological consequences associated with positive and negative responses to disclosure of sexual assault among college women: A prospective study. *Violence against Women, 21*(7), 803–823.

Orchowski, L. M., Untied, A. S., & Gidycz, C. A. (2013). Factors associated with college women's labeling of sexual victimization. *Violence and Victims, 28*(6), 940–958.

Orenstein, A. (2007). Special issues raised by rape trials symposium: Ethics and evidence: V. The use of prejudicial evidence. *Fordham Law Review, 76*(3), 1585–1608.

Page, A. D. (2007). Behind the blue line: Investigating police officers' attitudes toward rape. *Journal of Police and Criminal Psychology, 22*(1), 22–32.

Page, A. D. (2008a). Gateway to Reform? Policy implications of police officers' attitudes toward rape. *American Journal of Criminal Justice: AJCJ, 33*(1), 44–58.

Page, A. D. (2008b). Judging women and defining crime: Police officers' attitudes toward women and rape. *Sociological Spectrum, 28*(4), 389–411.

Page, A. D. (2010). True colors: Police officers and rape myth acceptance. *Feminist Criminology, 5*(4), 315–334.

Parratt, K. A., & Pina, A. (2017). From "real rape" to real justice: A systematic review of police officers' rape myth beliefs. *Aggression and Violent Behavior, 34*, 68–83.

Patterson, D. (2011a). The linkage between secondary victimization by law enforcement and rape case outcomes. *Journal of Interpersonal Violence, 26*(2), 328–347.

Patterson, D. (2011b). The impact of detectives' manner of questioning on rape victims' disclosure. *Violence Against Women, 17*(11), 1349–1373.

Patterson, D., Greeson, M., & Campbell, R. (2009). Understanding rape survivors' decisions not to seek help from formal social systems. *Health & Social Work, 34*(2), 127–136.

Paul, L. A., & Gray, M. J. (2011). Sexual assault programming on college campuses: Using social psychological belief and behavior change principles to improve outcomes. *Trauma, Violence, & Abuse, 12*(2), 99–109.

Paulhus, D. L. (1991). Measurement and control of response bias. *Measures of Personality and Social Psychological Attitudes.*, 17–59.

Payne, D. L., Lonsway, K. A., & Fitzgerald, L. F. (1999). Rape myth acceptance: Exploration of its structure and its measurement using the Illinois Rape Myth Acceptance Scale. *Journal of Research in Personality, 33*(1), 27–68.

Pease, B. (2014). Theorising men's violence prevention policies. In N. Henry & A. Powell (Eds.), *Preventing sexual violence: Interdisciplinary approaches to overcoming a rape culture* (pp. 22–40). Palgrave Macmillan UK.

Pease, B., & Flood, M. (2008). Rethinking the significance of attitudes in preventing men's violence against women. *Australian Journal of Social Issues, 43*(4), 547–561.

Pedersen, S. H., & Strömwall, L. A. (2013). Victim blame, sexism and just-world beliefs: A cross-cultural comparison. *Psychiatry, Psychology and Law, 20*(6), 932–941.

Persson, S., & Dhingra, K. (2020). Attributions of blame in stranger and acquaintance rape: A multilevel meta-analysis and systematic review. *Trauma, Violence, & Abuse.* https://doi.org/10.1177/1524838020977146

Persson, S., & Dhingra, K. (2021). Moderating factors in culpability ratings and rape proclivity in stranger and acquaintance rape: Validation of rape vignettes in a community sample. *Journal of Interpersonal Violence*, https://doi.org/10.1177/0886260521991294

Persson, S., & Hostler, T. J. (2021). When men who dislike feminists feel proud: Can self-affirmation and perspective-taking increase men's empathy toward feminists? *Psychology of Women Quarterly, 45*(3), 372–386.

Persson, S., & Pownall, M. (2021). Can open science be a tool to dismantle claims of hard-wired brain sex differences? Opportunities and challenges for feminist researchers. *Psychology of Women Quarterly, 45*(4), 493–504.

Peter-Hagene, L. C., & Ullman, S. E. (2018). Longitudinal effects of sexual assault victims' drinking and self-blame on posttraumatic stress disorder. *Journal of Interpersonal Violence, 33*(1), 83–93.

Peterson, Z. D., & Muehlenhard, C. L. (2004). Was it rape? The function of women's rape myth acceptance and definitions of sex in labeling their own experiences. *Sex Roles, 51*(3), 129–144.

Petty, R. E., & Cacioppo, J. T. (1986). The elaboration likelihood model of persuasion. In R. E. Petty & J. T. Cacioppo (Eds.), *Communication and Persuasion: Central and Peripheral Routes to Attitude Change* (pp. 1–24). Springer.

Phillips, A. (2010). *Gender and culture.* Polity.

Phillips, J. D., & Griffin, R. A. (2015). Crystal Mangum as hypervisible object and invisible subject: Black feminist thought, sexual violence, and the pedagogical repercussions of the duke lacrosse rape case. *Women's Studies in Communication, 38*(1), 36–56.

Phipps, A. (2009). Rape and respectability: Ideas about sexual violence and social class. *Sociology, 43*(4), 667–683.

Pinzone-Glover, H. A., Gidycz, C. A., & Jacobs, C. D. (1998). An acquaintance rape prevention program: Effects on attitudes toward women, rape-related attitudes, and perceptions of rape scenarios. *Psychology of Women Quarterly, 22*(4), 605–621.

Pithers, W. D. (1994). Process evaluation of a group therapy component designed to enhance sex offenders' empathy for sexual abuse survivors. *Behaviour Research and Therapy, 32*(5), 565–570.

Plesser, H. E. (2018). Reproducibility vs. replicability: A brief history of a confused terminology. *Frontiers in Neuroinformatics, 11*, 76.

Potter, S. J. (2012). Using a multimedia social marketing campaign to increase active bystanders on the college campus. *Journal of American College Health, 60*(4), 282–295.

Potter, S. J., Moynihan, M. M., Stapleton, J. G., & Banyard, V. L. (2009). Empowering bystanders to prevent campus violence against women: A preliminary evaluation of a poster campaign. *Violence Against Women, 15*(1), 106–121.

Potter, S. J., & Stapleton, J. G. (2012). Translating sexual assault prevention from a college campus to a united states military installation: Piloting the know-your-power bystander social marketing campaign. *Journal of Interpersonal Violence, 27*(8), 1593–1621.

Powell, A., & Henry, N. (2014). Framing sexual violence prevention. In N. Henry & A. Powell (Eds.), *Preventing sexual violence: Interdisciplinary approaches to overcoming a rape culture* (pp. 1–21). Palgrave Macmillan UK.

Progressive. (2008). *'This is not an invitation to rape me', research report.* https://www.rapecrisisscotland.org.uk/publications/TINAITRM-Testing-Report.pdf

Puthillam, A., Parekh, A., & Kapoor, H. (2022). Who are you to me? Relational distance to victims and perpetrators affects advising to report rape. *Violence Against Women, 28*(3–4), 780–800.

RAINN. (2021). *Victims of sexual violence: Statistics.* https://www.rainn.org/statistics/victims-sexual-violence

Rape Crisis England and Wales. (2019). *Rape crisis calls for sustainable funding for specialist services.* https://rapecrisis.org.uk/news/rape-crisis-calls-for-sustainable-funding-for-specialist-services/

Rape Crisis England and Wales. (2021). *Statistics–Sexual violence.* http://rapecrisis.org.uk/get-informed/about-sexual-violence/statistics-sexual-violence/

Reavey, P., & Warner, S. (2003). *New feminist stories of child sexual abuse: Sexual scripts and dangerous dialogue.* Routledge.

Reich, R. R., Ariel, I., Darkes, J., & Goldman, M. S. (2012). What do you mean 'drunk'? Convergent validation of multiple methods of mapping alcohol expectancy memory networks. *Psychology of Addictive Behaviors: Journal of the Society of Psychologists in Addictive Behaviors, 26*(3), 406–413.

Rich, M. D., Utley, E. A., Janke, K., & Moldoveanu, M. (2010). "I'd rather be doing something else:" male resistance to rape prevention programs. *The Journal of Men's Studies, 18*(3), 268–288.

Richardson, D. C., & Campbell, J. L. (1980). Alcohol and wife abuse: The effect of alcohol on attributions of blame for wife abuse. *Personality and Social Psychology Bulletin, 6*(1), 51–56.

Rippon, G. (2019). *The gendered brain.* Bodley Head.

Roberts, S. O., Bareket-Shavit, C., Dollins, F. A., Goldie, P. D., & Mortenson, E. (2020). Racial inequality in psychological research: Trends of the past and recommendations for the future. *Perspectives on Psychological Science, 15*(6), 1295–1309.

Rosenberg, M. (1979). *Conceiving the self.* Basic Books.

Rosenberg, M. (1956). Cognitive structure and attitudinal affect. *The Journal of Abnormal and Social Psychology, 53*(3), 367–372.

Rozee, P. D., & Koss, M. P. (2001). Rape: A century of resistance. *Psychology of Women Quarterly, 25*(4), 295–311.

Rumney, P., & Fenton, R. A. (2011). Judicial training and rape. *The Journal of Criminal Law, 75*(6), 473–481.

Rumney, P., & McPhee, D. (2020). The evidential value of electronic communications data in rape and sexual offence cases. *The Criminal Law Review*, 1–6.

Rumney, P. (2006). False allegations of rape. *The Cambridge Law Journal*, 65(1), 128–158.

Rumney, P., McPhee, D., Fenton, R. A., & Williams, A. (2019). A police specialist rape investigation unit: a comparative analysis of performance and victim care. *Policing and society*, 30(5), 548–568

Rung, N. (2021). *Stora porrboken*. Rebel Books.

Ruti, M. (2015). *The age of scientific sexism: How evolutionary psychology promotes gender profiling and fans the battle of the sexes*. Bloomsbury Academic.

Ryan, K. M. (2011). The relationship between rape myths and sexual scripts: The social construction of rape. *Sex Roles*, 65(11), 774–782.

Sakalli-Ugurlu, N., Yalcin, Z. S., & Glick, P. (2007). Ambivalent sexism, belief in a just world, and empathy as predictors of Turkish students' attitudes toward rape victims. *Sex Roles*, 57(11-12), 889–895.

Salazar, L. F., Vivolo-Kantor, A., Hardin, J., & Berkowitz, A. (2014). A web-based sexual violence bystander intervention for male college students: Randomized controlled trial. *Journal of Medical Internet Research*, 16(9), e3426.

Sales, D. (2021). Devoted father, husband and police officer who hid dark desire to rape and kill. *The Daily Mail*. https://www.dailymail.co.uk/news/article-9773105/Wayne-Couzens-Devoted-father-hid-dark-desire-rape-kill.html

Sanders, A., & Jones, I. (2007). The victim in court. In *Handbook of victims and victimology*. Willan.

Sanghani, R. (2015). Police rape prevention poster 'blames sexual assault victims'. *The Telegraph*, 8 April 2015. https://www.telegraph.co.uk/women/womens-life/11522485/Police-rape-prevention-poster-blames-sexual-assault-victims.html

Scheel, A. M., Schijen, M. R. M. J., & Lakens, D. (2021). An excess of positive results: Comparing the standard psychology literature with registered reports. *Advances in Methods and Practices in Psychological Science*, 4(2), 25152459211007468.

Schewe, P. A., & O'Donohue, W. (1996). Rape prevention with high-risk males: Short-term outcome of two interventions. *Archives of Sexual Behavior*, 25(5), 455–471.

Schlesinger, P., & Tumber, H. (1994). *Reporting crime: The media politics of criminal justice: office of justice programs*. Oxford University Press Address. https://www.ojp.gov/ncjrs/virtual-library/abstracts/reporting-crime-media-politics-criminal-justice

Schnopp-Wyatt. (1999). *Expert testimony in rape trials: Prejudicial or probative?* University of Illinois at Chicago.

Schuller, R. A., & Hastings, P. A. (2002). Complainant sexual history evidence: Its impact on mock jurors' decisions. *Psychology of Women Quarterly*, 26(3), 252–261.

Schuller, R. A., & Stewart, A. (2000). Police responses to sexual assault complaints: The role of perpetrator/complainant intoxication. *Law and Human Behavior*, 24(5), 535–551.

Schwartz, M. (2010). *Police investigation of rape-roadblocks and solutions*. National Institute of Justice Visiting Fellowship. https://www.ojp.gov/ncjrs/virtual-library/abstracts/national-institute-justice-visiting-fellowship-police-investigation

Schwartz, M. D., DeKeseredy, W. S., Tait, D., & Alvi, S. (2001). Male peer support and a feminist routing activities theory: Understanding sexual assault on the college campus. *Justice Quarterly*, 18(3), 623–649.

Schwendinger, H., & Schwendinger, J. (1977). Social class and the definition of crime. *Crime and Social Justice*, (7), 4–13

Schwendinger, J., & Schwendinger, H. (1974). Rape myths: In legal, theoretical, and everyday practice. *Crime and Social Justice*, 1, 18–26.

Scottish Executive/TNS System 3. (2007). *Findings from the wave 10 post-campaign evaluation of the domestic abuse campaign 2006/07*. Scottish Executive.

Scully, D. (1990). *Understanding sexual violence: A study of convicted rapists*. Routledge.

Scully, D., & Marolla, J. (1984). Convicted rapists' vocabulary of motive: Excuses and justifications. *Social Problems, 31*(5), 530–544.

Seta, J., & Seta, C. (1993). Stereotypes and the generation of compensatory and non-compensatory expectancies of group members. *Personality and Social Psychology Bulletin, 19*, 722–731.

Shaver, K. G., & Drown, D. (1986). On causality, responsibility, and self-blame: A theoretical note. *Journal of Personality and Social Psychology, 50*(4), 697–702.

Shaw, J., Campbell, R., Cain, D., & Feeney, H. (2017). Beyond surveys and scales: How rape myths manifest in sexual assault police records. *Psychology of Violence, 7*(4), 602–614.

Sheldon, J. P., & Parent, S. L. (2002). Clergy's attitudes and attributions of blame toward female rape victims. *Violence Against Women, 8*(2), 233–256.

Sidanius, J., & Pratto, F. (1999). *Social dominance: An intergroup theory of social hierarchy and oppression.* Cambridge University Press.

Siddique, H. (2020). We are facing the 'decriminalisation of rape' warns victims' comissioner. *The Guardian* https://www.theguardian.com/society/2020/jul/14/we-are-facing-the-decriminalisation-of-warns-victims-commissioner

Sims, C. M., Noel, N. E., & Maisto, S. A. (2007). Rape blame as a function of alcohol presence and resistance type. *Addictive Behaviors, 32*(12), 2766–2775.

Sinclair, C. H., & Bourne, L. E. (1998). Cycle of blame or just world: effects of legal verdicts on gender patterns in rape-myth acceptance and victim empathy. *Psychology of Women Quarterly, 22*, 575–88.

Skogan, W. G. (1977). Dimensions of the dark figure of unreported crime. *Crime & Delinquency, 23*(1), 41–50.

Sleath, E., & Bull, R. (2012). Comparing rape victim and perpetrator blaming in a police officer sample: Differences between police officers with and without special training. *Criminal Justice and Behavior, 39*(5), 646–665.

Sleath, E., & Bull, R. (2017). Police perceptions of rape victims and the impact on case decision making: A systematic review. *Aggression and Violent Behavior, 34*, 102–112.

Sleath, E., & Woodhams, J. (2014). Expectations about victim and offender behaviour during stranger rape. *Psychology, Crime & Law, 20*(8), 798–820.

Smith, D. E. (1989). *The everyday world as problematic: A feminist sociology.* Northeastern University Press.

Smith, O. (2009). *An investigation into the effects of court culture on barristers' opinions of responses to rape.* Dissertation (BSc), University of Bath.

Smith, O. (2018). *Rape trials in England and Wales: Observing justice and rethinking rape myths.* Springer.

Smith, O., & Skinner, T. (2012). Observing court responses to victims of rape and sexual assault. *Feminist Criminology, 7*(4), 298–326.

Söchting, I., Fairbrother, N., & Koch, W. J. (2004). Sexual assault of women: Prevention efforts and risk factors. *Violence against women, 10*(1), 73–93.

Spates, K. (2012). "The missing link": The exclusion of black women in psychological research and the implications for black women's mental health. *SAGE Open, 2*(3), 2158244012455179.

Spence, J. T., Helmreich, R. (1972). The attitudes toward women scale: An objective instrument to measure attitudes toward the rights and roles of women in contemporary society. *Catalog of Selected Documents in Psychology, 2*(66).

Spencer, B. (2016). The impact of class and sexuality-based stereotyping on rape blame. *Sexualization, Media, & Society, 2*(2), 1–8.

Spohn, C., & Tellis, K. (2012). The criminal justice system's response to sexual violence. *Violence Against Women, 18*(2), 169–192.

Spohn, C., White, C., & Tellis, K. (2014). Unfounding sexual assault: Examining the decision to unfound and identifying false reports. *Law & Society Review, 48*(1), 161–192.

Sprankle, E., Bloomquist, K., Butcher, C., Gleason, N., & Schaefer, Z. (2018). The role of sex work stigma in victim blaming and empathy of sexual assault survivors. *Sexuality Research and Social Policy, 15*(3), 242–248.

Stabile, B., Grant, A., Purohit, H., & Rama, M. (2019). "She lied": Social construction, rape myth prevalence in social media, and sexual assault policy. *Sexuality, Gender & Policy, 2*(2), 80–96.

Stanko, B., & Williams, E. (2009). Reviewing rape and rape allegations in London: What are the vulnerabilities of the victims who report to the police? In M. A. H. Horvath & J. M. Brown (Eds.), *Challenging contemporary thinking.* (pp. 207–225). Willan.

Stanko, E. A. (1996). Warnings to women. Police advice and women's safety in Britain. *Violence Against Women, 2*(1), 5–24.

Stanko, E. A., & Hohl, K. (2018). Why training is not improving the police response to sexual violence against women: A glimpse into the 'black box' of police training. In E. Milne, K. Brennan, N. South, & J. Turton (Eds.), *Women and the criminal justice system: Failing victims and offenders?* (pp. 167–186). Springer International Publishing.

Stanley, N., Barter, C., Wood, M., Aghtaie, N., Larkins, C., Lanau, A., & Överlien, C. (2018). Pornography, sexual coercion and abuse and sexting in young people's intimate relationships: A European study. *Journal of Interpersonal Violence, 33*(19), 2919–2944.

Steblay, N., Hosch, H. M., Culhane, S. E., & McWethy, A. (2006). The impact on juror verdicts of judicial instruction to disregard inadmissible evidence: A meta-analysis. *Law and Human Behavior, 30*(4), 469–492.

Steiner, P. M., Atzmüller, C., & Su, D. (2017). Designing valid and reliable vignette experiments for survey research: A case study on the fair gender income gap. *Journal of Methods and Measurement in the Social Sciences, 7*(2), 43.

Stephens, K. A., & George, W. H. (2004). Effects of anti-rape video content on sexually coercive and noncoercive college men's attitudes and alcohol expectancies. *Journal of Applied Social Psychology, 34*(2), 402–416.

Stephens, K. A., & George, W. H. (2009). Rape prevention with college men: Evaluating risk status. *Journal of Interpersonal Violence, 24*(6), 996–1013.

Stern Review. (2010). *A report by baroness vivien Stern CBE of an independent review into how rape complaints are handled by public authorities in England and Wales.* Home Office.

Stanko, B., & Williams, E. (2009). Reviewing rape and rape allegations in London: What are the vulnerabilities of the victims who report to the police? In M. A. H. Horvath & J. M. Brown (Eds.), *Rape: Challenging contemporary thinking* (pp. 207–225). Willan.

Stevenson, K. (2000). Unequivocal victims: The historical roots of the mystification of the female complainant in rape cases. *Feminist Legal Studies, 8*(3), 343–366.

Strömwall, L. A., Alfredsson, H., & Landström, S. (2013a). Blame attributions and rape: Effects of belief in a just world and relationship level. *Legal and Criminological Psychology, 18*(2), 254–261.

Strömwall, L. A., Alfredsson, H., & Landström, S. (2013b). Rape victim and perpetrator blame and the Just World hypothesis: The influence of victim gender and age. *Journal of Sexual Aggression, 19*(2), 207–217.

Stuart, S. M., McKimmie, B. M., & Masser, B. (2019). Rape perpetrators on trial: The effect of sexual assault–related schemas on attributions of blame. *Journal of Interpersonal Violence, 34*(2), 310–336.

Stubbs-Richardson, M., Rader, N. E., & Cosby, A. G. (2018). Tweeting rape culture: Examining portrayals of victim blaming in discussions of sexual assault cases on Twitter. *Feminism & Psychology, 28*(1), 90–108.

Suarez, E., & Gadalla, T. M. (2010). Stop blaming the victim: A meta-analysis on rape myths. *Journal of Interpersonal Violence, 25*(11), 2010–2035.

Suler, J. (2004). The online disinhibition effect. *CyberPsychology & Behavior, 7*(3), 321–326.

Süssenbach, P., Albrecht, S., & Bohner, G. (2017). Implicit judgments of rape cases: An experiment on the determinants and consequences of implicit evaluations in a rape case. *Psychology Crime & Law, 23*(3), 291–304.

Süssenbach, P., Bohner, G., & Eyssel, F. (2012). Schematic influences of rape myth acceptance on visual information processing: An eye-tracking approach. *Journal of Experimental Social Psychology, 48*(3), 660–668.

Swim, J. K., Aikin, K. J., Hall, W. S., & Hunter, B. A. (1995). Sexism and racism: Old-fashioned and modern prejudices. *Journal of Personality and Social Psychology, 68*(2), 199–214.

Sykes, G. M., & Matza, D. (1957). Techniques of neutralization: A theory of delinquency. *American Sociological Review, 22*(6), 664–670.

Tajfel, H. (1981). *Human groups and social categories.* Cambridge University Press.

Taslitz, A. E. (1999). *Rape and the culture of the courtroom.* New York University Press.

Taylor, N., & Joudo, J. (2005). *The impact of pre-recorded video and closed circuit television testimony by adult sexual assault complainants on jury decision-making: An experimental study.* Australian Institute of Criminology. Available from: https://www.aic.gov.au/publications/rpp/rpp68

Taylor, S., & Johnson, K. C. (2007). *Until proven innocent: Political correctness and the shameful injustices of the Duke lacrosse rape case.* St. Martin's Press.

Temkin, J., & Ashworth, A. (2004). The sexual offences act 2003:(1)-Rape, sexual assaults and the problems of consent. *Criminal Law Review,* 328–346.

Temkin, J. (2010). And always keep a-hold of nurse, for fear of finding something worse: Challenging rape myths in the courtroom. *New Criminal Law Review, 13*(4), 710–734.

Temkin, J., Gray, J. M., & Barrett, J. (2018). Different functions of rape myth use in court: Findings from a trial observation study. *Feminist Criminology, 13*(2), 205–226.

Temkin, J., & Krahé, B. (2008). *Sexual assault and the justice gap: A question of attitude.* Bloomsbury Publishing.

Tharp, A. T., DeGue, S., Valle, L. A., Brookmeyer, K. A., Massetti, G. M., & Matjasko, J. L. (2013). A systematic qualitative review of risk and protective factors for sexual violence perpetration. *Trauma, Violence, & Abuse, 14*(2), 133–167.

The Gillen Review. (2019). Report into the Law and Procedures in Serious Sexual Offences in Northern Ireland. https://www.justice-ni.gov.uk/publications/gillen-review-report-law-and-procedures-serious-sexual-offences-ni

The National Center for Victims of Crime. (2004). *Spousal rape laws: 20 years later.* http://www.ncdsv.org/images/NCVC_SpousalRapeLaws20YearsLater_2004.pdf

Thelan, A. R., & Meadows, E. A. (2021). The Illinois Rape Myth Acceptance Scale-Subtle Version: Using an Adapted Measure to Understand the Declining Rates of Rape Myth Acceptance. *Journal of interpersonal violence,* 8862605211030013. Advance online publication. https://doi.org/10.1177/08862605211030013.

Thiara, R. K., & Gill, A. K. (2010). *Violence against women in South Asian communities: Issues for policy and practice.* Jessica Kingsley Publishers.

Thomas, C. (2020). The 21st century jury: Contempt, bias and the impact of jury service. *Criminal Law Review,* (11), 987–1011.

Thompson, M. (2000). Life after rape: A chance to speak? *Sexual and Relationship Therapy, 15*(4), 325–343.

Thornhill, R., & Palmer, C. T. (2000). *A natural history of rape: Biological bases of sexual coercion.* MIT Press.

Tillman, S., Bryant-Davis, T., Smith, K., & Marks, A. (2010). Shattering silence: Exploring barriers to disclosure for African American sexual assault survivors. *Trauma Violence & Abuse, 11*(2), 59–70.

Tversky, A., & Kahneman, D. (1973). Availability: A heuristic for judging frequency and probability. *Cognitive Psychology, 5*(2), 207–232.

Uji, M., Shono, M., Shikai, N., & Kitamura, T. (2007). Rape Myth Scale: Factor structure and relationship with gender egalitarianism among Japanese professionals. *Psychiatry and Clinical Neurosciences, 61*(4), 392–400.

Ullman, S. E. (1996). Social reactions, coping strategies, and self-blame attributions in adjustment to sexual assault. *Psychology of Women Quarterly, 20*(4), 505–526.

Ullman, S. E. (1999). Social support and recovery from sexual assault: A review. *Aggression and Violent Behavior, 4*(3), 343–358.

Ullman, S. E. (2010). *Talking about sexual assault: Society's response to survivors.* American Psychological Association.

Ullman, S. E., & Brecklin, L. R. (2002). Sexual assault history, PTSD, and mental health service seeking in a national sample of women. *Journal of Community Psychology, 30*(3), 261–279.

Ullman, S. E., Townsend, S. M., Filipas, H. H., & Starzynski, L. L. (2007). Structural models of the relations of assault severity, social support, avoidance coping, self-blame, and PTSD among sexual assault survivors. *Psychology of Women Quarterly, 31*(1), 23–37.

UN Women. (2021). *Facts and figures: Ending violence against women.* https://www.unwomen.org/en/what-we-do/ending-violence-against-women/facts-and-figures

Van Lange, P. A. M. (2008). Does empathy trigger only altruistic motivation? How about selflessness or justice? *Emotion, 8*(6), 766–774.

Van Valkenburgh, S. P. (2021). Digesting the red pill: Masculinity and neoliberalism in the manosphere. *Men and Masculinities, 24*(1), 84–103.

Venema, R. M. (2016). Police officer schema of sexual assault reports: Real rape, ambiguous cases, and false reports. *Journal of Interpersonal Violence, 31*(5), 872–899.

Vera-Gray, F., McGlynn, C., Kureshi, I., & Butterby, K. (2021). Sexual violence as a sexual script in mainstream online pornography. *The British Journal of Criminology, 61*(5), 1243–1260.

Vetten, L. (2011). III. Politics and the fine art of preventing rape. *Feminism & Psychology, 21*(2), 268–272.

Viki, G. T., & Abrams, D. (2002). But she was unfaithful: Benevolent sexism and reactions to rape victims who violate traditional gender role expectations. *Sex Roles, 47*(5), 289–293.

Walker, S. P., & Louw, D. (2005). The court for sexual offences: Perceptions of the victims of sexual offences. *International Journal of Law and Psychiatry, 28*(3), 231–245.

Waltman, M. (2021). Pornografins koppling till prostitution och våld mot kvinnor. In N. Rung (Ed.), *Stora porrboken.* Rebel Books.

Waterhouse-Watson, D. (2013). *Athletes, sexual assault, and trials by media: Narrative immunity.* Routledge.

Webster, S. D., Akhtar, S., Bowers, L. E., Mann, R. E., Rallings, M., & Marshall, W. L. (2004). The impact of the prison service sex offender treatment programme on minority ethnic offenders: A preliminary study. *Psychology, Crime and Law, 10*(2), 113–124.

Wennstam, K. (2002). *Flickan och skulden: En bok om samhällets syn på våldtäkt.* Albert Bonniers Förlag.

Wentz, E., & Archbold, C. A. (2012). Police perceptions of sexual assault victims: Exploring the intra-female gender hostility thesis. *Police Quarterly, 15*(1), 25–44.

West, C. M. (2008). Mammy, Jezebel, Sapphire, and their homegirls: Developing an 'oppositional' gaze toward the images of Black women. In J. Chrisler, C. Golden, & P. Rozee (Eds.), *Lectures on the psychology of women* (4th ed., pp. 287–299). McGraw-Hill.

Westmarland, N., Aznarez, M., Brown, J., & Kirkham, L. (2012). *The benefits of specialist rape teams: A report commissioned and funded by the Association of Chief Police Officers (ACPO).* Routledge.

Westmarland, N., & Bows, H. (2018). *Researching gender, violence and abuse: Theory, methods, action.* Routledge.

Whatley, M. A. (1996). Victim characteristics influencing attributions of responsibility to rape victims: A meta-analysis. *Aggression and Violent Behavior, 1*(2), 81–95.

Wheatcroft, J. M., Wagstaff, G. F., & Moran, A. (2009). Revictimizing the victim? How rape victims experience the UK legal system. *Victims & Offenders, 4*(3), 265–284.

White, A. M., Strube, M. J., & Fisher, S. (1998). A black feminist model of rape myth acceptance: Implications for research and antirape advocacy in Black communities. *Psychology of Women Quarterly, 22*(2), 157–175.

WHO. (2021). *Violence against women.* https://www.who.int/news-room/fact-sheets/detail/violence-against-women

Wiley, S., Srinivasan, R., Finke, E., Firnhaber, J., & Shilinsky, A. (2012). Positive portrayals of feminist men increase men's solidarity with feminists and collective action intentions. *Psychology of Women Quarterly, 37*(1), 61–71.

Wilson, L. C., & Miller, K. E. (2016). Meta-analysis of the prevalence of unacknowledged rape. *Trauma, Violence, & Abuse, 17*(2), 149–159.

Winkel, F. W., & de Kleuver, E. (1997). Communication aimed at changing cognitions about sexual intimidation: Comparing the impact of a perpetrator-focused versus a victim-focused persuasive strategy. *Journal of Interpersonal Violence, 12*(4), 513–529.

Wright, L. A., Zounlome, N. O. O., & Whiston, S. C. (2020). The effectiveness of male-targeted sexual assault prevention programs: A meta-analysis. *Trauma, Violence, & Abuse, 21*(5), 859–869.

Wright, P. J. (2011). Mass media effects on youth sexual behavior. *Annals of the International Communication Association, 35*, 343–386.

Wright, P. J., Tokunaga, R. S., & Kraus, A. (2016). A meta-analysis of pornography consumption and actual acts of sexual aggression in general population studies. *Journal of Communication, 66*(1), 183–205.

Wyatt, G. E. (1992). The sociocultural context of African American and White American women's rape. *Journal of Social Issues, 48*(1), 77–91.

Xue, J., Fang, G., Huang, H., Cui, N. X., Rhodes, K. V., & Gelles, R. (2019). Rape Myths and the cross-cultural adaptation of the Illinois Rape Myth Acceptance Scale in China. *Journal of Interpersonal Violence, 34*(7), 1428–1460.

Yeater, E. A., & O'Donohue, W. (1999). Sexual assault prevention programs: Current issues, future directions, and the potential efficacy of interventions with women. *Clinical Psychology Review, 19*(7), 739–771.

Yule, K., Hoxmeier, J. C., Petranu, K., & Grych, J. (2022). The chivalrous bystander: The role of gender-based beliefs and empathy on bystander behavior and perceived barriers to intervention. *Journal of Interpersonal Violence, 37*(1–2), 863–888

Zidenberg, A. M., Wielinga, F., Sparks, B., Margeotes, K., & Harkins, L. (2021). Lost in translation: A quantitative and qualitative comparison of rape myth acceptance. *Psychology, Crime & Law,* 1–19.

Zydervelt, S., Zajac, R., Kaladelfos, A., & Westera, N. (2017). Lawyers' strategies for cross-examining rape complainants: Have we moved beyond the 1950s? *The British Journal of Criminology, 57*(3), 551–569.

Index

Note: Page numbers followed by "*n*" indicate notes.

www.ingramcontent.com/pod-product-compliance
Lightning Source LLC
Chambersburg PA
CBHW070340270326
41926CB00017B/3931